TRUE NORTH

EMERGING
LEADER
EDITION

Foreword by David Gergen

BILL GEORGE
AND ZACH CLAYTON

TRUE NORTH

EMERGING
LEADER
EDITION

Leading Authentically in Today's Workplace

WILEY

Published by John Wiley & Sons, Inc., Hoboken, New Jersey.
Published simultaneously in Canada.

For general information on our other products and services or for technical support, please contact our Customer Care Department within the United States at (800) 762-2974, outside the United States at (317) 572-3993 or fax (317) 572-4002.

Wiley publishes in a variety of print and electronic formats and by print-on-demand. Some material included with standard print versions of this book may not be included in e-books or in print-on-demand. If this book refers to media such as a CD or DVD that is not included in the version you purchased, you may download this material at http://booksupport.wiley.com. For more information about Wiley products, visit www.wiley.com.

Library of Congress Cataloging-in-Publication Data is Available:

ISBN 9781119886105 (Hardback)
ISBN 9781119886129 (ePDF)
ISBN 9781119886112 (ePub)

Cover Design and Illustration: Wiley

SKY10045467_040723

Bill's Dedication

This book is dedicated to my family. First to my wife, Penny, whose love, passion for life, and wisdom have brought me great joy and made it all possible. To our sons, Jeff and Jon, and our daughters-in-law, Renee and Jeannette, who are making such important contributions to the world as emerging leaders. And finally, to our grandchildren, Dylan, Freeman, Stella, and Jade—future leaders who will make the world better for everyone.

Zach's Dedication

To my wife, Katie—who has brought greater joy, meaning, and love to my life than I ever dreamed—and to our wonderful children, Jack, Kent, Charlie, and Mary Katherine. We hope they will live authentically and find purpose in their lives through service to others.

TRUE NORTH SERIES

Authentic Leadership: Rediscovering the Secrets to Creating Lasting Value (2003)

True North: Discover Your Authentic Leadership with Peter Sims (2007)

Finding Your True North: A Personal Guide with Nick Craig and Andrew McLean (2008)

7 Lessons for Leading in Crisis (2009)

True North Groups with Doug Baker (2011)

Discover Your True North: Becoming an Authentic Leader (2015)

The Discover Your True North Fieldbook with Nick Craig and Scott Snook (2015)

Emerging Leader Edition of True North: Leading Authentically in Today's Workplace

    Bill George and Zach Clayton (2022)

Emerging Leader's Guide to True North with Josh Hall and Lauren Schwenk (2022)

Contents

Foreword

When Peter Drucker was in his prime, CEOs often traveled across the country to California to seek his counsel on how to lead and manage their companies. He was an iconic figure in the business world, the father of management studies, whose 30 books were highly influential in shaping modern global companies. As I found in conversation late in his life, he had a wisdom about him that was spellbinding.

Upon his death 10 years ago, people naturally asked, "Who will carry on Peter's work?" Soon it became apparent that the most obvious candidate was Warren Bennis, and once again, CEOs made the trek to California to meet quietly with one of the sweetest, wisest men I have been blessed to know. Warren was the father of leadership studies in American universities, the man who gave them academic legitimacy through his two dozen books, and the best mentor and friend one could possibly have.

Upon his death a year ago, the question naturally arose again: "Well, who will now carry on Warren's work?" With the publication of his most important book, the *Emerging Leader Edition of True North*, we may well have our candidate: Bill George. There are obvious differences: Bill himself would modestly point out that both Drucker and Bennis were lifelong scholars deeply schooled in theory; by contrast, Bill first made his mark as a highly successful CEO of a large company before becoming a major thought leader. Yet all three have been at the forefront in shaping leadership and management practices of successive generations.

By chance, Warren introduced me to Bill at the World Economic Forum in 2001. Bill was coming off his years as CEO of Medtronic and was beginning to pull together his thoughts and experiences about leadership so that he could share them with younger business leaders.

Soon Bill published his first book, essentially a memoir, titled *Authentic Leadership*, and it was quickly a best seller. Without realizing it, he had launched an entirely new career, one with even greater impact than his first. In reading the *Emerging Leader Edition* of *True North*, you will find not only a distillation of his ideas about leadership but also revealing portraits of a galaxy of more diverse leaders and what they have learned on their own journeys toward True North. This *Emerging Leader Edition* of *True North* bids to be a classic, standing alongside *The Effective Executive* by Peter Drucker and *On Becoming a Leader* by Warren Bennis. I am proud to call Bill a friend and trusted adviser—and to salute him on the completion of his best book.

Here's what is essential for a reader to understand: Most books that come from the academy are intended for a small audience of specialized scholars. That is the way advances in knowledge are often made. But non-scholars wonder how they apply to them. Bill's ideas work well in practice *and* apply across the board, helping not only business leaders but those in the civic and public sectors as well.

Bill George's work—like Warren's and Peter's—intentionally crosses the bridge between the academy and practice. Through writing, teaching, and mentoring, he is helping leaders become better at leading themselves and, in turn, their organizations. At present more than two dozen CEOs of major global companies are calling on him regularly for counsel and advice.

The evidence shows that leaders from across the world are hungry to discover their True North and lead toward their North Star. At the Harvard Business School, Bill introduced his course, Authentic Leadership Development, as a second-year elective in 2005. Students embraced it with growing enthusiasm, such that it has become one of the most popular courses at the school and attracts a growing number in executive education.

Bill's course has migrated to the Harvard Kennedy School (HKS), where I am a professor of practice and co-director of our Center for Public Leadership. Dana Born, a retired air force general and the first woman in any military branch to gain flag rank while at a military academy, has just started teaching it, and once again students are responding with gusto. Moreover, Bill has introduced True North to an annual training program at the HKS for Young Global Leaders chosen by the World Economic Forum. They love it, especially the deep-dive, small-group conversations every morning over breakfast.

Altogether, some 10,000 men and women have now been trained at Harvard alone in Bill's ideas about authentic leadership. Longitudinal studies are not yet possible on how much it may have shaped lives and leadership, but anecdotal evidence points to encouraging results.

One group that has had lots of exposure to Bill and his work is students who have pursued joint degrees at HBS and HKS and in their third year have received scholarships from Bill and Penny George. These George Fellows, typically in their late 20s, have a home at our Center for Public Leadership and meet frequently, often with Bill and Penny. Bill generously mentors a number of them and remains close long after they have graduated. Altogether, the George Fellowship now has 100 alumni.

To be sure, many had transformative experiences that strengthened their leadership before they became George Fellows. Even so, their recent achievements have been impressive. Here are a few whom Bill continues to mentor:

- Seth Moulton is the U.S. representative for Massachusetts 6th congressional district where he has served since 2015.
- Maura Sullivan is vice president of operations for Ginkgo Bioworks, making COVID-19 tests accessible to kids across America.
- Jonathan Lee Kelly is founder at Asymmetric Holdings, a firm focused on delivering meaningful customer experiences in the restaurant industry.

- Rye Barcott is cofounder and CEO of With Honor, a nonprofit dedicated to promoting veteran leadership to public service, and is author of *It Happened on the Way to War*.
- John Coleman is managing partner at Sovereign's Capital and coauthor of *Passion & Purpose*.
- Peter Brooks is cofounder and CEO of Sylmar Group, a water and wastewater company that protects public health and the environment.
- Nate Fick is general manager of security for Elastic, an enterprise security company, and author of *One Bullet Away*, a *New York Times* best-seller.
- Brian Elliott is founder of FriendFactor, advocacy platform for LGBTQ+ rights, and InReach Capital, a real estate investment firm.
- Stephen Chan is chief of staff for Northeastern University and former vice president of strategy and operations at The Boston Foundation.
- Claude Burton is cofounder and partner at SkyKnight Capital, a private equity company investing in market-leading businesses.

Can there be any doubt that the ideas here apply to emerging leaders from every sector of life and across national boundaries?

As this *Emerging Leader Edition* is being published, the world faces a leadership crisis. Authoritarians have consolidated greater global power. Polarization defines our U.S. politics. Inequality threatens our economy and capitalism itself. Racial progress has stalled. The pandemic made apparent deep cleavages in society. For people everywhere, life becomes ever more volatile and unpredictable. Instead of putting a firm hand on the wheel, many leaders seem unable to steer toward safe ports in the storm. A 2021 Global Leadership Forecast survey from DDI found that only 11 percent of surveyed organizations reported having a "strong" or "very strong" leadership bench, the lowest rating in the past 10 years.

This book can help us find our way. If individual leaders can recognize when they have drifted away from True North and make successful course corrections, as Bill George argues, nations can as well. Surely, authentic leadership beats what we have now.

David Gergen, Cambridge, Massachusetts

Introduction

A Clarion Call to Emerging Leaders

> Crises are hitting us from all directions.
> It is increasingly clear we need an infusion
> of strong, new leaders to help us navigate safely.
> —David Gergen, *Hearts Touched with Fire*

The first two decades of the 21st century have careened from one crisis to the next. It started with the September 11, 2001, attack on the World Trade Center, followed by the bankruptcies of Enron and WorldCom, and many other unethical firms and the 2008 global financial meltdown. The second decade featured the demise of General Electric (GE), Boeing's mishandling of the 737 MAX crashes, the COVID-19 pandemic, George Floyd's murder, the devastation of climate change, and, most recently, Russia's invasion of Ukraine.

At their core, these tragic events can all be traced to failed leadership.

The *Emerging Leader Edition of True North* is not an analysis of these crises or the leaders who caused them. Rather, this is a calling to you as emerging leaders of the next generations—Gen X, Millennials, and Gen Z—to step up and lead authentically by discovering your True North and following your North Star to make this world a better place.

In this book, we feature numerous stories of emerging leaders who are already making a difference, like Kabir Barday, Abby Falik, Tracy Britt Cool, and Rye Barcott, along with pioneers from the

Baby Boomer generation, like Indra Nooyi, Ken Frazier, Mary Barra, Satya Nadella, Ursula Burns, John Donahoe, and Chip Bergh.

We are confident your cohort of emerging leaders will create a better world. We wrote this book to enable you to realize your full potential as an authentic leader who has a positive impact on others through your life and work. This book will challenge you to reflect on your leadership, your humanity, your values, and your purpose in life.

Wherever you live, whatever you do, this is your calling:

Make a positive impact on the world as an authentic leader: Discover your True North, and follow your North Star.

Your True North and North Star

Your True North is the moral compass that guides your actions, derived from your most deeply held beliefs, your values, and the principles you lead by. It is your internal compass, unique to you, that represents who you are at your deepest level.

Just as a compass points toward a magnetic pole, your True North points toward your North Star. Your North Star is the purpose that you pursue to make this world better for everyone.

When you discover your True North, you know yourself at the deepest level and can be authentic. When you have found your North Star, you are ready to pursue your purpose as your calling. This inner journey of knowing yourself is a prerequisite to the great outer journey of leading others. We challenge you to make this journey, both achieving your full potential and having a lasting positive impact on society.

The hardest person you will ever have to lead is yourself.

Many people do not know who they are. They are so focused on trying to impress others that they let the world shape them rather than shaping themselves into the kind of leaders they want to be. When you follow your True North, your leadership will be authentic and people will naturally want to associate with you.

As philosopher William James wrote a century ago,

The best way to define a man's character is to seek out the particular mental or moral attitude in which he felt himself most deeply and intensely alive. At such moments there is a voice inside which says, "This is the real me!"

Can you recall a time when you felt most intensely alive and could say with confidence, "This is the real me"? I had that feeling from the first time I walked into Medtronic and joined a group of talented people dedicated to the mission to "alleviate pain, restore health, and extend life." I felt I could be myself and be appreciated for who I was and what I could contribute. I sensed immediately that my values aligned with the organization's values.

Whether you are leading a small team or a large organization, you will inevitably face pressure from external forces that challenge your values or attempt to seduce you with rewards. These pressures and seductions may pull you away from your True North. When you get too far off course, your moral compass tells you something is wrong. That's when you need to reorient yourself, which requires resolve to resist the constant pressures and expectations confronting you. As you are tested in the world, you yearn to look in the mirror and respect the person you see and the life you are leading.

This is not to say that authentic leaders are perfect. Far from it. All leaders have weaknesses, make mistakes, and are subject to human frailties. By acknowledging their shortcomings and admitting their errors, the humanity and vulnerability of authentic leaders comes through, and they connect with and inspire others to reach their full potential.

The End of Command-and-Control

In the 20th century, business schools instructed managers to build competencies such as leadership style and communication skills. Some authors took these ideas to the extreme, writing nonsense such as "strike a power pose when presenting" or "fake it until you make it." What the competency-based models missed is the importance of character. While your title makes you a *manager*, your character makes you a *leader*.

Most Baby Boomers accepted the rules of hierarchy, waiting their turn for senior leadership positions. They valued a company's financial stability, and their net worth grew as the postwar American economy soared. This era was particularly hard for professional women, since they often faced higher standards with little flexibility or acknowledgment of their lives outside the workplace.

In business, the 1980s and 1990s were typified by Jack Welch, the mastermind who made GE the most valuable company in the world and the epitome of 20th-century leadership. Jack was passionate, competitive, financially driven, and highly successful. He spawned countless imitators who sought to copy his style. Search firms aggressively recruited GE managers to transform organizations, although many GE alumni who became chief executive officers (CEOs) ultimately failed.

When I was CEO of Medtronic, I felt at odds with many of my fellow CEOs who seemed to be more interested in their stock price and the amount of money they were making. As I concluded my term as CEO in 2001, I felt the predominant model of leadership was deeply flawed, as the media primarily judged leaders based on their charisma, leadership style, stock price, and compensation packages.

In 2008, public trust of business leaders fell to a 50-year low following the global financial collapse. The harm the financial community caused for so many woke us up to the need to rethink capitalism—not just as a vehicle to make financiers wealthy but also as a way to create value for all stakeholders.

These crises taught emerging leaders lessons on what *not* to do. They watched as those in control chased money, fame, and power instead of serving others. They learned the perils of putting self-interest ahead of the best interests of the institutions they led.

Authenticity: The Gold Standard for Leaders

When I wrote *Authentic Leadership* in 2003, I was surprised how often people asked, "What do you mean by *authenticity*?" In that era of charismatic leaders, many people were fearful of being themselves. The reality is that *no one can be authentic by trying to be like someone else*. You can learn from others' experiences, but you cannot be successful trying to be *like* them. People will trust you only when you are genuine and authentic.

The crises of the early 21st century led to a rethinking of leadership. By 2015, the *Harvard Business Review* heralded, "Authenticity has become the gold standard for today's leaders." Now the hierarchical, directive leadership style so prevalent in the past century has been replaced by empowerment, collaboration, and authenticity. The old notion of leaders being the smartest guys in the room, as typified by Enron CEO Jeff Skilling, has been superseded by leaders with high levels of self-awareness and emotional intelligence, such as Microsoft's Satya Nadella.

No longer is leadership about developing charisma, emulating other leaders, looking good externally, and acting in your self-interest. Nor should you conflate leading with your leadership style, managerial skills, or competencies. These capabilities are but the outward manifestation of who you are. If you create a false persona or hide behind a mask, people will quickly see through you.

Authentic leaders are true to themselves and their beliefs. They engender trust and develop genuine connections, which enables them to motivate people to achieve high levels of performance. Rather than letting the expectations of others guide them, they are their own person and go their own way. As servant leaders, they are more concerned about helping others succeed than about their own success or recognition.

The rise of authentic leadership coincides with the arrival of emerging leaders. Gen X (born 1965–1980), Millennials (born 1981–1996), and Gen Z (born 1997–2012) expect different things from work and have different values, such as greater transparency and increased diversity. Whereas previous generations hesitated to openly discuss their personal lives or mental health in the workplace, emerging leaders cannot imagine closing off these parts of themselves.

Newer generations won't conform to a conventional work schedule: 9 of 10 Millennials say they prioritize work-life balance. COVID-19 only accelerated this trend, particularly with regards to increasing flexibility. In the post-pandemic world, people insist on working for leaders who focus on their employees' well-being, addressing such vital subjects as employee engagement, work-life integration, mental health, workplace flexibility, and the social impact of their work.

Purdue researchers summarize the desires of the emerging generations:

> *They want companies to act more human. To have a greater purpose that speaks to connection and support. Meet their expectations for flexible working, better health care, but most importantly, help them keep the personal energy they need to survive and thrive when times get tough.*

Dov Seidman, author of *How* and founder of LRN and The HOW Institute for Society, describes why these changes are necessary. He says leadership has morphed in recent centuries from "hands to heads to hearts." In the industrial revolution, companies strove to maximize the output of people using their *hands*. In the past 50 years, the information revolution shifted the focus to data analysis, maximizing people's use of their *heads*. In the era that's developing, we are focusing on using our *hearts*.

Artificial intelligence will supplement the way we use our heads, but it will never take the place of essential leadership qualities of the heart such as empathy, passion, courage, values, intuition, and purpose. As leaders we must develop our hearts to grapple with complex challenges and dilemmas. Do you have these qualities of the heart? You need to cultivate them throughout your lifetime to be an authentic leader in today's world.

Ralph Lauren CEO Patrice Louvet summarizes the distinction between 20th- and 21st-century leaders:

We have gone from leaders who expect everyone to serve them to servant leaders who see their role as serving the people they lead and represent. Our job as leaders is to create the conditions for our people to thrive and realize their full potential. Twentieth-century leaders felt they had all the answers and knew exactly what to do. Twenty-first-century leaders are constantly learning, even if they have been on top for many years.

The big shift is from "command-and-control" to "empowerment with personal accountability." The emerging generations won't tolerate the command-and-control model anymore. We drive the decisions down as close as possible to the customer and then hold people accountable for outcomes.

Figure I.1 clarifies the differences between 20th- and 21st-century leaders.

To summarize the differences in a word—it's *authenticity*. Authentic leaders are characterized by *truth-telling, transparency,* and *trust.*

- **Truth-telling.** Of all the qualities required for authentic leaders, the one indispensable value is integrity: telling the truth. Without truth between people, there can be no authentic relationships. Organizations cannot function without integrity and the common basis that truth provides. Without honesty, or-

Characteristics	20th-Century Leaders	21st-Century Leaders
Philosophy	Command-and-control	Authentic leadership
Organizational approach	Hierarchical management	Empowering leadership
Image	Charismatic	Purpose-driven
Motivation	Self-interest	Institution's best interest
Experience	Perfect resume	Learning through crucibles
Time frame	Short-term	Long-term
Greatest strength	IQ	EQ
Personal measurement	External validation	Intrinsic contribution

Figure I.1   Differences in 20th- and 21st-Century Leaders

ganizations devolve into political jungles where charisma takes precedence over character—a guaranteed route to failure.

- **Transparency.** In the 20th century, senior leaders often shared with their teams on a need-to-know basis. The internet and social media have completely changed people's access to information and expectations of transparency. No longer can leaders keep important information away from their stakeholders, as everything tends to come out eventually. To have an effective organization, information must flow freely—up, down, and sideways. Authentic leaders share the complete picture with colleagues. They don't expect perfection; they insist on openness.

- **Trust.** Trust emanates from truth-telling and transparency as well as admitting your mistakes and exposing your vulnerabilities. Author Stephen M. R. Covey says high-trust organizations earn a "trust dividend" because when people trust each other they make decisions and reach alignment faster. An essential part of your job as a leader is to build the trust of your employees and your customers in the quality of your products and services. Trust is not created by your words alone, but by your actions. To use the cliché, you must "walk the talk."

By developing these three qualities—telling the whole *truth*, being fully *transparent*, and building *trust* with all your stakeholders—you gain credibility as an authentic leader.

Navigating the Emerging Leader Edition

To write the *Emerging Leader Edition of True North*, my coauthor Zach and I interviewed 50 leaders with an emphasis on the new generation of leaders. These interviews are in addition to the 172 leaders we spoke with for previous versions of the book. In our total of 222 interviews, we tapped into a collective wisdom about the art of leading people.

In this book, we describe leadership principles I learned during my career, starting as an individual contributor, then growing into a leader, and eventually rising to CEO of Medtronic. For the last 2 decades, I have been teaching leadership to executives and MBA students, coaching and mentoring leaders, and serving on corporate boards—experiences that have given me a deeper appreciation for authentic leaders in all walks of life. Zach, a 37-year-old Millennial, has spent the last 12 years in a different phase of his career—creating a digital media startup and growing it into a successful company with several hundred employees.

As a note, I'll use the pronoun "I" when sharing personal stories or reflections. "We" reflects the points that Zach and I believe are essential to your development.

This book does not contain "six easy steps" or other simple formulas. Rather, discovering your True North requires introspection, support, and feedback from family, friends, and colleagues. Ultimately, *you must take responsibility for your own development.* Like musicians or athletes born with great abilities, you must devote yourself to a lifetime of intentional practice to realize your full potential.

Part I: Discover Yourself focuses on your journey through life. It begins with deep exploration of your life story, which is more powerful than any set of leadership skills or characteristics. By exploring your crucibles, you learn how to turn your challenges into inspiration to accomplish extraordinary things. During their journey many leaders lose their way. To understand how you could derail, we analyze five types of leaders who were caught in the trap of leading without their True North to chase money, fame, and power.

Part II: Develop Yourself outlines the four elements of your personal development that comprise your internal compass: developing self-awareness, living your values, finding your sweet spot, and leading an integrated life. These elements enable you to develop as an authentic leader, and cultivate the ability to stay true to who you are as you confront challenges in the world around you.

Part III: Lead People describes your transformation from an *I* leader focused on yourself to a *We* leader focused on serving others. Only then will you be ready to discover your North Star—the purpose of your leadership. Purpose-driven leaders COACH their teammates to achieve their full potential by Caring, Organizing, Aligning, Challenging, and Helping.

Part IV: Navigate Today's Challenges guides you on leading through today's challenges. We examine the importance of creating inclusive cultures. We explore how to lead through crises. Finally, we challenge you to be moral leaders serving society by committing to solving the world's most difficult problems (Figure I.2).

Each chapter begins with the life story of a featured leader who exemplifies the key points of that chapter. Then we introduce leadership principles and frameworks that help you apply the concept, illustrating them through the deep insights of the leaders we interviewed. At the end of each chapter, we profile an emerging leader as well as my take on these ideas. Each Idea in Brief section recaps the chapter's main points, offers specific actions for you to implement, and poses probing, introspective questions to ask yourself in your leadership development process. We encourage you to spend time journaling your answers. Even better, purchase the *Emerging Leader's Guide to True North*, which provides additional exercises for deeper reflection.

The *Emerging Leader Edition of True North* enables you to embark on the most exciting journey of your life by discovering your True North and following your North Star.

My coauthor, Zach, adds: When I began working with Bill as a 24-year-old student, I didn't fully understand how much I would draw on his wisdom during all the twists and turns of my journey ahead. So let me share a message for other emerging leaders reading this book:

- *True North* contains a lifetime of wisdom that can unlock your success.

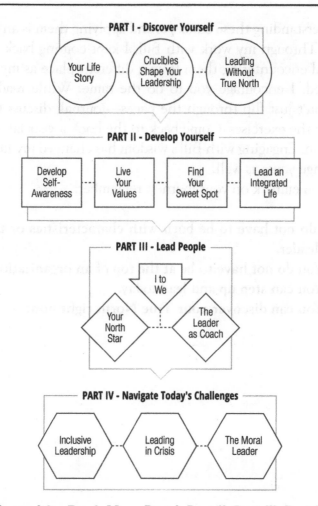

Figure I.2 Book Map: Part I, Part II, Part III, Part IV

- It provides a road map for figuring out who you are and what you are meant to do.
- The self-knowledge you gain and mindset you develop will positively change your relationships.
- The inner journey of understanding and developing yourself will prepare you for the outer journey of making your most meaningful contribution to the world.

Understanding these concepts and applying them is an ongoing process. Through my work with Bill, I kept coming back to these ideas and encountering them from a different place as my journey progressed. I encourage you to do the same. While reading this book, don't just flip through the pages—journal, discuss the concepts, do the exercises. Come back to the book a year later and do it all again. Engaging with Bill's wisdom has changed my life, and it can change yours as well.

As you embark on your journey, remember:

You do not have to be born with characteristics or traits of a leader.

You do not have to be at the top of an organization.

You can step up and lead today.

You can discover your True North right now.

Part One

Discover Yourself

In our interviews with leaders about their development, the most striking commonality was the way their life stories influenced their leadership. Your life story is your foundation. It shapes how you see the world, and it can propel you forward or hold you back.

In Part I, we examine three topics:

1. *How you frame your life story.* Your journey through life will take you through many peaks and valleys as you face the world's trials, rewards, and seductions. Reflection and introspection will help you understand your life experiences and, in some cases, reframe them.

2. *The role crucibles play in shaping your leadership.* The way you deal with your greatest adversities will shape your character far more than the adversities themselves. Much like iron is forged by heat, your most significant challenges and your most painful experiences present the greatest opportunities for your personal growth.

3. *The risk of losing your way.* Everyone experiences pressures and difficulties in life, and all of us deal with fears and uncertainties. In your life journey, you will be confronted with seductions that threaten to pull you off course from your True North. We examine five archetypes that can cause you to lose your way.

As you gain greater clarity and insight about your life's journey, you will discover the focus of your True North.

1

YOUR LIFE STORY

> The reservoir of all my life experiences
> shaped me as a person and a leader.
> —*Howard Schultz, CEO, Starbucks*

The journey to authentic leadership begins with understanding yourself: your *life stories* and *crucibles*. The life stories of the 222 leaders we interviewed cover the full spectrum of experiences, including the impact of parents, teachers, coaches, and mentors; support of their communities; and leadership in team sports, scouting, student government, and early employment. Many leaders were influenced by difficult experiences, such as personal illness or illness of a family member; death of a loved one; or being discriminated against by peers.

These leaders found their passion to lead through their unique life stories:

- *None* were born as leaders.
- *None* had innate characteristics, traits, or styles of a leader.
- *None* succeeded by emulating other leaders.

Rather, by being their authentic selves, they became great leaders, using their gifts to help others. This could happen only if they first understood themselves and their life stories.

All great myths pay tribute to the winding journey of the human condition. For instance, Homer's Odysseus spends a decade traversing the world before he comes to know himself. Though each journey is unique, the patterns are similar. Life involves suffering and hardship. We learn as we struggle and stumble along the way. Through these encounters, *our character is formed*. We gain wisdom, and we find clues about how we can fulfill our purpose in the world.

As former secretary of health and human services John Gardner once said, "I guess I had certain leadership qualities that life was just waiting to pull out of me." Have you examined what leadership qualities life wants to pull out of you? As you read the following stories, think about the ways your life story inspires you and defines your leadership.

Kabir Barday: A Phoenix Arises from a Hospital Bed

Kabir Barday's parents immigrated from India to Atlanta, Georgia, before he was born. Despite facing harassment and discrimination after 9/11, they believed in the American dream and instilled that dream in Kabir. Indeed, the feeling of a destiny of greatness burned so strong in him that Kabir, a brilliant student, was surprised when Stanford University and Massachusetts Institute of Technology (MIT) rejected his college applications. Upon graduating from Georgia Institute of Technology (Georgia Tech), he faced additional rejections when Google and Facebook passed over his job applications. "I was very used to getting exactly what I wanted," he says. "That feeling of rejection was unfamiliar to me."

At first, this rejection inspired Kabir to work intensely, perhaps too much so. After working several years as a software consultant, Kabir founded OneTrust, an enterprise software platform that helps companies do good for people and the planet by managing privacy, ethics, ESG, and security. To jump-start the business, he flew 500,000 miles a year to meet with customers internationally. Often, the only familiar meals when arriving late evening in an unfamiliar city would be Starbucks and McDonald's. Kabir saw his fiancée just about 30 days that first year. He says, "I alienated my friends and personal relationships. I didn't show up at two of my closest friends' bachelor parties or weddings."

On Thanksgiving, Kabir traveled to London to keep working because the British did not celebrate the holiday. While in London, Kabir spent an evening lying in bed in excruciating pain. The next day he saw a doctor who told him, "Your lymph nodes are fully inflamed, which usually means cancer." The doctor recommended immediately checking into a hospital, but instead Kabir traveled to Brussels for his next meeting. Arriving in Brussels, he faced overwhelming pain and was forced to find a hospital in the middle of the night.

Kabir ultimately spent two months at the Mayo Clinic where, given the complexity and severity of his symptoms, even after 300 tests, doctors could not precisely diagnose his issue. The prognosis seemed grim, as he had no platelets in his blood with extremely low hemoglobin and received blood transfusions almost daily. Against all odds, he began to improve.

The doctors still don't know what it was, but they suspect an autoimmune related issue. For a few years following the initial hospitalization, a number of additional auto-immune related issues would surface and remind me your health is something that needs to be constantly respected.

Kabir's crucible could have been devastating, but instead it cracked him open to a new phase in his life.

Today, he meditates to reduce stress and cherishes spending time with his wife and children. "What no medical practice has mastered," he says, "is the connection between stress, diet, the exposome, and the importance of these things working together. Just like you manage your goals in business, you must manage your well-being."

This is a dream job and so much fun, but I never admitted the impact of the stress of being switched on all the time. Looking back, was it all worth it? The company flourished and we dominated the market, but at what cost? I was young enough to rebuild those relationships and prioritize those parts of my life, but the ultimate sacrifice was myself.

Kabir's experiences as a self-described "intense leader" early in his career gave way to a more integrated approach. He learned that "self-forgiveness is the ultimate skill that somebody in my position needs to develop." His life experience also prepared him to lead through the turbulence of 2020, including the COVID-19 pandemic and racial unrest that gripped the country. He explains,

> As brutal as the last 2 years have been, everything has made me a better leader. Going through my own health crisis, I now realize that everyone faces some challenge. Our Black, Latinx, and Asian employees walked me through the experiences they had growing up. Their stories were so powerful that they changed me as a leader.

Today Kabir is achieving even greater success because he is focused on living a more grounded, balanced, and integrated life. Only 6 years old and already valued at more than $5 billion, OneTrust has experienced a staggering 48,337 percent 3-year growth rate and was ranked as the fastest-growing startup in the country by *Inc.* magazine. Kabir reflects, "The only successful way to run a company today is people first with empathy and authenticity."

Reframing Your Life Story

Kabir Barday, as well as all the leaders we interviewed, found inspiration to lead through their life stories. By understanding the formative experiences of their early lives, they reframed their life stories to shape their leadership around fulfilling their passions and following their True North.

You may be asking, "Doesn't everyone have a life story? What makes leaders' stories different?" Many people with painful stories see themselves as victims, feeling the world has dealt them a bad hand. Some get so caught up in chasing the world's esteem to fill a wound that they never reflect on what they want. Others lack the introspection to connect the dots between their life experiences and the goals they are pursuing, which can lead to repeating their mistakes.

The difference with authentic leaders lies in the way they interpret their life stories. Their stories provide context for their desire to have a positive impact in the world. By reflecting on their stories, leaders understand how important events and interactions with people have shaped their approach to the world. Discerning our stories, and then reframing them as necessary, enables us to recognize that we are not victims but people shaped by experiences that provide the impetus for us to become leaders.

Novelist John Barth once said, "The story of your life is not your life. It is your story." In other words, it is how you understand yourself through your story that matters, not the facts of your life. You must actively process your life story to gain meaning and inspiration from it.

Can you connect the dots between your past and your future to find your inspiration to lead authentically? What people or experiences have shaped you? What have been the key turning points in your life? How does your past inspire you or hold you back? Where in your story do you find your passion to lead? How can you leverage your gifts and life story to make a difference?

Howard Schultz: Building a People-Based Business

When Howard Schultz was 7, his father fell on ice and lost his job and the family's health care. With no savings to fall back on and his mother 7 months pregnant, Howard realized the trap that working-class people were facing. He vowed he would do things differently, dreaming of building "a company my father would be proud to work at" that treated employees well and provided healthcare benefits. Little did he realize that one day his company would have more than 380,000 employees working in 32,000 stores worldwide.

Howard's life experiences provided the motivation to build Starbucks into the world's leading coffeehouse. "My inspiration comes from seeing my father broken from 30 terrible blue-collar jobs, where an uneducated person didn't have a shot," Howard says. These memories led Howard to provide health coverage for everyone, even part-time employees.

> *That event is directly linked to the culture and values of Starbucks. I wanted to build a company where you would be valued and respected, no matter where you came from, your skin color, or education. Offering health care was a transforming event that created unbelievable trust with our people. We wanted to build a company that linked shareholder value to the Starbucks culture.*

Howard is proud of his roots. He credits his life story with giving him the motivation to create one of the great business successes of our lifetime. But understanding the meaning of his story took deep thought because, like nearly everyone, he had to confront fears and ghosts from his past.

Born in the Bayview Housing projects in Brooklyn, Howard never forgets where he came from or lets his wealth go to his head: "I was surrounded by people who felt there was no hope, and just couldn't get a break."

> *That's something that never leaves you—never. From my earliest memories, I remember my mother saying I could do anything I wanted in America. In contrast, I watched my father break down while complaining bitterly about not having opportunities or respect. What drives me is fear of failure. I know all too well the face of self-defeat.*

Howard first encountered Starbucks Coffee in 1982 while making a sales call in Seattle's Pike Place Market. Learning he could acquire Starbucks from its founders, Howard rounded up financing from private investors despite 200 rejections. Then his largest investor proposed to buy the company himself, telling him, "If you don't go along with my deal, you'll never work in this town again. You'll be dog meat." Leaving the meeting, Howard broke into tears. Eventually, he raised $3.8 million and staved off the investor.

The saddest day of Howard's life came when his father died. Instead of seeing him as a failure, he realized his father had been crushed by the system. Then Howard channeled his drive into building a company where his father would have been proud to work.

Among Howard's greatest talents is his ability to connect with people from diverse backgrounds. He says, "Starbucks gave me the canvas to paint on."

> Starbucks is the quintessential people-based business, where everything we do is about humanity. The culture and values of the company are its signature and its competitive difference. People are hungry for human connection and authenticity, and coffee is the catalyst for that connection.

Recently, when two Black men were arrested for "loitering" at Starbucks in Philadelphia, Howard immediately flew there, apologized to the men, compensated them financially, and spoke openly to the media about the shame and disgust he felt. "This was contrary to everything Starbucks stands for," he says.

Read More
Howard Schultz, Founder, Starbucks

Go deeper on how Howard turned searing early life experiences, including growing up in poverty and frequently clashing with his father, into the motivation to build Starbucks into a great employer.

Sally Jewell: Advocating for the Environment

Sally Jewell says her favorite proverb, "We don't inherit the earth from our ancestors, we borrow it from our children" inspires her passion for nature and the environment.

As a young child, Sally moved from England to Seattle when her father was offered a medical fellowship at the University of

Washington. Asking colleagues what people did in Seattle, her father was told, "They camp, hike, and join this little co-op called REI above the Green Apple Pie Market on Pike Street downtown." Sally says,

> My introduction to the outdoors—and REI for that matter—came because my parents asked, "What do people do around here?" Seattle is a beautiful place. It's a place where we were able to enjoy the outdoors.

Sally studied engineering at the University of Washington, where she was one of only a few women in her class. Upon graduation, she received 15 job offers, choosing Mobil Oil. Sally's passion for the outdoors influenced this decision, as the job eventually moved her to Denver where she could spend more time skiing and hiking. Those were challenging days for women in the oil fields. She describes regular meetings in men's offices with *Hustler* centerfolds pinned to the walls, and men who told female colleagues, "I love it when you wear tight sweaters to work."

These experiences toughened Sally, who doesn't mince words or put up with nonsense. Once she got a call about an oil leak flowing into a creek. Flicking his lighter, the contractor told her, "I can take care of that leak real fast." Sally responded tartly, "Don't ever suggest anything like that again or your company will never again do business with Mobil." She says,

> I was getting tested all the time by people trying to take shortcuts or people trying to intimidate me or see what I was made of—just bad behavior that's inconsistent with good business practices. I was fortunate that Mobil is an ethical company and that people would back me up.

After 3 years with Mobil, Sally returned to Seattle to join Rainier Bank to review energy loans and became more invested in community volunteer work—a time she says was the "connective tissue to the rest of the things in my career." Her love for the environment and reputation as an "outdoor adventurer, with an inclination toward environmentalism" led her into roles on nonprofit boards, including as founding member of Mountains to Sound Greenway Trust and later to the board of the outdoor retail co-op Recreational Equipment Inc. (REI).

During her 19 years in banking, she rose to executive vice president of Security Pacific, CEO of West One Bank Washington, and CEO of Washington Mutual's Western Bank subsidiary. When REI faced a liquidity crisis in 2000, she answered the call to become COO. In 2005, the REI board elected her CEO.

As CEO, Sally and her team reshaped REI's mission to "inspire, educate, and outfit for a lifetime of outdoor adventure and stewardship." She endeavored to bring the outdoors into all people's lives, and support volunteerism and outdoor stewardship. She established REI's goal of being carbon neutral by 2020, one of the first organizations to do so.

Sally's passion and tenacity brought her to the attention of President Barack Obama, who appointed her secretary of the interior in 2013. Sally views public service as a high calling:

> For the future of our nation's public lands, we need to establish deep, meaningful connections between young people—from every background and every community—and America's great outdoors. We created "Every Kid in a Park" to give four million fourth graders free access to all of America's public lands. I'd like to see 10 million children learning on public lands.

Sally's life demonstrates that leaders can apply their gifts to all sectors—for-profit, nonprofit, and government—if they have a throughline that motivates them. In Sally's case, the essential challenge of protecting the environment has propelled her to have meaningful impact through different roles across diverse organizations.

Read More
Wendy Kopp, Founder, Teach for America

Discover how Wendy developed resilience that helped her navigate multiple crises to build the most successful educational reform program of the past 25 years.

Alan Page: Changing the World through Education

Most people know Alan Page as one of the best professional football players of all time—a member of the College Football All-America team who led Notre Dame to the 1966 national championship, a Hall of Famer who played in four Super Bowls, and the first defensive player ever named the NFL's most valuable player. But if that is all you know about Alan, you have missed the amazing human being within.

Alan was born in Canton, Ohio. His father worked at the steel mill, and his mother worked as a club attendant. He and his family faced constant racial discrimination. He observes, "If you were Black, you knew your place. You knew which side of the tracks you belonged on." In the face of this discrimination, Alan's parents had one nonnegotiable goal: their children would get a good education.

While still playing pro football, Alan attended law school and joined a local law firm. Later, he was elected to the Minnesota Supreme Court, where he served for 20 years before reaching mandatory retirement at age 70. Fighting the discrimination he had known as a child motivated Alan. He believes in the principle of equal justice under the law for everyone but recognizes we are far from that goal. "Our justice system is grounded in discrimination," he says.

> Go back to our original constitution: Blacks were three-fifths of a person. We fought a civil war over slavery, but we did not end the racial animus connected to slavery. People who died during the civil rights struggle of the '50s and '60s gave their lives so someone like me could have the opportunity to do the things I've done. Whatever I've done pales in comparison.

While Alan is known for his football achievements, the greatest lesson he uncovered from interpreting his life story was that education is the best antidote to discrimination—and that his real purpose is to *enable everyone to obtain a quality education*. In his acceptance speech at the NFL Hall of Fame in Canton, Alan said,

I don't know when children stop dreaming. I have seen the cloud of resignation as they travel through school without making any progress. They know they are slipping through the net in the huge underclass our society seems willing to tolerate. At first, kids try to conceal their fear with defiance. Then the defiance turns into disregard for our society and its rules. It's then we have lost them—maybe forever. We can make a difference if we go back into the schools before they've given up on the system and before the system gives up on them.

Alan's passion clearly comes through when he speaks about racial justice or education, but his actions are even more powerful. The Page Education Foundation, which he and his wife, Diane, founded in 1988, has provided college scholarships for 8,000 students, mostly young minorities, many of whom would not have gone to college without financial support. In return for their scholarships, Page Fellows have given back 500,000 hours in volunteer community service, primarily in mentoring young people in secondary schools.

Now Alan is working with Neel Kashkari, president of the Federal Reserve Bank of Minneapolis, to amend the Minnesota state constitution to give every child a civil right to quality public education as opposed to "an adequate education system." Alan notes, "The most basic rights—voting, freedom of speech, freedom of religion, freedom of the press—are fundamental. We have the chance to be the founding fathers and mothers of the future."

Alan's life story is a living testament to what dedicated leaders can achieve when they focus on changing the world through their passion. In 2018, he was awarded the Presidential Medal of Freedom, the nation's highest civilian honor.

Read More

Reatha Clark King, Former President, General Mills Foundation

Follow Reatha's journey from the cotton fields to the boardroom as she works to help others overcome poverty and discrimination.

Phases of Authentic Leadership

When I graduated from college, I had the naive notion that the journey to leadership was a straight line to the top. I learned the hard way that leadership is not a singular destination—it is a marathon that progresses through many stages with lots of ups and downs and surprises along the way as you progress to your peak leadership and continue leading through the final stage.

Former Vanguard CEO Jack Brennan believes that the worst thing people can do is to manage their careers with a career map: "The most dissatisfied people I have known and those who experienced ethical or legal failures all had a clear career plan." Jack recommends being flexible and venturesome in stepping up to unexpected opportunities. "If you're only interested in advancing your career, you'll wind up dissatisfied," he says. The idea of a career ladder places tremendous pressure on leaders to keep climbing ever higher. Instead, Facebook's Sheryl Sandberg favors the metaphor of a career "jungle gym" where you can move up, down, or across.

The leader's journey follows the span of life, which now can extend well into the 90s. Individuals move through three periods of leadership with different types of leadership opportunities unfolding in each (Figure 1.1). There will be differences in the pace at which leaders navigate the timeline, but there are many commonalities among their experiences.

- Phase I is *Preparing for Leadership*, where leaders develop through education and studying, as well as extracurricular experiences and early work as individual contributors.

- Phase II is *Peak Leadership*, which begins as individuals take on more responsibility for leading others and culminates in their peak leadership experience.

- Phase III is *Generativity*, a stage of human development coined by psychologist Erik Erikson. It begins when leaders have completed their principal career leadership roles, and it continues for the rest of their lives. In this phase, authentic leaders

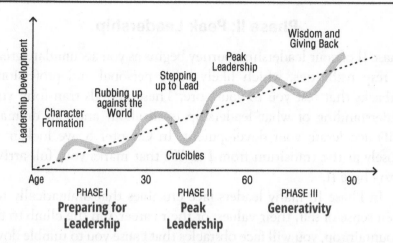

Figure 1.1   A Sketch of Bill's Leadership Journey

look for opportunities to spread their knowledge and wisdom across many people and organizations, even as they continue active learning.

Phase I: Preparing for Leadership

In Phase I, your character is formed as an individual contributor or team leader. There is a natural amount of self-absorption in this phase. In your teens and 20s, measures of success such as college acceptance or early career assignments are based primarily on individual accomplishments. Venture capitalist and author Randy Komisar describes how life begins to further progress:

> We begin life on a linear path where success is based on clear targets. Life gets complicated when the targets aren't clear, and you must set your own.

Gradually you begin to realize that individual achievement alone will not take you where you want to go. Randy says that by "rubbing up against the world," you begin to know yourself and see opportunities to chart your own unique path.

Phase II: Peak Leadership

Phase II of your leadership journey begins as you accumulate great-er responsibilities, which likely bring personal and professional setbacks that test you to your core. These periods transform your understanding of what leadership is all about and can dramati-cally accelerate your development. In Chapter 8, we look more closely at the transition from *I* to *We* that marks your full arrival into Phase II.

In Phase II, many leaders face crucibles that dramatically test their sense of self, their values, or their career. On the climb to the mountaintop, you will face obstacles that cause you to tumble down into the valley. With time, many leaders process these setbacks and move their sights from success to lasting significance. That's when the shift from an "I"-centric worldview to a "We"-centric approach of servant leadership occurs. It will unlock your passions, values, and capabilities to address meaningful problems and make a lasting difference. Whether you are CEO of a large company, founder of a small nonprofit, or leader of an inside team, peak leadership is find-ing your stride as you lead others to achieve a fulfilling purpose.

Phase III: Generativity

Phase III, the last phase of your leadership journey, can be the most rewarding of all. As we saw in the stories of Howard Schultz, Sal-ly Jewell, and Alan Page, many leaders are forgoing conventional retirement to share their leadership and wisdom with multiple organizations. They serve on for-profit or nonprofit boards, mentor young leaders, or take up teaching. Many leaders work across all three sectors: for-profit, nonprofit, and public service.

Warren Bennis described his philosophy of the third phase of leadership with the little-known term *neoteny*, "the retention of all those wonderful qualities we associate with youth: curiosity, playful-ness, eagerness, fearlessness, warmth, energy." Older people with neoteny continue to grow while retaining the youthful qualities of joy, exploration, and discovery. It is a philosophy worthy of consideration throughout our lifetimes, but especially in the final third.

Let's now look at Erskine Bowles's journey and how he has navigated these three phases of leadership.

Erskine Bowles: A Life That Outlived His Dreams

Erskine Bowles has woven together multiple careers throughout the private, public, and educational sectors. In his 20s, he prepared by working at Wall Street investment bank Morgan Stanley. In his 30s and 40s, Erskine built one of the first mid-market investment banks.

Then Erskine served in government, becoming President Bill Clinton's chief of staff, where he led negotiations with Speaker Newt Gingrich to produce the first federal balanced budget in 40 years and later coordinated the Tsunami Recovery for the United Nations. Then he was called back home to serve as president of the 16-institution University of North Carolina (UNC) system. Erskine says, "I never imagined doing the things I did, not one of them. My life has outlived my dreams."

The most striking element of his life is the throughline of service that runs through each chapter. Erskine's father told his children the measure of their lives would be what they did for others. "My dad told us about our responsibility to add to the community woodpile. As it turns out, all four of us were deeply involved in some form of public service. I never considered *not* doing public service. It was just part of my life."

Erskine bought into the idea of adding to the community woodpile. Even while building his company with three young children, he accepted opportunities to serve. "I was leading a rural prosperity task force for Governor Hunt, chairing a project on early childhood education, serving on the community hospital board, and becoming president of the Juvenile Diabetes Research Foundation," he says.

When an important community obligation came along, Erskine told himself he could make time to take on the challenge by doing one less business deal.

He explains, "Money didn't drive me. I had no desire to be the richest guy in the graveyard." Erskine's desire to add to the community woodpile led to his transitioning from finance to the federal government instead of simply pursuing "more." Instead, Erskine sees money as a tool.

> Having made money before Washington gave me freedom to speak truth to power, which is a rarity. When President Clinton got pissed at me, I said, "Look, it's fine. I know my way back to Charlotte, but this is what I think." That formed a real relationship where he knew that he could trust that I always told him what I really thought.

Like so many leaders we interviewed, Erskine also faced adversity, navigating major crises like Clinton's impeachment, the 2004 tsunami, and the Great Recession. He also ran for the U.S. Senate twice and lost.

Yet his greatest regret is not spending more time with his children when they were young. "Raising kids is not a movie. You can't see it again. Once it's done, it's done. I missed a lot of things I'd give a lot to do over now." Today, Erskine makes family his top priority, striving to be fully present with his children and nine grandchildren. "For the first time in my life I'm not just physically with them, I'm all in—I'm mentally and emotionally with them too. Save time for your family. When you're with them, you've got to be all there."

At 76, Erskine is most excited about his philanthropic work, which he approaches with the same data-driven ardor he applies to everything he does. Though his immediate purposes have changed as he transitioned from building a business to working in Washington to leading the UNC system, Erskine's pull to add to the community woodpile has stayed constant. "To be happy, I need to have purpose in my life," he says. "My legacy is what my children do for others."

Emerging Leader: Zach Clayton's Take

My passion for entrepreneurship started as a young child. I launched my first business at age 9, selling yeast rolls based on my grandmother's recipe. Early imprints of entrepreneurship, business, and leadership were instilled in me by my father, a banker who saw banking as a noble profession that made communities stronger.

When I enrolled at Harvard Business School as a 22-year-old, I was one of the youngest in my class. I earned a place there because of my drive to achieve, and I intended to keep it up. A Henry Wadsworth Longfellow quote scribbled on a notecard by my desk reminded me that great men's heights were achieved when "they, while their companions slept, toiled upward in the night."

At Harvard, I met Professor Bill George, who cut an impressive figure on campus. In our early interactions, he asked deeper, more probing questions than anyone I had ever met.

After graduating, I founded a digital media company. To save money, I moved back in with my parents while I was bootstrapping the business—pouring my life savings into the company, working more than 80 hours each week, and trying to create a make-things-happen culture. Meanwhile, Bill invited me to collaborate with him on his writing. Could an ambitious young entrepreneur ask for a more enriching "side gig" than research for one of the world's foremost leadership experts?

Ironically, at the time many people on my team at Three Ships would have called me a poor leader. This isn't false humility. While I had read biographies of the great leaders, while I had heard speeches from top CEOs, while I was personally working with Bill George—I hadn't yet figured out how to be a servant leader who builds strong organizations by helping build up others. There was a gap between what I knew intellectually about leadership and what I believed in my heart.

At age 27, I went to a 3-day leadership workshop and received a 360-degree review based on input from 10 of my colleagues. I opened the envelope excited to read about how much they admired my strengths but instead learned I ranked in the 19th percentile of leadership effectiveness. Comments included things such as, "You tend to be extremely impatient, at times creating unnecessary panic or fire drills," "You can come across angry or abrasive when you don't get what you're looking for," and "Sometimes you're not clear about what you want, and we unnecessarily work long hours at the last minute."

Initially, I considered if I wasn't meant to be a leader and should instead focus my energy on being a high-impact individual contributor. "Maybe I'm not cut out for this," I grumbled. Gradually, the cold water in my face started to wake me up. I shared the results with my team and asked for their help improving, which is still an ongoing process. I realized I needed to transform from a pacesetter competing into a leader who seeks the best from each person.

My own business crucible occurred in 2017, after I sold one of Three Ships' subsidiaries to a company owned by a private equity firm. I joined the acquirer's executive team as chief digital officer. The company had 1,300 employees and was a leader in direct-to-consumer insurance sales. The executive team had semiannual planning meetings in a Park Avenue tower with Jack Welch, the retired CEO of General Electric. We flew around in chartered jets to meet clients and look at acquisitions. It was heady stuff for "a kid" who still paid $1,000 a month to rent an apartment in my hometown of Raleigh, North Carolina.

In preparation for the company's executive offsite, I sent the CEO a 10-page memo laying out the state of our digital operations, recommending growth strategies, and encouraging us to adopt a mission of helping people secure their financial future through high-quality insurance products. At the offsite, the CEO lectured me that I just didn't get it, saying, "The real reason we are here is to make money and play golf. We'll sell whatever makes the most money." He declared he would "rewire the molecules in my brain" to help me understand that we just needed to squeeze operations harder to drive up contribution margin, sell the business, make three times our money, and get rich.

Our conversation that day flipped a switch. I had arrived excited and energized, ready to make the company better, but I left deflated and disappointed. I vowed to remember that experience as I led other businesses in the future. Shortly thereafter, I walked away from the company despite forfeiting several million dollars in guaranteed payments had I remained.

I wish I could say it's been smooth sailing ever since. As I returned my full focus to Three Ships, I pivoted from our professional services business model into owning our own marketplace websites. We resigned many of our largest client accounts, fired more than a dozen people, and funded operating losses while we waited for the new marketplace business model to take off.

I worked hard each day to make the transition successful, but I tossed and turned at night. Many days were dispiriting. The employees I fired felt betrayed, and those who remained almost certainly wondered if they were following the right leader. Some days I wondered myself: Was I making a catastrophic mistake? Did I know what I was doing? Was I balancing respect for all those I worked with and the need to make sound business decisions?

The wisdom I learned from Bill helped propel me through the dark days. "I am more than my business's income statement," I told myself. "The measure of my life is not the success of this business."

During this time, the outcome of our pivot was uncertain, and I had to let go of my attachment to achievement. While facing hardship, I could feel myself growing. I let go of the need to have a perfect resume. I learned to name and accept my weaknesses. When I faced adversity, I shared it with my team and asked for their ideas and support. I talked more openly about my mistakes. I laughed more. While still hard-charging, I gave up on the idea that I needed to show up first in the office to set the pace and now enjoy playing with my four children at breakfast time before I head in to work. Most importantly, I became more comfortable that I am a work in process.

As the weeks and months went on, I could gradually feel the power of the new business model take root. The business purpose came into sharper focus—simplifying the ways people discover, research, and buy. We adopted clear values and made them the cornerstone of how we hired and managed. We stepped up the ways we were investing in employees and the community—getting the Mattress Advisor team to donate truckloads of mattresses or the House Method team to build Habitat for Humanity homes. Our team increased its trust, engagement, and alignment. As we did so, our performance improved—we grew revenue 20 times, expanded from 20 to more than 300 employees, achieved some of the highest profit margins in our industry, and significantly increased employee engagement.

I know my journey will have many more twists and turns. Bill reminds me that many people find their 40s the most testing decade. Through working with him, I have come to understand the power of listening to your life and authoring your story.

Bill's Take: My Journey to Leadership

Growing up in a middle-class family in Grand Rapids, Michigan, I dreamed of making an impact on the world, but for years I had no idea how.

As the only child of older parents, I was much closer to my mother than my father, who traveled 4 days a week and played golf every weekend. My mother epitomized unconditional love. She never spoke ill of another person. All she asked of me was to be true to my values, which I have tried to do throughout my life. She was the matriarch of her modest Dutch family, taking care of my grandfather and bringing her family together every holiday.

When I was 9, my father told me, "Son, I want you to be the leader I never became." Believe it or not, he even named the companies I could lead, starting with Coca-Cola and adding Procter & Gamble and IBM. While I was way too young for these thoughts, the idea of leadership was implanted deeply in my brain.

In high school, I joined many organizations, but my classmates never chose me for leadership. When I ran for class president my senior year, I lost by a 2:1 margin because my classmates did not see me as a leader. I hadn't yet learned that leadership is about relationships with people.

Eager for a fresh start, I chose engineering at Georgia Tech, an outstanding school with a special culture where I felt at home and could play tennis year-round. Once again, I joined many organizations and ran for office six times—and lost all six. I felt like a real loser!

Then some seniors pulled me aside and told me, "Bill, no one is going to want to work with you—much less be led by you—because you are moving so fast you never take time for other people." That was tough to hear, yet they were spot-on. I spent the next year reflecting on this feedback and changing my approach. By my junior year, I was elected to lead many organizations and began to take the first steps to leadership.

Idea in Brief: Your Life Story

Recap of the Main Idea

- Leadership is not a destination—it is a long journey with many stops along the way.
- Everyone has a life story that shapes them and provides the basis for their leadership.
- Everyone faces challenges on their journeys. Those challenges shape our character, which define our leadership because leadership *is* character.
- By processing our stories, we find meaning in the setbacks and craft narratives about our story that shape our leadership.
- While we do not control the circumstances and events of our lives, we do control the narrative we create about them.

Questions to Ask

1. Looking at patterns from your childhood and teenage years, what people, events, and experiences have had the greatest impact on you and your life?

2. In what life experiences have you found the greatest inspiration and passion for your leadership?

3. Do the failures or disappointments you experienced earlier in your life constrain you, or have you been able to reframe them as learning experiences?

4. What is holding you back from advancing further on your leadership journey?

5. What adjustments to your personal and leadership development will you make?

Practical Suggestions for Your Development

- Chart your "Lifeline" by mapping out highs vs. lows on the y-axis and time on the x-axis (see Figure 1.1 as an example). What are the most important high and low experiences on your lifeline?

- Ask a trusted friend to do the same, and share your lifelines with each other in an open, honest, and nonjudgmental dialogue.

2

CRUCIBLES SHAPE YOUR LEADERSHIP

> The crucible is an essential element in the process of
> becoming a leader. Whatever is thrown at them, leaders
> emerge from their crucibles stronger and unbroken.
> —*Warren Bennis, On Becoming a Leader*

Most of the leaders we interviewed were shaped by *crucibles*—the significant trials in their lives. Psychologist Abraham Maslow found that tragedy and trauma were the most important human learning experiences leading to self-actualization. Crucibles teach people that life is uncertain, and they have limited control. Through crucibles, you learn life's most difficult lessons: that life is not always fair and that bad things can happen to good people.

This new reality empowers individuals to challenge old assumptions and understand they must demonstrate personal agency to deal with their world. On the other hand, crucibles can launch people into despair, crisis, and doubt. During a crucible, pain and suffering may overwhelm you. If you bury your crucible—if you refuse to face it—it can bury you too.

Your crucible can also catalyze a breakthrough in your life. When the façade of impressing the external world is stripped away, you become open to deeper introspection and a clearer understanding of your True North. With sufficient resilience, you can emerge from these challenges stronger and more authentic.

Ping Fu's life illustrates how leaders can overcome the most severe crucibles to make a difference through their leadership.

Ping Fu: Bend but Not Break

Ping Fu rose from horrendous circumstances during China's Cultural Revolution under Mao Zedong to pioneer the revolution of 3D printing technology. At age 8, Ping was taken from her home in Shanghai and sent with her younger sister to a dormitory in Nanjing, where she was physically, emotionally, and sexually abused. Yet Ping overcame these horrific beginnings, earned her master's degree in computer science, and founded Geomagic, a pioneering company in 3D imaging and printing. Her story illustrates that with courage and perseverance, people can transform the pain of severe crucibles into the foundation for *posttraumatic growth*.

Ping's first 8 years of life were happy and untroubled. But then, foreshadowing what could happen under Mao's Cultural Revolution, her father took her into his garden one day and taught her about "three friends of winter: the pine tree, plum blossom, and bamboo."

> In the unbearable heat of summer and severe cold of winter, pine trees stand unperturbed. The plum blossom blooms in the midst of misfortune, suggesting dignity and forbearance under harsh circumstances. Bamboo is flexible, bending with the wind but never breaking, capable of adapting to any circumstance, suggesting resilience. . . .the ability to bounce back from the most difficult times.

Ping never forgot her father's lessons: to be unperturbed by harsh circumstances, show forbearance, resilience, and flexibility—*to bend but not break*.

When Mao's Red Guards seized Ping and took her to Nanjing, she was handed her baby sister and thrown into a small room with no bed, toilet, or sink. There she was belittled for her bourgeois upbringing. She observes, "During the Cultural Revolution, I lost my childhood, the mother who raised me, the mother who bore me, and I became surrogate mother to my younger sister."

I went from a beloved child to nobody. No parents around, no teachers. I had no food, we're being fed chickenshit, dirt, tree trunks. That reality was shoveled into my life, and I had to accept it. Yet I had to take care of my little sister as we held each other for human touch. I couldn't leave her as she couldn't live without me. Together we created collective courage.

When she was 10, Ping heard children screaming that her sister was drowning in the canal. Although she didn't know how to swim, she jumped in the water and dragged her sister out. Nearby, a group of teenage boys were laughing at her. They carried her to a nearby soccer field, where they beat her and kicked her so hard that she flew in the air and broke her tailbone. Then they pinned her down, ripped off her clothes, knifed her in the stomach, and raped her. She explains, "They brought great shame on me, calling me 'broken shoe.' I was a ruined woman. The only thing that kept me from killing myself was my responsibility to my little sister. I responded by trying to treat everyone with kindness."

The Cultural Revolution ended in 1976 when Mao died. Having missed K–12 education, Ping entered college where she researched how China's One Child Policy led to widespread infanticide of baby girls. Her writing was published anonymously in *China Daily*, the Chinese government's newspaper. When the publication was traced to her, Ping was thrown into jail and deported, penniless, to the United States, where she studied computer science. Ping says these challenges taught her to overcome barriers:

I never get desperate if I'm hitting big problems. I have overdeveloped self-confidence that collectively we can find the solution. When I hit a wall, I believe there is always an open space behind it and another opportunity. I learned from my journey that entrepreneurship requires self-learning.

In 1997, Ping founded her company Geomagic with a $2 million investment from her family and friends. "My goal was not to make $1 billion, but to touch a billion people," she explains. "Since we live in a 3D world, I wanted to blur the line between our physical world and the digital world." When the company received a $6 million venture capital infusion, she and the investors recruited a CEO with big company experience who spent fast and left the company in debt. At this point Ping returned as CEO. She took no salary, put her own house up as collateral for a loan, and rebooted Geomagic into its most successful period.

In 2005, *Inc.* magazine named Ping Entrepreneur of the Year, writing, "Geomagic has defined and dominated the field of 3D printing." Among its accomplishments, Geomagic improved product modeling in the hearing aid and dental industries and provided software to repair space shuttle Discovery's damaged tiles. Describing her success, Ping observes, "As an immigrant, you come here with nothing, so you have courage because you have nothing to lose."

> *It takes courage to leave your country for another country, and it broadens your perspective on life. As an immigrant entrepreneur, you need the qualities of courage and tenacity with an explorer mentality to succeed, because you must fight to win. Now I am focused on generosity, devoting my time, care, and influence on the younger generation.*

Ping's story illustrates how crucibles can open you up to new frontiers because you believe, "if I got through that experience, I can get through anything."

Crucibles of Leadership

No one goes through life without experiencing serious challenges. In his 1953 play about the Salem witch trials, *The Crucible*, playwright Arthur Miller popularized the term. Leadership guru Warren Bennis says the crucible is an essential element in the process of becoming a leader.

Some magic takes place in the crucible of leadership, whether a transforma-tional experience like Mandela's years in prison, or a painless experience such as being mentored. Whatever is thrown at them, leaders emerge from their crucibles stronger and unbroken.

All of us have had or will have crucibles, whether they were as painful as Ping's or as basic as being rejected by your social group in school. Some crucibles are dramatic and life-changing, whereas others seem insignificant until you reflect on the influence they had in your life.

Crucibles are the real test of your character. If you explore your crucible deeply, it can be a transformative experience that enables you to reframe your life's meaning. You can look back and draw strength from a crucible experience and use its meaning to shape your path going forward.

Crucibles may come early in your life, such as losing a loved one, dealing with illness, facing your parents' divorce, growing up in poverty, facing discrimination, being rejected by peers, or experiencing early failures. Later in life, crucibles can be triggered by events such as divorce, illness, losing a loved one, or being fired from your job. Quite often, crucibles occur when you least expect them.

A crucible is measured not by the severity of the trauma you face but rather by the impact it has on you, which you may not fully comprehend until years later. Even ordinary setbacks can be a cru-cible. This is especially true for crucibles in your youth.

Left unaddressed, crucibles can leave you feeling like a victim or paralyzed by roadblocks. Unresolved anger, grief, or shame may cause you to deny your experiences, shut down your feelings, avoid pain in confronting difficult issues, or struggle to develop intimate relationships.

Crucibles are hardest to address when you are in the midst of them and cannot envision the outcome. You may feel so much pain that you cannot see the learning that comes from the experience. To navigate through it, you need to believe in yourself and your purpose in life and summon the inner strength and courage to endure. These difficult times also require the affirmation and support of those closest to you. Ultimately, it is essential to face these difficult times; as we said before, if you bury your crucible, it can bury you.

In *The Second Mountain*, David Brooks describes life as two mountains:

> *The first mountain puts the desires of the ego at the center. We establish an identity, separate from our parents, cultivate our talents, build a secure ego, and try to make a mark in the world. People climbing that first mountain spend a lot of time thinking about reputation management. They are always keeping score. Their goals are those our culture endorses—to be a success, to be well-thought-of, to get invited into the right social circles.*

Life often knocks us off that first mountain. Perhaps a tragedy, or we just stumble and realize we won't reach the summit we were seeking. Perhaps we reach the summit and wonder, "Is that all there is?" David explains, "People in the valley have been broken open. There is another layer to them they have been neglecting, a substrate where the dark wounds and most powerful yearnings live."

In the valley, we finally accept that we don't have to impress the world. When we learn the wisdom from our crucible, we are prepared to go in a new direction that the world is calling us. From the valley we can begin the journey to the second mountain anew—but this time with relationships, the heart, and the soul guiding the way.

Personal Illness Leads to Purpose

Former Novartis CEO Dan Vasella followed a path to leadership that was one of the most difficult and unusual of all our interviewees. His emergence from extreme challenges in his youth to reach the pinnacle of the global pharmaceutical industry illustrates the transformation many leaders undergo on their journeys.

Born in 1953 to a modest family in Fribourg, Switzerland, Dan's early years were filled with medical problems that stoked his passion to become a physician. Suffering from asthma at age 5, he was sent alone to the mountains of eastern Switzerland for two summers where he lived on a farm with three alcoholic brothers and their niece.

At age 8, Dan had tuberculosis followed by meningitis, which forced him to spend a full year in a sanatorium. He suffered not only from illness but also from loneliness. His parents never visited him, and his two sisters came only once. He still remembers the pain and fear of lumbar punctures as the nurses held him down "like an animal" so that he couldn't move.

One day a new physician took time to explain each step of the procedure to him. Dan asked the physician whether he could hold the nurse's hand rather than being held down. Dan recalls, "This time the procedure didn't hurt, so I reached up and gave him a big hug. These human gestures of forgiveness, caring, and compassion made a deep impression on the kind of person I wanted to become."

Even after recovering from his illnesses, Dan's life was unstable. When he was 10, his older sister passed away from cancer. The following year, his younger sister died in an automobile accident and his father died in surgery. To support the family, his mother worked in a distant town. Left alone at 14, Dan rebelled, joined a motorcycle gang, and got into frequent fights.

Inspired by the compassionate physician at the sanatorium as a role model, Dan decided to become a physician. During medical school, Dan sought psychoanalysis to come to terms with his early experiences. "I wanted to understand myself and not feel like a victim," he says. "I learned I did not have to be in control all the time."

After residency, Dan realized he wanted to help people by running an organization that restored people to health. Joining pharmaceutical company Sandoz, Dan moved to America where he flourished in marketing. Shortly after returning to Switzerland, he became CEO of the pharmaceutical division, a position in which he led negotiations to merge with crosstown rival Ciba-Geigy.

Just 43 years old, Dan was named CEO of the merged company called Novartis.

As CEO, Dan blossomed as a leader, integrating the two companies and creating a new Novartis culture built on compassion, competence, and competition to empower leaders throughout the organization. His greatest success came from the drug Gleevec, which he found languishing in Novartis' research labs. He convinced his team to get the drug to market within two years, breaking all records for Food and Drug Administration (FDA) approval. Gleevec became Novartis' best-selling drug with $6 billion in revenues.

Dan used his crucible experiences to guide him to a purpose that animated his leadership.

My childhood illnesses, the deaths of my father and sisters, and experiences of dying patients had a powerful impact. As CEO, I have the leverage to impact the lives of many more people and follow my moral compass. Ultimately, the only thing that matters is what we do for others.

Read More

Mike Sweeney, Former CEO, Steinway

Find out how Mike's early cancer diagnosis prompted him to reexamine his life and career—dedicating himself to only working for companies that make a positive difference in the world.

Reframing Your Childhood Crucible in Midlife

Oprah Winfrey uses her voice and her empathy to impact people rather than lead an organization, but it wasn't until she was 36 that she fully understood the impact of her childhood crucible. When Oprah interviewed a woman named Truddi Chase who had been sexually abused as a child, she was overcome with emotion. "I thought I was going to have a breakdown on television," she says.

"I yelled, 'Stop! Stop! You've got to stop rolling cameras!'" But the cameras kept rolling as feelings roiled inside her.

Truddi's story triggered many traumatic memories from Oprah's own childhood. "That was the first time I recognized that I was not to blame," she said, as her demons had haunted her without explanation until that day.

> I was a sexually promiscuous teenager. As a result, I got into a lot of trouble and believed I was responsible. It wasn't until I was 36 years old that I connected the fact, "Oh, that's why I was that way." I always blamed myself.

Born out of wedlock, Oprah grew up in poverty in rural Mississippi. When she was young, her mother moved north to find work. "I went to live with my grandmother, which probably saved my life," she says. Yet even as a young child, she had a vision she could make something of her life, recalling when she was 4 watching her grandmother boiling the laundry in a large cauldron. "I remember thinking, 'My life won't be like this. It will be better.' It wasn't from arrogance. It was just a place of knowing things could be different for me."

Oprah recalled the trauma of being raped by her cousin after she relocated to Milwaukee when she was 9. She was molested numerous times by family members during the five years she lived with her mother. "It was an ongoing, continuous thing, so much so that I started to think, 'This is the way life is.'" At age 14, she gave premature birth to a child who lived only 2 weeks.

Today, Oprah has built one of the most respected media empires in the world, but it was not until the Truddi Chase interview that she realized her broader mission. Ever since the traumatic experiences of her youth, she had felt the need to please people and could never say no. That day she finally understood why.

Since then, Oprah's mission has gone far beyond pursuing personal success to empowering people all around the world, especially young women.

I was always searching for love and affection and attention, and somebody to look at me and say, "Yes, you are worthy." My greatest lesson has been to recognize that I am solely responsible for my life, not living to please other people, but doing what my heart says.

Until we spoke for 3 hours at the Nobel Peace Prize dinner in Oslo, I saw Oprah as a celebrity and missed her greater calling. As she described how passionate she is about emboldening millions of people to take responsibility for their lives, I realized the real impact of her leadership. Asked about her show's theme, Oprah says, "The message has always been the same: You are responsible for your life. I hope my show and my speeches help young people get the lesson sooner than I did."

Given the abuse and poverty she experienced earlier in her life, it would have been easy for Oprah to feel like a victim. Yet she rose above her difficulties, reframing her story in positive terms: first by converting her crucible into the strength to take responsibility for her life, then in recognizing her mission to empower others to take responsibility for theirs. Her transformation did not occur until her mid-30s. Often the gestation period takes that long because we need real experiences to see where we fit in the world and help us understand the meaning for our lives.

One person influenced by Oprah's wisdom is her friend Prince Harry, Duke of Sussex, who grappled with his own crucible after the death of his mother, Diana, Princess of Wales. Harry used military service and wild partying to avoid thinking about the loss of his mum. His reality and that of others who experience significant crucibles in their early years is they cannot avoid thinking about them—*all the time*. Just when they think they have moved onto the next phase of their lives, memories of that excruciating experience come flooding back. In response, they shut down their emotions and avoid people trying to help them.

Burying your emotions and your crucible doesn't work because the active mind can't be buried. Even if you could stop thinking about your crucible, this wouldn't resolve anything. Prince Harry describes his efforts to escape the pain saying, "I would drink a week's worth in one day on a Friday or Saturday night, trying to mask something, or take drugs to feel less like I was feeling."

Harry first had to deal with his loss and his anger. He reflects,

> When I think of my mum, the first thing that comes to mind is always the same. Strapped in the car, seatbelt across, my mother driving, chased by paparazzi on mopeds, unable to drive because of tears. I felt helpless, being too young to help my mother. That happened every day until the day she died.

In-depth introspection allows you to deal with your crucible, whether it seems large or minor. As you come to terms with your crucible, you can choose how to move forward. As Harry processed his mother's death with the help of a therapist, he resolved to take greater agency with his own family life. When his wife, Meghan, Duchess of Sussex, faced her own encounters with paparazzi, Harry said,

> It takes me back to what happened to my mum and what I experienced when I was a kid. After what happened to my mum, I didn't want to lose another woman in my life.

Ultimately, he and Meghan resigned their positions as senior royals to chart their own path in Los Angeles.

Although perhaps not as dramatic as Oprah Winfrey's or Prince Harry's experiences, all of us encounter crucibles in our lives. It is naive to think that you can go through life without difficulties or spend your entire life trying to avoid them. The important thing is how you frame and use your crucibles to develop as a person and leader. One of the most important impacts of your crucible is that the experience enables you to overcome your need for external gratification and focus on who you are, your unique gifts, and how you can help others.

Daron Babcock transformed his life after he hit the bottom of a crucible that threatened to swallow him whole. A year after moving from Texas to Oregon to start his own company, Daron's wife was diagnosed with breast cancer and died 2 years later. Up to this point, Daron believed hard work enabled him to control his universe, but his wife's death shattered this illusion.

Daron's loss left him rudderless, and he became deeply depressed. He recalls, "I didn't care whether I lived or died." To dull his pain, Daron self-medicated. He remembers, "I shot cocaine for the first time and felt no pain. Using drugs and alcohol to avoid facing my grief destroyed me. Substance abuse numbs you and blinds you to reality."

One day at the ocean, while his young boys played in the sand dunes, Daron pushed through the waves on his surfboard. He explains, "There was this deep internal pull to keep paddling further as I didn't want to be here anymore, but looking back and seeing my boys I just couldn't do it. I was deeply wounded, but my boys saved me."

Daron's family and friends intervened and took him to rehab, but he escaped through the window the first night. Eventually they got him to stay. He says, "Transformation is too soft to describe my experience."

> It was the difference between life and death, getting the help you need and learning how to frame your experience. My wound is an engine inside me that propels me to this day. In my recovery I went on a spiritual journey and reconciliation with God. I was like the prodigal son wallowing with pigs, when I finally cried out and said, "God, if you're real, I quit."

Daron was ashamed and humbled by his addiction. He says, "Absent humility, life is really shallow; you may die with lots of toys, but they are meaningless." Eventually, a friend who did prison ministry introduced Daron to the Bonton community in South Dallas, Texas. One of the most impoverished communities in the city, Bonton has only a 51 percent high school graduation rate, second highest teen birth rate, highest infant mortality rate in Dallas County, and double the rate of cancer, stroke, heart disease, diabetes, and childhood obesity. Daron says,

We walked up to this house and a guy opened the door with a federal GPS ankle monitor on and this beautiful smile. It was a providential collision, as if my whole life was preparing me for this time. I met my purpose in life with people who had never been told they could make something of their lives.

Starting with a garden in a small lot, Daron formed Bonton Farms and has grown it to two fully functioning farms, farmer's market, café, and coffee house. Daron says, "We are addressing barriers Bonton residents face, so they have a fighting chance at life."

In spite of all the prejudice, racism, and systemic oppression, people here are beautiful people who want to build bridges and be inclusive, so they have an equitable place in this world. Bonton is a metaphor for thousands of other places like it. If we can make it work here, we can do it elsewhere.

Reflecting on his life, Daron says, "Realizing the fragility of life enabled me to search inwardly to find my real values."

When your time on this earth is up, what did your life stand for? It's easy to fall into the trap of gaining the most status or income. Facing tragedy as a young person shifts that paradigm forever. By losing things that were an illusion, I was given a gift of real things that can't be taken away. I don't have much money anymore, but I'm the richest man in Dallas.

Life experiences like Oprah's, Prince Harry's, and Daron's reveal that the pain of crucibles can create capacity for a reorientation of our lives to service for others.

Posttraumatic Growth

After the publication of *True North* in 2007, I received a moving letter from Pedro Algorta, one of 16 survivors of the airplane crash in the Andes Mountains chronicled by Piers Paul Read in his book and movie *Alive*. Pedro and his colleagues spent 70 days in the mountains struggling to stay alive without food or water.

For 35 years, Pedro buried his crucible. However, the experiences kept coming back. From his experience, Pedro cites three ways to deal with trials:

1. Be the victim by living your life looking backward, with anger and blame about what happened to you.
2. Live your life as if nothing happened, while the memories and pain remain buried inside you.
3. Use the event to transform your wound into a pearl.

If you follow either of the first two approaches Pedro describes—being angry about your crucible or burying it—you may experience posttraumatic stress disorder (PTSD). With PTSD, the event is commonly relived through recurrent recollections, nightmares, and flashbacks. The sad thing about being the victim or pretending nothing happened is that you never feel you can trust others and lead a normal life.

The third approach—Pedro's metaphor of the oyster pearl—calls on you to use your pain as a catalyst for renewal, which psychologist Carol Dweck refers to as *posttraumatic growth*. The key to experiencing positive growth after trauma is processing your experience, recognizing the uncertainties in life, and then using a sense of agency to exercise responsibility for the choices you make going forward.

Many people refuse to address or even acknowledge their crucible, saying, "That's in the past; I don't want to dig it up." Burying your crucible doesn't work, as it will constantly resurface. Reframing the event to turn its pain into a growth experience can enable you to use your hardships to help others.

Using Your Crucible to Help People and Transform Organizations

Valerie Keller is a remarkable leader who spent the first 25 years of her life in a religious cult with rigid rules about everything from the woman's role to serve her husband to the clothes they wear. Her parents were "hippies for Jesus," part of the charismatic revival. She says that while the cult gave people a sense of belonging, it had a "fear-based culture of 'us versus the world.'"

As a young girl, Valerie left her home in the Louisiana bayous with her parents and moved to the corn fields of Indiana to join cult leader Dr. Hobart Freeman. When he died, the cult fell apart and her parents moved back to Louisiana, but their belief systems stayed the same. At 19, Valerie married a man she met through the church, and was advised by church elders not to excel beyond him. Although she scored off the charts on standardized tests, Valerie attended the same community college as her husband.

Upon graduation, she realized her real passion was volunteering at shelters for the homeless. When the shelters ran into financial problems, Valerie quit her job as public relations manager for a leading financial institution to save the organization. When she found out her husband was having an affair, she says, "I escaped both the church and my marriage, causing the fundamentalist church members to turn on me. I was all alone."

That courageous move enabled Valerie to devote herself fully to using her gifts to serve others. In the aftermath of Hurricane Katrina, she transformed the homeless shelter into a center for chemical treatment, housing development, and continuum of care. She explains, "I decided to turn my experience in the cult and the church into a positive crucible by working for a higher purpose that was more fulfilling for people." She went on to get her MBA from Oxford University.

For her work on Katrina, she was chosen as a Young Global Leader by the World Economic Forum (WEF), where she says she "found her tribe" in young leaders committed to transforming the world. Her purpose morphed into making purpose-driven business the norm for companies, as she saw the opportunity to help companies do purpose-driven transformations. At WEF's meeting in Davos, she got to know Mark Weinberger, CEO of Ernst & Young (EY), who invited her to join EY as an entrepreneur. Based on her experience as a social entrepreneur, she conceived of creating a new EY organization called Beacon that would work to redefine business as a force for good as she led purpose-driven transformation globally for EY. A year later she launched Beacon at a high-profile event in Davos that included Virgin Airlines' founder Richard Branson, Unilever's Paul Polman, and Huffington Post's Arianna Huffington.

When Polman retired from Unilever, Valerie created the idea to form a new organization called IMAGINE to help companies become fully sustainable, and invited Paul to partner with her. She explains, "We are working with leading food and apparel companies to create sustainable enterprises and transform their supply chains for sustainability for true systems change." She is also helping other emerging leaders accelerate their work through transformational courses at Oxford by creating a community of purpose-driven former CEOs.

Valerie is a remarkable leader whose life is an example of post-traumatic growth. She did not let herself feel trapped by the cult or her church, but used the experience of her crucible to devote herself to a life of service by enabling people and organizations to focus on transformative purposes.

Chad Foster initially denied his crucible, then dealt with it. When he did so, like Pedro and Valerie, he also found posttraumatic growth. When he was 3, Chad's parents noticed he had problems seeing in dark areas. They took him to Duke University, where he was diagnosed with retinitis pigmentosa, a degenerative eye disease.

The doctors told Chad's parents to put him in a special school for the blind; instead, they signed him up for soccer. He played football, basketball, and soccer; wrestled; and ran track. He didn't see himself as blind or visually impaired because his self-image refused to acknowledge his disability. When he lost all his eyesight in his early 20s, he says, "my imagined future-self died."

That was incredibly painful. I was in shock, in denial. I saw myself as a hard-charging young man ready to make a difference in the medical field. After

I went blind, I wasn't even sure if I could help myself, let alone other people. I felt afraid, ashamed, and embarrassed with fears of dependency and disability. I was angry, sad, and bitter.

Chad's story is one not of victimhood but rather of posttraumatic growth. Stripped of delusion, self-deception, and unnecessary pride, he learned to accept his condition. He says, "We need to see ourselves for *who we are*, which is the foundation for self-acceptance."

Not accepting ourselves takes us down the path of defeat, depression, and victimhood. Life is like a game of cards: no one controls their hand, but everyone controls how they play their cards. Instead of asking, "Why me?" with a victim's tone, I learned to ask, "What can I learn from it?" Eventually, the answer came to me: I can give back to others through my speaking, writing, and interpersonal interactions.

Chad goes on, "I refuse to let my lack of eyesight limit my vision."

I could tell myself I went blind because I have terrible luck or that I went blind because I'm one of the few people on the planet with the strength and toughness to overcome it and help others. Both stories are correct, but one frames me as a victim, the other reframes my struggle into a strength. We become the stories we tell ourselves.

He concludes, "We all have fears, whether fear of failing or not reaching our full potential. Courage is not the absence of fear. It is acting despite fear, stepping through that fear. I could live with failing in pursuit of my goals, but I couldn't live without reaching my full potential."

None of us controls the circumstances in our lives, but we control how we show up and how hard we try. If you don't own your life, who will? Excuses are for losers. We can find legitimate reasons to fail, but how do they serve us? It's scary to hold yourself accountable for getting what you want out of life, but if we don't, we are the losers.

Are you a victim or someone who overcomes adversity? Are you letting fears hold you back? How can you reframe the adversity you have faced to realize your dreams?

Emerging Leader: Abby Falik

For Abby Falik, early encounters with poverty seared her. At age 13, Abby's parents took her to Southern Africa, where she encountered extreme poverty. She was confused, overwhelmed, and highly aware of her own privilege. "Once the social justice nerve gets exposed," she says, "you cannot ignore it." Her interactions with kids her own age were especially formative. "I had been told I could do and be whatever I want. Talking to a 10-year-old who had talent and aspirations, I understood she had none of the opportunities I had because of where she was born."

During college, Abby took a year off to live and work in Latin America. In Nicaragua, she returned to the community where she lived during high school. On her initial visit, she observed that despite high literacy rates, there were virtually no books in the community—so she decided to raise funds to build a library.

> Building the library was the hardest and most humbling experience of my life. I felt like I was failing. I had no business being forewoman on a construction project in a foreign language and culture. I remember being deflated at the end of each day that more progress wasn't being made.

Looking back, Abby frames these feelings of impatience and exhaustion as foundational to her learning. She says, "I learned constructive failure. It was a failure to arrive thinking that I, as a foreigner, was going to rally the community and make something happen on my timeline. It took letting go and being humble to let the project emerge on its own."

For the second half of her gap year, Abby moved to Brazil.

I was overwhelmed as a young person in a huge city with a culture so different from anything I had experienced. I had to find friends, a job, and an apartment. It was lonely, disorienting, and ultimately transformative. My experiences that year broke me down. It is deeply humbling when the approach you have taken in one context falls flat in another where norms are different.

Abby's crucible experiences in Nicaragua and Brazil enabled her to see herself through a fresh lens and reflect on her purpose in life. She asked herself, "What of my crucible experience was a useful challenge, and what were the obstacles that were necessary for growth to happen?" The roots of that experience inspired Abby to found Global Citizen Year, a nonprofit that uses the formative transition between high school and college to launch a new generation of leaders with curiosity, conviction, and courage. Abby's organization has funded more than $30 million in scholarships for more than 1,000 fellows to live and work in Asia, Africa, and Latin America.

When COVID-19 hit, Abby had to reimagine her organization since students could not travel. Together with her team, she created the Global Citizen Year Academy to provide 17- to 21-year-old students from 80 countries an intensive leadership experience, delivered virtually. She was able to adapt so quickly because her crucibles gave her resilience, yet she never wavered from her commitment to forge new pathways for diverse young people on the cusp of adulthood.

Today, Abby is an influential voice on social innovation, leadership, and the future of education. Her story proves that painful experiences have the potential to unlock new growth by processing them.

Bill's Take: Coping with Tragedy

Bad things happen in life that we cannot anticipate. In my mid-20s, I faced crucibles that brought me face-to-face with the meaning of life, its pain, and injustices. I was on top of the world as I started my first job. I loved my work, friends, and new environment. Just 4 months later, I received an emergency telephone call from my father, who could barely speak as he told me my mother died that morning of a heart attack. She was my role model, supporter, and source of unconditional love. I was closer to her than anyone else in the world. Arriving home that afternoon, I realized my father couldn't cope with my mother's death. In a real sense, I lost two parents in one day.

The following year I fell in love and got engaged. Weeks before the wedding, my fiancée started experiencing severe headaches, double vision, and loss of balance. I took her to a leading neurosurgeon for a week of tests. All her exams were negative, but severe headaches continued.

When the neurosurgeon told her coldly that she was emotionally disturbed, I knew intuitively this was a misdiagnosis. Something was seriously wrong, but it definitely was not psychological. I was desperate but didn't know where to turn for help, with the wedding only 3 weeks away. When we talked by telephone on Saturday, we were paralyzed about what to do. Returning home from church the next morning, I noticed our Georgetown house was dark with the curtains pulled.

One of my roommates met me at the door and asked me to sit down. Sensing the worst, I exclaimed, "She's not dead, is she?" I felt searing pain as he nodded affirmatively. She died that morning from a malignant brain tumor—a glioblastoma. Once again, I tumbled into the well of grief, alone in the world and unable to comprehend the deeper meaning of what had happened. Thankfully, my friends gathered around me to provide the love and support I so desperately needed.

This was a crucial time in my life when I could have become bitter and depressed and even lost my faith. The grace of God, power of faith, and support of friends provided my basis for healing. Tragic as these events were, they opened my heart to the deeper meaning of life and thinking more deeply about what I could contribute during my lifetime. I recognized there are many things in life we can never explain. The words of St. Paul in 1 Corinthians 13:12 provided the greatest comfort: *"Now we see through a glass, darkly; but then face to face."*

Sometimes in life when one door closes, another one opens. Months after my fiancée's death, I met my future wife, Penny, who supported me in my grief. We fell in love and married a year later. Penny is the best thing that has ever happened to me: an amazing mother, grandmother, leader, counselor, and wife for 53 years.

Idea in Brief: Crucibles Shape Your Leadership

Recap of the Main Idea

- Each of us will experience a crucible in our life, whether it is life-threatening like Ping Fu's or a deep hurt from our youth that leaves a scar inside you.
- Your crucible offers a unique opportunity to understand what is truly important in your life and discover your True North.
- Through posttraumatic growth, we can use our crucible to transform our lives.

Questions to Ask

1. Write about your greatest crucible, and describe:
   a. How you felt at the time
   b. The resources you called upon to get through it
   c. How you resolved the issues if you have done so
   d. How this experience shaped you and your views about the world
2. How can you use these experiences to reframe your life story and understand yourself and your life more fully?
3. Are there ways these experiences are holding you back today?

Practical Suggestions for Your Development

- Think back over your life and recall the experience that involved the greatest pressure, stress, or adversity. That is your crucible.

- Reflect on its meaning for your life and the calling it presents for you.

- Share your crucible with a close friend, mentor, or loved one, and seek their wisdom and guidance on how to reframe it.

3

LEADING WITHOUT TRUE NORTH

Without a moral compass, you will swim in chaos.
—*James Burke, former CEO, Johnson & Johnson*

In the first two chapters, we explored the role that your life story and your crucible have in discovering your True North—your moral compass. In this chapter, we explore the risks and consequences of trying to lead if you haven't discovered your True North.

As a young leader, there are great risks in trying to get ahead too fast, as I know from my own experience. This is especially true if you jump into major leadership roles without first knowing *who you are*. You are subject to being driven by external gratification—money, fame, and power—and these great tempters can control you and your decisions, even if you aren't aware of their impact. In this chapter, four of the leaders we profile are young leaders who tried to lead without a moral compass: Mark Zuckerberg, Adam Neumann, Travis Kalanick, and Elizabeth Holmes. Each of them wound up way off track.

Before you move too fast to get ahead, take the inner journey to know who you are by understanding your life story. Why do so many leaders avoid grounding themselves in their life stories? They may fear vulnerability or lack close friends who can help them reflect on their experiences. They try to bury their past and put on a new mask. Or they get caught up in chasing the world's esteem by trying to accumulate money, fame, and power rather than pursuing their intrinsic motivations.

The consequence of denying or repressing your life story and your crucible can be severe. This can magnify your shadow side—the dark parts of your personality you find less desirable and try to repress.

While the shadow operates hidden from view, it shapes your behavior. Many leaders with great potential lose their way because they do not face their shadow side and find themselves off course from their True North.

Mark Zuckerberg: Leading without a Moral Compass

Facebook founder Mark Zuckerberg publicly touts the company mission of "giving people the power to build community and bring the world closer together," but Mark's actions contradict that noble goal.

Mark founded Facebook as a 19-year-old amid controversy that he stole the idea from Divya Narendra and brothers Cameron and Tyler Winklevoss. In instant messages, Mark describes intentionally stalling his work on their website to secretly develop his own competitive site, writing to one confidant, "Yeah, I'm going to f— them." He later settled a lawsuit with his one-time cofounders for $20 million in cash and $65 million in Facebook stock. In a mediation meeting with the Winklevoss twins, Mark rationalized his actions by claiming that he had done nothing wrong in copying their idea.

A year later, Mark pushed out cofounder and chief financial officer Eduardo Severin. Eduardo's father provided Mark's initial funding for Facebook, in exchange for significant ownership. Ultimately, Mark settled with Eduardo for a reported $5 billion in Facebook stock.

When I first saw the movie *The Social Network*, I was inclined to cut Mark some slack as an inexperienced 19-year-old. As he grew more powerful and continued similar behaviors, I realized this pattern was just a prologue. Today Mark continues his deceptive and unethical behavior—now with global consequences. In 2016, Facebook executive Andrew Bosworth's internal memo rationalized the company's aggressive growth tactics as the price of winning:

> *The ugly truth is that anything that allows us to connect more people more often is justified. All the questionable contact importing practices, the subtle*

language that helps people stay searchable by friends. The best products don't win. The ones everyone uses win. Growth tactics are how we got here.

Increasingly, Facebook's efforts to win came at higher costs. In March 2018, voter-profiling company Cambridge Analytica revealed it harvested private information from more than 50 million Facebook users without their permission. Facebook knew about this in December 2015 but concealed it from users and regulators.

In 2018, the *Wall Street Journal* revealed that Facebook's task force studying user behavior found its "algorithms exploit the human brain's attraction to divisiveness. If left unchecked, the platform would feed users more and more divisive content to gain user attention and increase time on the platform." Mark's response? He ignored the research and axed efforts to recalibrate the platform.

For example, in August 2020 Facebook refused to remove an adulterated video of Nancy Pelosi that was slowed down to appear she was intoxicated. In early 2021 when the *Wall Street Journal* reported a Mexican drug cartel used Facebook to recruit and pay hit men, the company took no action to stop the cartel from posting. In the Middle East, human traffickers recruited women for sex work under false pretenses. In Ethiopia, armed militants advocated violence against ethnic minorities. Other misuses included organ harvesting and pornography.

Former employee Frances Haugen says Facebook prioritized growth over safety because "Facebook realized if they change the algorithm to be safer, people will spend less time on the site, they'll click on less ads, they'll make less money."

Wall Street Journal's investigative report "The Facebook Files" revealed:

Documents show in the U.S. and overseas Facebook's researchers have identified the platform's ill effects, including teen mental health, political discourse, and human trafficking. Despite congressional hearings, its own pledges, and numerous media exposés, the company didn't fix them.

Following the release of "The Facebook Files," Facebook executives were somber: "We created the machine, and we can't control the machine."

In testimony to Congress about the Capitol riot, Mark denied claims that the platform's advertising-driven business model amplified polarizing speech, taking no responsibility, and instead blaming the company's issues on "a political and media environment that drives Americans apart."

Mark claims he is pursuing a more connected world—yet his actions focus on promoting a more valuable stock price. He has ignored the dangerous realities of the social infrastructure he created, feigning optimism and naivety to the darker side of the platform and explaining away issues to factors outside his control.

In early 2022, Mark's flawed business model finally bit the company, when Facebook lost 200 million users in the prior quarter, causing its stock to decline $230 billion (26 percent) in a single day—the most in American history. Mark blamed Apple CEO Tim Cook, who strongly advocates user privacy, for enabling Apple users to "opt in" to have your personal information sold to advertisers or "opt out" to deny its use. In Facebook's case, 74 percent of Apple users opted out of Facebook targeting.

The tragic reality is that Mark Zuckerberg has no True North to follow in making decisions, leaving Facebook swimming in chaos.

Why Leaders Lose Their Way

Ask yourself, "Could this happen to me? Am I vulnerable to being seduced by money, fame, or power? What blind spots do I have that might cause me to lose sight of my True North? Do I have a moral compass guiding my actions?" These questions trouble every authentic leader.

People who lose their way do not start off as bad people, yet somewhere along the way they get pulled off course. Little by little, they get caught up in their own success and are emboldened to push the limits even further. Eventually, they overstep, and it all falls apart.

What motivates you to lead? If your honest answers are power, prestige, and money, you are at risk of derailing. If you have a deeper desire to serve something greater than yourself, eventually these rewards will come to you without seeking them. Sole pursuit of extrinsic rewards can never completely fulfill you because you will always want more, and you will be pulled further from your True North.

Even Abraham Lincoln acknowledged his extrinsic motivations in his 1858 Senate campaign, stating simply, "I claim no extraordinary exemption from personal ambition." He had the moral principles necessary to keep him focused on his True North and his purpose to combat "a powerful plot to make slavery universal and perpetual." Lincoln transcended desire for external gratification by devoting himself to a noble cause that ultimately cost him his life.

Leaders who focus on external gratification instead of inner satisfaction have trouble staying grounded. They reject the honest critic who holds up a mirror and speaks the truth. Instead, they surround themselves with sycophants—supporters telling them what they want to hear. Over time, they lose perspective and capacity for honest dialogue, and people learn not to confront them.

Derailing: Fearing Failure yet Craving Success

Underlying these tendencies may be a fear of failure. Many leaders advance by imposing their will on others and stepping on their competitors. By the time they reach the top, they are paranoid that someone is waiting in the wings to knock them off their pedestal. Underneath their bravado lies the fear they aren't qualified for such leadership roles and that someone is going to unmask them.

To overcome their fears, some leaders drive so hard for results that they lose touch with reality and become incapable of acknowledging their weaknesses. Confronted with their failures, they try to cover them up or rationalize that problems aren't their fault. Often, they look for scapegoats to blame, either within their organization or outside. By combining power, charisma, and charm, they convince others to accept their distortions, causing their organizations to lose touch with reality. In the end, their organizations suffer the greatest harm.

The fear of failure's other side is an insatiable craving for success. Most leaders want to do a good job, gain recognition, and be rewarded accordingly. Achieving success, they enjoy added power and prestige, which can go to their heads and breed entitlement. At the height of their power, their success creates a deep desire to keep it going, so they are prone to pushing the limits, thinking they can get away with it.

Former Novartis' CEO Dan Vasella describes this process:

> *Being successful is intoxicating, but it creates a pattern of celebration leading to belief, leading to distortion. When you achieve good results, you are celebrated, and you begin to believe that you are at the center of all that champagne toasting.*

Five Archetypes of Derailing

In observing leaders who have derailed, we identified five archetypes of leaders who lead without their True North (Figure 3.1).

Can you see yourself in any of these archetypes? Could these patterns of derailment pull you off track?

Imposters

Imposters rise through the organizational ranks with a combination of cunning and aggression. They understand the politics of getting ahead and let no one stand in their way. They are often unabashed students of Machiavelli, determining every angle to advance as they execute their game plan. They are the ultimate political animals, adept at figuring out who their competitors are and then eliminating

Archetype	Pattern of Derailment	Antidote
Imposters	Lack self-awareness and self-esteem	Build self-awareness (Chapter 4)
Rationalizers	Fail to establish and uphold clear values, then self-deceive with a story about why it's okay	Establish clear values (Chapter 5)
Glory seekers	Motivated by the world's acclaim	Seek intrinsic meaning in your work (Chapter 6)
Loners	Fail to build personal support structures, lack the grounding of an integrated life	Build trusted relationships that ground you (Chapter 7)
Shooting stars	Build shallow foundations and keep moving to the next thing	Commit to an enduring purpose that makes a difference in the world, and measure progress against that purpose (Chapter 9)

Figure 3.1   Five Archetypes of Derailing

them one by one. They have little appetite for self-reflection or developing self-awareness.

Abraham Lincoln once said, "If you want to test a man's character, give him power." Having acquired power, Imposters lack confidence about how to use it. They are beset with doubts about their leadership and are often paranoid that underlings are out to get them.

Prior to founding WeWork in 2010, Adam Neumann sold high-end baby clothing. His insight about New York real estate was that Millennials would accept higher density commercial office space in exchange for better perks. Adam pushed this idea to the max, raising $10.4 billion in the following decade, largely from tech investor Masayoshi Son of SoftBank.

WeWork grew rapidly and so did Adam's ego. *The Cult of We* by Eliot Brown and Maureen Farrell describes Adam's behavior as CEO, as he installed an ice plunge pool in his personal office, had the company acquire a $63 million corporate jet, and put friends and family in executive roles.

Adam alienated colleagues through dehumanizing antics. Adam often asked employees to ride in his chauffeured $200,000 luxury car when he was going to a meeting. Once Adam was done speaking with them, he dropped them off and told them to take alternative transportation to their destination.

When WeWork attempted to go public in 2019, Adam's behavior as CEO and his controlling position came under fire. The *Wall Street Journal's* investigative journalism portrayed Adam's darker sides—drug use, shirking work for surfing, and his erratic management style. When the IPO failed, Adam negotiated an eye-dropping $185 million fee for himself as part of an even larger exit package. Existing employees and shareholders were left with huge losses as WeWork announced thousands of job cuts.

A charismatic pitchman, Adam succeeded at selling visions of transforming the real estate industry, but his model never proved financially viable. When he departed a billionaire, everyone else was left with the remains of a broken business.

Rationalizers

Rationalizers always appear on top of the issues. When things don't go their way, they blame external forces or subordinates. Masters of denial, they rarely take responsibility themselves. As they advance and face greater challenges, they transmit pressure to their subordinates instead of modulating it. When pressuring subordinates fails to produce the numbers, they try to hit financial expectations by cutting funding for research, growth initiatives, or organization building. Eventually, these short-term actions catch up with them. Then they borrow from the future to make today's numbers look good, or stretch accounting rules, rationalizing that they can make it up further down the road.

Unfortunately, their actions only make the future worse. Then they turn to more aggressive schemes, such as reporting future revenue streams in quarterly sales or filling customer warehouses with inventory. When these short-term actions fail to stem the tide, they resort to desperate measures that often cross into illegal actions. Ultimately, they become victims of their rationalizations, as do their depleted organizations.

The misdeeds of rationalizers have become all too apparent in recent years. Pressures from shareholders caused many executives to play the game of meeting stock market expectations while sacrificing the long-term value of their companies. Even years later, many rationalizers cling to denial, unwilling to take responsibility for problems they caused. As Warren Bennis said, "Denial and projection are the enemies of reality."

Rajat Gupta was a close professional colleague of mine. We served together on three boards: Goldman Sachs, World Economic Forum USA, and Harvard Business School Board of Dean's Advisors. Rajat was also a board member of Procter & Gamble and American Airlines. He was one of the world's most accomplished leaders— intelligent, savvy, and well connected with the most prominent people.

Rajat was the first worldwide managing partner of McKinsey born outside America. He built a global powerhouse during 9 years at the helm, growing McKinsey's revenue by 280 percent to $3.4 billion. Rajat led philanthropically as well, chairing the Global Fund and founding the Indian School of Business. For the Indian community, he was a role model of the American dream fulfilled, a symbol that an Indian immigrant could make it to the top in America.

On October 24, 2012, Rajat was sentenced to 2 years in federal prison. He was convicted on four criminal counts for providing inside information to Galleon Fund founder Raj Rajaratnam. He shared privileged information he learned at Goldman board meetings during 2008, which Rajaratnam used to make insider trades. In the crucial board meeting to approve Warren Buffett's $5 billion investment in Goldman, Rajat called Rajaratnam at 3:52 p.m., just 16 seconds after the board meeting ended, to advise him the transaction was approved. Rajaratnam then bought $90 million in stock before the market's 4:00 p.m. closing.

How could such an exceptional leader at the peak of his success fall so far, so fast? We may never know the full story since Rajat still denies his misdeeds, but his life story offers clues. Rajat's father was a journalist and freedom fighter jailed by the British when India was fighting for independence. Young Rajat faced a crucible when he was orphaned as a teenager as his father died when he was 16, and his mother passed away 2 years later. With no money to live on, he took responsibility for raising his two younger siblings. Despite these challenges, he gained admission to the famed Indian Institute of Technology and immigrated to America to attend business school before joining McKinsey in 1973.

What caused Rajat to cross the line to provide Rajaratnam with inside information? On paper, Rajat had it all—talent, wealth, power, and respect—but apparently none of this was enough.

As a Goldman Sachs director, I was subpoenaed by the U.S. government to testify in his trial. Throughout the trial, Rajat maintained his innocence, suggesting he was a victim of Rajaratnam, who had already been sentenced to 11 years in prison. Although his net worth was $120 million, Rajat seemed to have an unquenchable thirst for more. A 2013 article in *New York Times* magazine speculated, "Teaming up with Rajaratnam seemed to be his plan for a spectacular career finale—to establish himself in the elite circle of billionaires."

Rajat reflected on this weakness in a 2005 speech at Columbia University, saying, "When I look at myself, yeah, I am driven by money," adding:

When I live in this society, you do get fairly materialistic. I am disappointed. I am probably more materialistic today than I was before. Money is very seductive. You have to watch out for it, because the more you have it, you get used to comforts, big houses, vacation homes. However much you say that you won't fall into the trap of it, you do fall into its trap.

When we sat together at board meetings, there were no outward signs of Rajat's inner struggle, but my intuition tells me he was deeply scarred by his teenage crucible and never resolved his need for financial security. His thirst for money may have been his shadow side, controlling him more than he understood. His story shows how vulnerable we are to temptation if not guided by our moral compass.

Glory Seekers

Glory seekers define themselves by the acclaim of the external world. Money, fame, and power are their goals. Often it seems more important to appear on lists of the most powerful business leaders than it does to build organizations of lasting value. Their thirst for fame is unquenchable. No achievement is sufficient because there are always people with more money, more accolades, and more power. Inside, glory seekers feel empty and envy those who have more.

Greg Lindberg's story is one of Horatio Alger lore. The fifth child of a middle-class family, Greg was first to graduate from college. Starting a trade publication, *Home Care Week*, as a college student, he invested $5,000 in making the newsletter his full-time work upon graduation. He says, "I rented office space for $285 a month and lived there, sleeping under my desk for 10 years." His mantra was "6 to 6 by 6"—working from 6:00 a.m. to 6:00 p.m., 6 days a week.

Greg paid himself just $40,000 annually and poured his earnings into acquisitions, first to expand his publishing business and then to expand into other industries. His formula for acquiring broken businesses was to find a business in distress, buy it cheaply, use offshoring to reduce costs, and grow revenue. When he was limited by Alabama law in funding related-party transactions of an insurance company he owned, Greg moved the company to North Carolina to secure different regulatory treatment.

To ensure this favorable treatment, Greg and his team contributed extensively to the North Carolina insurance commissioner's campaign and formed a super PAC to donate $425,000 in advertising. When a new insurance commissioner was elected, Greg pressured him to approve extremely aggressive related-party deals. He offered to donate $500,000 to the North Carolina Republican Party, with $250,000 directed to the commissioner's campaign fund—violating campaign finance limits. The commissioner contacted the FBI, which wired him up for a conversation in which Greg promised him $2 million in campaign donations to remove a regulator.

The trial made national headlines, as the media chronicled Greg's $35 million in luxury homes, expensive Gulfstream jets, and $45 million yacht. To reward women he met through matchmaking services, Greg provided jewelry, extravagant trips, and, in one case, a $90,000-per-month Manhattan apartment. In 2020, a federal jury convicted Greg of bribery. At his sentencing, Judge Max Cogburn said, "It was shocking that so much could be done in terms of buying and selling government, like sacks of potatoes."

In 2001, Greg Lindberg was a smart, creative, and hard-charging entrepreneur, but he never cultivated the moral character he desperately needed. Greg's glory seeking transformed him into a bully who ran over regulators. Did his lack of true friends blind him to feedback? Why did he shut down those who challenged him, forcing people to fall in line to keep his loyalty?

Today, he lives in a small prison cell. Greg hit his financial goals year after year until his lack of True North led to massive disaster.

Loners

Loners avoid forming close relationships, seeking out mentors, or creating support networks. They believe they can make it on their own. Not to be confused with introverts, loners often have myriad superficial friends and acolytes but don't listen to them. They reject honest feedback, even from those who care about them.

Without wise counsel, loners are prone to making major mistakes. When results elude them and criticism of their leadership grows, they circle the wagons. They are rigid in pursuing their objectives, not recognizing their behavior makes it impossible for them to reach their goals. Meanwhile, their organizations unravel.

Lehman Brothers CEO Dick Fuld was a loner who denied the deep trouble his firm was in. From March to September 2008, his associates warned him that the firm was overleveraged, lacked liquidity, and was inadequately capitalized, making it vulnerable to market volatility. Treasury secretary Hank Paulson had 50 discussions with Dick, telling him Lehman had "to recognize its losses, raise equity and strengthen liquidity." In his book Hank wrote, "My conversations with Dick were very frustrating. Although I pressed him to accept reality and operate with a greater sense of urgency, I suspected that despite my blunt style, I wasn't getting through."

On Friday, September 12, 2008, Hank called the heads of the big investment banks to a meeting to address the implications of Lehman's pending bankruptcy. Dick was not present, choosing to stay in his office behind closed doors, perhaps hoping for a government bailout. He was still waiting at 8:00 pm on Sunday evening when Securities and Exchange Commission (SEC) commissioner Chris Cox called to tell him there would be no bailout. In the early hours of September 15, Lehman filed for bankruptcy, putting Dick and most of his employees out of work, making their Lehman stock worthless, and triggering the greatest financial crisis since the Great Depression.

As a leader, you need to listen to your colleagues, accept honest feedback, and be willing to face reality when your strategy is going awry.

Shooting Stars

The lives of shooting stars center entirely on their careers. To observers, they are perpetual motion machines, always on the go, traveling incessantly to get ahead. They rarely make time for their family, friendships, communities, or even themselves. Much-needed sleep and exercise routines are expendable. As they run ever faster, their stress mounts. Kabir Barday found himself in this situation as he built OneTrust, but his health crisis prompted him to reevaluate his life and his leadership.

Unlike Kabir, many shooting stars move up so rapidly in their careers that they never take time to learn from their mistakes. A year or two into any job, they are ready to move on, before they have to confront the results of their decisions. When they see problems of their making coming back to haunt them, their anxiety rises, and so does the urgency to move to a new position. If their employer doesn't promote them, they are off to another organization. One day they find themselves at the top, overwhelmed by intractable problems. At this point, they are prone to irrational decisions.

Shooting stars place their success above any deeper purpose for their organization, as Uber founder Travis Kalanick's story demonstrates. Travis grabbed headlines for the extraordinary international growth of his ride-sharing app. With profanity-laced tirades, he willed the company to success, often encouraging employees to drive the competition into the ground. As Uber grew to 12,000 employees, 40-year-old Travis explained his management style as pushing himself to the limit. "In a car, you can go fast, but there is a red line. You want to push into that red line and see what that engine's made of."

Red-lining CEOs are not fun to watch. By 2017, Uber was enmeshed in controversy over workplace culture issues, including a floodgate of sexual harassment complaints, issues with regulators claiming Uber broke transportation laws, and a Google lawsuit alleging Uber stole its intellectual property. A video of Travis lashing out at an Uber driver went viral.

While he admitted to arrogant outbursts, Travis saw them as a strength, boasting about Uber's tough culture. He dismissed internal survey data showing his employees' negative view of his leadership, saying he had a public relations issue, not a culture issue.

He lacked confidantes who provided honest feedback. Ultimately, five board members requested his resignation.

Travis had a brilliant app that transformed transportation, but he lacked the leadership to develop a company around the app. His replacement, Expedia CEO Dara Khosrowshahi, reset the culture, established new values, and apologized for the company's mistakes. Dara streamlined the company's sprawling investments, grounded the company in making transportation simple by giving people access to vehicles, and made respect the culture's cornerstone.

The Loneliness of Leaders

It is lonely at the top. For leaders, talking with their subordinates or their boards about their biggest problems and deepest fears is risky. Leaders know they are ultimately responsible, and the well-being of many rests in their hands. If they fail, many people will be harmed.

Because of this loneliness, many leaders deny their fears, shutting down their inner voice because it is too uncomfortable to hear. Instead, they try to satisfy external voices pressuring them. Because the advice of outsiders is often too painful to face, some leaders listen only to people who reinforce their views. As Apple founder Steve Jobs advised, "Don't let the noise of others' opinions drown out your own inner voice."

Meanwhile, their work lives and personal lives grow more unbalanced. Fearing failure, they favor their work life, even saying, "My work *is* my life." Eventually, they lose touch with those closest to them—their spouses, children, and best friends—or coopt them to their point of view. Over time, little mistakes turn into major ones, and no amount of hard work can correct them. Instead of seeking wise counsel, they dig a deeper hole. When the collapse comes, it is unavoidable.

Who are *they*? They could be one of those executives facing prosecution for their actions. Or a CEO forced to resign for personal reasons. But they could also be you, me, or any one of us. We may not have faced a plight as severe as these leaders, but we should all recognize in ourselves the capacity to lose our way.

Emerging Leader: Elizabeth Holmes

In 2015, Elizabeth Holmes appeared on the cover of *Inc.* magazine as "The Next Steve Jobs." *Forbes* called her the youngest woman to become a self-made billionaire and estimated her net worth at $3.6 billion. Six years later, it appears "The Next Bernie Madoff" might have been more fitting.

Like many tragic stories, this one started well. Elizabeth was a young entrepreneur who started a computer business in high school. As a promising chemical engineering student at Stanford University, she worked at the Genome Institute of Singapore, testing blood samples for SARS-CoV-1. After her freshman year, Elizabeth dropped out of college and used her tuition money to found blood testing company Theranos.

A young and relentlessly focused CEO, Elizabeth studied Silicon Valley founders and modeled herself after them. Associates say she deepened her voice to increase her gravitas. Like the late Steve Jobs, she wore black turtlenecks. She built a board of political luminaries—including former secretaries of state George Shultz and Henry Kissinger and former defense secretary general Jim Mattis. They brought connections and star power but—tellingly—no knowledge of medicine.

Powered by enormous fundraising rounds and breathless press, Elizabeth became the darling of Silicon Valley as Theranos' valuation peaked at $9.1 billion. In interviews, she cast herself as a disruptive leader who aimed to personalize health care with revolutionary blood tests. *Fortune, Bloomberg Businessweek,* and *Forbes* put her on their covers. She hired a celebrity photographer to send portraits to journalists, lived in a rented mansion, and traveled by private jet.

Elizabeth claimed her testing device Edison would diagnose terminal illnesses early, creating "a world in which no one has to say goodbye too soon." In pitching a deal with Walgreens, she falsely claimed Theranos devices powered U.S. military's battlefield testing. She later admitted to doctoring investor reports by adding pharmaceutical company logos, so it appeared these companies had vetted Theranos' technology.

Internally, Theranos was a calamity. Her chief operating officer (COO), who became her boyfriend as well, described the lab in 2014 to her as a "f—ing disaster zone." Most shockingly, Theranos' supposedly groundbreaking medical device didn't work. According to the *Wall Street Journal*, patients were given inaccurate diagnoses on cancer and HIV. Many employees resigned, questioning the efficacy of the technology, and rejecting Theranos' toxic culture.

Elizabeth ignored serious patient health risks presented by these issues, treating them as a public relations problem. Obsessed about her image, she directed employees to edit her Wikipedia page and hired law firms to threaten anyone who publicly challenged Theranos. In 2015, I was personally threatened by her vice president of communications for a critical article I wrote questioning her leadership.

The rules in medical technology are different from software products. If Pinterest gets a product update wrong, people don't die. If a testing company misdiagnoses cancer or HIV, the consequences are life-threatening. That's why medical technology has a high threshold for risk. While Elizabeth embraced the role of celebrity CEO, she lacked the medical expertise required to build a medical technology company.

Elizabeth was not guided by a moral compass, nor did she try to develop herself as an authentic leader. Now at age 37, Elizabeth Holmes is paying the price for placing business success ahead of patient safety. In 2018, the SEC banned her from serving as an officer or director of a public company for 10 years. On January 3, 2022, she was convicted on four counts of criminal fraud.

Theranos? It is bankrupt with a valuation of zero.

Elizabeth Holmes' tragic tale is a lesson to emerging leaders: "Fake it until you make it" doesn't work, nor does its cousin, "Fake it until you become it," which is equally dangerous. People will see through you.

Bill's Take: My Moral Compass Kept Me in Check

I was the kid who tried too hard to get ahead, be recognized, and be loved by others. I went straight from college to business school, graduating at age 23. Then I took an intentional detour into the U.S. government, serving as assistant to the Defense Department's chief financial officer (CFO) and as special assistant to the Secretary of Navy. I loved my 3 years there, learning from amazing leaders and contributing to my country.

Next, I accepted a position as head of strategic planning for Litton Industries, working for a wonderful mentor who taught me about business realities. Nine months later, I became general manager of Litton's microwave oven division with the mission to launch Litton into the consumer appliance market.

We grew the business at 50 percent per annum the next 9 years, built our organization from 200 to 2,000 people, and attracted a top-flight executive team. Externally, there was never-ending pressure—from our parent company for financial results, from competitors like GE and Sears, and from external regulators like the FDA.

I loved it, but it was stressful. In retrospect, I may have moved too fast in innovating to stay ahead of the competition and tried too hard to be Litton's best-performing unit, which led to quality issues. I was young, aggressive, and brash in dealing with our corporate bosses.

Luckily, I had a strong sense of my moral compass. Penny's wisdom and support, the insights of my men's group, and learning to meditate provided guardrails to my life and leadership. I was fortunate that these tools helped me avoid the types of ethical lapses that can cause derailment.

Idea in Brief: Leading without True North

Recap of the Main Idea

- There are five archetypes of leading without True North: imposters, rationalizers, glory seekers, loners, and shooting stars.

- Derailing occurs when you fail to follow your True North, beginning the ethical drift which can culminate in behavior that is universally condemned and damages your reputation.

- Although it's relatively easy to rebound from a business failure, it's considerably harder to recover from a significant character failure.

- The seeds of such disaster are sown when we don't understand our journey and our motivations and we place too much emphasis on external measures of success or fame.

- As a leader, it is important to understand our shadow sides, which can pull us away from our True North.

Questions to Ask

1. Have you seen leaders lose their way or worked with someone who fits these archetypes? Which of the qualities of the five archetypes do you see in yourself?

2. Do you have a fear of failing? Do you fear what other people would think about you if you did? Are you avoiding situations in which there is a risk of failing? How could the experience of failing help you achieve your ultimate goals?

3. In what ways do you crave success? How is this affecting your decisions about leadership and your career? Do you only choose situations that give you a high probability of success?

4. What steps can you take to prevent being derailed during your career?

Practical Suggestions for Your Development

- Write down the most difficult ethical dilemma you are currently facing and chronicle the "least generous" interpretation of your actions.
- Project forward a decade and assume the worst: you have derailed in a major failure. Envision the situation in which you could lose your way.

Part Two

Develop Yourself

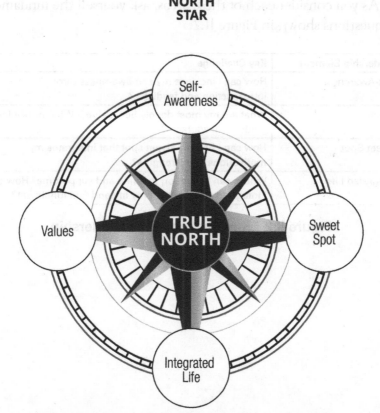

Figure II.1   A Compass for the Journey

Having examined your life story in detail, you are now prepared to pursue your development as an authentic leader. In our interviews, we learned that there are four essential elements in your personal development: self-awareness, values, sweet spot, and integrated life (Figure II.1). With one chapter devoted to each area, Part II challenges you to engage in continuous personal growth as you develop authenticity.

Taken together, these four elements form the compass that guides you to your True North. After each experience, you need to calibrate your compass to ensure the steps you are taking on your leadership journey are consistent with your True North and the way you want to lead your life. Because your circumstances, your opportunities, and the world around you are constantly changing, this is a never-ending process.

As you consider each of these areas, ask yourself the fundamental questions shown in Figure II.2.

Leadership Element	Key Challenge
Self-Awareness	How can I increase my self-awareness through introspection and feedback?
Values	What are my most deeply held values? What principles guide my leadership?
Sweet Spot	How can I find my sweet spot that integrates my motivations and strengths?
Integrated Life	Whom can I count on to guide and support me? How can I integrate all aspects of my life and find fulfillment?

Figure II.2   Key Challenges of Leadership

4

DEVELOP SELF-AWARENESS

Know Thyself.
—Inscribed on temple wall at Delphi, 6th century BCE

Self-awareness is the foundation of authenticity. You develop it by exploring your life story and your crucible, and by understanding how these experiences shape you as a person and leader. You enhance it as you seek honest feedback from others. You refine it by adopting practices that help you remain mindful and aware, even amidst life's chaos.

When the Stanford Graduate School of Business surveyed its advisory council on the leader's most important quality, their answer was unanimous: self-awareness. It is the sine qua non of knowing your values, discerning your passions, staying balanced, and discovering your purpose. In this chapter, we'll discuss how to become self-aware through mindfulness, honest feedback, and self-acceptance of yourself and compassion for yourself and others, which leads to self-actualization.

Satya Nadella: "Know-It-Alls" to "Learn-It-Alls"

When Satya Nadella took over as Microsoft chief executive officer (CEO) from Steve Ballmer in 2014, the company was suffering from a dysfunctional political culture that had missed every significant high-tech innovation in the past decade, including internet search, mobile phones, e-commerce, social media, and the cloud. In my own interactions with Steve, I found him abrasive, arrogant, and domineering. Satya observes, "People would walk around our campus thinking we are God's gift to mankind. Whether it's in ancient Greece or modern Silicon Valley, there's only one thing that brought companies, societies, and civilizations down—hubris."

Upon taking the helm, Satya rapidly transformed Microsoft's strategy and culture, exiting its failed acquisition of Nokia mobile phones, moving into social media with the acquisition of LinkedIn, broadening into games with Minecraft and Activision Blizzard, and expanding its cloud business, Azure. Under Ballmer, Microsoft's stock had been flat for 14 years. Since Satya became CEO, it has grown nine times to a valuation of $2.5 trillion, making Microsoft one of the world's two most valuable companies.

For all his success, Satya is extremely humble with unusually high levels of self-awareness and empathy, shaped by his life experiences and his crucibles. Ironically, a lack of empathy nearly cost him the chance to join Microsoft. During his interview, Microsoft's Richard Tait asked him, "Imagine you see a baby lying on the street, and the baby is crying. What do you do?" Satya immediately responded, "You call 911." Richard put his arm around Satya and said, "You need to get some empathy. If a baby is lying on the street crying, you pick up the baby."

Satya's crucible came during his first child's birth. His son Zain was born with cerebral palsy caused by utero asphyxiation, confining him to a wheelchair. In his book *Hit Refresh*, Satya observes how this experience became the catalyst for his empathy.

> *I was devastated, but mostly I was sad for how things turned out for me and Anu. Thankfully, Anu helped me to understand that it was not about what happened to me. It was about deeply understanding what had happened to Zain and developing empathy for his pain and his circumstances.*
>
> *Being an empathetic father and bringing that desire to discover what is at the core, the soul, makes me a better leader. An empathetic leader needs to be out in the world, meeting people where they live.*

Zain lived for 26 years until he passed away in February 2022.

Satya's first experience with grief and loss occurred at age 6 when his 5-month-old baby sister died. His journey led to the discovery of Buddha's teachings about suffering and impermanence—that life's problems cannot always be solved. Accepting this reality enabled him to develop greater equanimity and compassion.

After he was named CEO, Satya spoke passionately about the aspects of his life stories that had enabled him to develop self-awareness.

> As a child in India, a young man immigrating to this country, a husband and the father of a child with special needs, and an engineer designing technologies that reach billions of people worldwide, all these came together in this new role that would call upon all my passions, skills, and values.
>
> We spend far too much time at work for it not to have deep meaning. If we can connect what we stand for as individuals with what this company is capable of, there is very little we can't accomplish. My personal philosophy and passion are to connect new ideas with a growing sense of empathy for other people.

Microsoft's culture had become dogmatic because everyone had to prove they knew it all and were the smartest people in the room. Satya committed to change Microsoft's culture from "know-it-alls" to "learn-it-alls." He sees the CEO's chief job as being the curator of the organization's culture. The key to culture change is empowerment that brings out the best in everyone. He asks all employees to adopt psychologist Carol Dweck's growth mindset, observing that "a fixed mindset will limit your growth and a growth mindset can move you forward, centered on the belief that everyone can grow and develop."

Satya believes that, with a growth mindset, all Microsoft employees could identify their innermost passions and connect them to Microsoft's mission of empowering every person and every organization on the planet to achieve more. To enable his team members to improve their self-awareness, Satya brought in a psychologist who specialized in mindfulness training. At a remote spot on the Microsoft campus, his senior leadership team shared at a deep level who they are, their life stories, guiding beliefs, and struggles.

"Everybody talks about change, but everybody wants the other person to change and not change themselves. The reality is that the inner change is the hardest one," Satya remarks. "That applies to human beings, societies, countries, and the world." Satya also speaks about his own weaknesses, including a fascination with new ideas and a propensity to move to the next idea too soon. He acknowledges, "I'm blessed to have a very capable team surrounding me who complement my strengths and weaknesses."

How many business leaders can you name who put empathy at the center of their leadership? Who guide their executive team in mindfulness exercises? Satya could only lead in this way because he possessed high levels of self-awareness and self-acceptance. He uses the empathy learned from dealing with his family crucibles to be a more vulnerable and open leader.

Satya recognized that without empathy, Microsoft would never succeed in understanding customer needs and delivering solutions to meet those needs. He has transformed one of the world's great businesses by refocusing it on the needs of customers, rebuilding the culture, and reinvigorating its mission to make a difference in the world.

The Journey to Self-Awareness

Developing self-awareness by understanding your life story and reframing your crucibles should be the starting point on every person's path to becoming a leader. Early in their careers, many leaders try so hard to establish themselves that they never take time for self-exploration. As they mature, they find something is missing in their lives or realize something is holding them back from being the person they want to be. Multiple stressors emerge as they take on more challenges, like getting married, having children, buying a home, managing teams, or losing a loved one. Too often these choices lead to detachment, addiction, infidelity, or other derailers.

How can you avoid these reactions when faced with stress? Understanding your life story allows you to better understand your vulnerabilities, fears, and longings. Reframing your crucibles gives you greater control of your emotional reactions. If you don't undertake this deep introspection, you are vulnerable to being manipulated because you don't have the self-awareness to recognize your triggers.

Self-awareness is the first step of your journey to self-acceptance and self-compassion, which ultimately lead to self-actualization (Figure 4.1).

When you gain self-awareness, you realize that you don't have to emulate other people to be successful. Nor do you have to live in envy of them. You can admire them and learn from them without wanting to be like them. That ultimately frees you up to be yourself.

The psychologist Carl Jung said the greater the light you have, the greater the shadow you cast—meaning people with extraordinary strengths often have corresponding weaknesses. Your shadow side comes from the imprints of your life story and represents the parts of your personality you don't want to admit. One's natural tendency is to hide their shadow side, but it becomes illuminated through self-awareness.

In many cases our strengths, when overused, turn into weaknesses. For instance, a wise, discerning person whose strength is good judgment may have a shadow side that manifests itself through petty criticism. Alternatively, an energetic person who is open to change may have a shadow side that encompasses impulsiveness or inconstancy. By accepting both your light and your shadow, you can become a more integrated human being who can consciously choose the middle ground between these poles.

To accept all of yourself unconditionally, you must directly confront your shadow side and learn to love your weaknesses just as you revel in your strengths. When you accept your light and

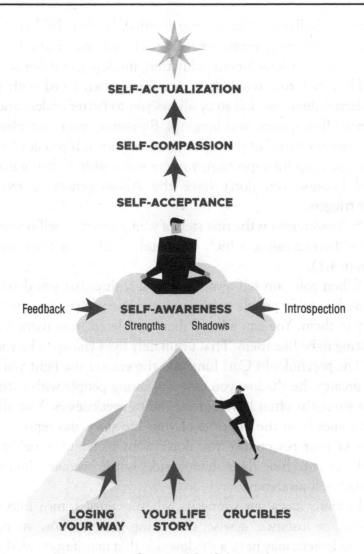

Figure 4.1   Gaining Self-Awareness

shadow, you can accept who you are and be comfortable in your own skin. This self-acceptance leads to the development of self-compassion, which enables you to have genuine compassion for yourself and others, as well as the challenges they face. Self-compassion ultimately frees you up to be yourself and become fully self-actualized.

Self-actualization is the full realization of your talent and potential. Psychologist Abraham Maslow refers to it as "the desire to become more and more what one is, to become everything that one is capable of becoming." Self-actualization is the highest form of self-awareness in knowing who you are as a person and leader.

Confronting Your Shadow Sides

Without the self-awareness that comes from accepting your shadow sides, it is easy to lose your mooring and pursue notoriety and external symbols of success rather than becoming the person you desire to be. Anxious to bury unpleasant memories altogether, people drive extremely hard to achieve success in tangible ways that are recognized by the external world. While their drive may enable them to be successful, it leaves them vulnerable to derailing, as their lack of self-awareness leads to self-deception and errors in judgment.

Randy Komisar was forced to face his shadow side when he left his role as CEO of LucasArts to become CEO of rival company Crystal Dynamics, which turned out to be his worst decision ever. "I couldn't find my reason for being there," he says. "The business floundered and ultimately succeeded, but I failed. I had to ask myself, 'What do I want out of life?'"

Randy resigned after a year and began practicing meditation to gain clarity on what he wanted to do and who he wanted to be. After reflection, he realized his inner struggles between material success and intrinsic fulfillment traced back to his father, who gambled constantly. "When he lost money, we feared we couldn't pay our college tuition. Insecurity about money was ingrained in me as a child," he says. Randy realized he had to release himself from his father's influence and stop climbing a success ladder to live his own life.

Self-Awareness Grounds You

Angela Ahrendts had a wake-up call on her journey to self-awareness as she neared the top of Liz Claiborne. When the Liz Claiborne board was considering her as successor to CEO Paul Charron, corporate leaders and consultants tried to mold Angela into their own image of a successful leader. The head of human resources told her, "We are concerned about your style and think you could dress more seriously. We'd like you to work with consultants to learn to become more corporate."

In what was supposed to be a 3-day workshop, the consultants told her after 1 hour of filming, "You talk too much with your hands. Try and hold them this way. You talk too fast; you need to talk slower and deeper, like a news announcer." Then they filmed her again. She says,

> By lunchtime that first day, I was so upset that I got teary-eyed and started to cry. I told the consultants, "I like me. I want to be the best version of me. I don't like the person you're trying to make me become. I never want to be that way, so I'm leaving." Back in New York, I told the head of HR [human resources], "I don't care if you want me to be CEO; I am not changing." That experience hurt me, but I had to get over it.

Just a week later, Angela was asked to become Burberry's CEO, where she attributes her success to being herself. "We became this incredible team. Our energy, passion, and love for one another enabled us to succeed. With me it always begins and ends with people. That's why I have opted not to change."

Had Angela adopted a more corporate style to get ahead, would she have been as successful at Burberry? I doubt it. I had similar experiences at Litton and Honeywell, where senior managers repeatedly told me to be less passionate and to hide my feelings. Had I done so, I too would have sacrificed my greatest strengths. After 9 years as CEO of Burberry, Angela was recruited by Tim Cook to join Apple to lead retail, online stores, and "Today at Apple." Today she serves on the boards of Ralph Lauren, Airbnb, and WPP and is chair of Save the Children.

Angela's story illustrates the importance of being yourself and *blooming where you're planted*—growing from your life story, your crucibles, and your values. By building on that solid foundation and being comfortable with who you are, there are no limits to what you can achieve. This is not a static way of being. Rather as an authentic leader, you are constantly growing by trying new things and taking on new challenges. We are constantly evolving as we test ourselves in the world, are influenced by it, and adapt to it—all to find our unique place.

Arianna Huffington also had a wake-up call on her journey to self-awareness. Several years after starting the *Huffington Post*, Arianna's celebrity was rising, as *Time* magazine chose her as one of the world's 100 Most Influential People.

Then she found herself lying on the floor of her home office in a pool of blood, having collapsed from exhaustion. She explains,

> *On my fall, my head hit the corner of my desk, cutting my eye and breaking my cheekbone. I went from doctor to doctor, from brain MRI [magnetic resonance imaging] to CAT [computed tomography] scan to ECG [electrocardiogram], to find out if I had an underlying medical problem beyond exhaustion. There wasn't, but doctors' waiting rooms were good places to ask myself deeper questions about the kind of life I was living.*

Arianna's collapse forced her to confront reality: "I was working 18 hours a day, 7 days a week, trying to build a business, expand our coverage, and bring in investors. My life was out of control. I asked myself, 'Is this what success looks like? Is this the life I want?'"

In her book *Thrive*, Arianna notes our capacity for well-being truly enriches our lives. "Society has a widespread longing to redefine success and what it means to lead the good life," she writes. "Recently, we shifted our attention to how much money we make, how big a house we buy, and how high we climb the career ladder. As I discovered painfully, these are not the only questions that matter in creating a successful life. It must go beyond money and power, and include well-being, wisdom, wonder, and giving."

Like many of us, Arianna's journey to self-awareness took many turns. Until her wake-up call, money, fame, and power distracted her from her True North. How can the woman who frequently discussed her yearning for wisdom sacrifice her health and well-being?

This is a common occurrence for high performers, who walk a tightrope between the drive that makes them successful and the perspective that keeps them grounded. Self-awareness acts as an internal ballast between intensity and reflection. Arianna recognized she had to change her behavior before something more dramatic occurred. Her ability to step back and observe the dichotomy between her vision and her behavior serves as a useful model for us all.

Acknowledge Your Imperfections

The hardest part of being self-aware is facing our weaknesses. To do so, you need honest feedback to identify your blind spots and acknowledge your imperfections.

Former Charles Schwab CEO Dave Pottruck set the pace with his aggressiveness and long hours. He recalls, "I thought my accomplishments spoke for themselves." Dave was shocked when his boss told him, "Your colleagues don't trust you." He recalls, "That was like a dagger to my heart. I was in denial, as I didn't see myself as others saw me."

Dave found changing was a very difficult process. "The more stress you are under, the more you revert to your old patterns." Then how do leaders change? They find the space between a stimulus and their response, then observe themselves in that space. When you observe that moment, you begin to realize you can change your response.

After his second divorce, Dave realized he still had large blind spots. He says, "When my first marriage ended, I was convinced it was all her fault. After my second marriage fell apart, I thought I had a wife selection problem." Then he worked with a counselor, who told him, "I have good news and bad news. The good news is you don't have a wife selection problem; the bad news is you have a husband behavior problem."

Dave explains, "Denial is the biggest challenge we face. To overcome it, you must be honest with yourself and not make excuses or blame others." Dave learned not to mask his natural self, but rather bring forth parts of his true self that he had previously cloaked.

He did this by sharing stories that showed his vulnerabilities and imperfections. As a result, his colleagues connected with him more authentically.

Peeling Back the Onion

As you search for your true self, you are essentially peeling back the layers of an onion (Figure 4.2). The outer layers are the ways you present yourself to the world—how you look, your facial expressions,

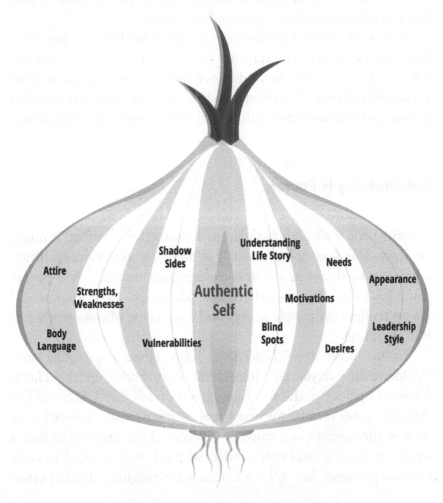

Figure 4.2   Peeling Your Onion

body language, attire, and leadership style. Often these outer layers are hardened to protect you from criticism of your inner self. I once asked a mentee why he spent so much time in front of the mirror. His answer was telling: "I need to look good on the outside, because I feel rotten on the inside."

Peeling the onion further, you reach your inner core where you gain a deeper understanding of your strengths, weaknesses, values, and motivations. Underneath these layers lies your understanding of your life story. As you approach your inner core, you find your shadow sides, blind spots, and vulnerabilities. At the core of your being is who you really are—your True North.

Your inner layers feel tender and vulnerable because they have not been exposed to the scrutiny of the outside world. When you don't feel safe, you hide your inner layers to protect them from exposure and harm. Too often, this leads to developing a false self or persona, which interferes with your ability to form genuine connections with others.

Vulnerability Is Power

What if we were willing to be vulnerable and expose our full selves to other people without false layers of protection? At first, it might be scary. We fear being rejected if we show our vulnerabilities, admit our weaknesses, and acknowledge our mistakes. Will people think less of us? Will they try to take advantage of our weaknesses? As we realize that people accept and love us for who we really are, it is liberating.

In his book *Love Leadership*, John Hope Bryant declares, "Vulnerability is power." John's life story backs up the claim. Growing up poor in the rough neighborhood of South-Central Los Angeles, John recalls, "When I was 5, my parents divorced over money, the number one cause of divorce." That instilled in him a strong work ethic and entrepreneurial spark that resulted in early business successes, but by his teens, he was struggling. "I didn't know my True North and didn't have any role models to help me figure it out," he explains.

> I faked it, acting like a big cheese, wearing sunglasses at night to feel important. It was just low self-esteem. Then I lost an investor's money and couldn't pay him back and wound up homeless. I went from having a beach house in Malibu to homeless, living in my leased Jeep. Everybody knew I lost everything because I was so arrogant. People were literally cheering for my failure.

When the police officers who beat Rodney King were found not guilty, people rioted in John's neighborhood. "I remember asking Reverend Jesse Jackson what I can do to help," he says. "He told me, 'We need businesspeople with investment to rebuild this community. Take your business skills and put them to work.'"

The next day, 19-year-old John organized a group of bankers to take a bus tour through South-Central Los Angeles. That eventually led to the founding of Operation HOPE, a nonprofit that focuses on financial literacy and mobility. As CEO, John has partnered with former president Bill Clinton and *Fortune 500* CEOs on a bold goal of building one million Black businesses by 2030.

In realizing his shortcomings and building self-awareness, John had the resilience to bounce back from adversity and the courage to share his story.

> Being self-aware without being vulnerable leads to depression and schizophrenia because there's no expression. We're looking for love in all the wrong places. Our addictions are caused by emotions we can't handle, so we medicate ourselves with drugs, alcohol, shopping, overworking, or sex.
>
> There are three ways to live: suicide; coping, which most of society does; and healing. Healing is the only path forward. It takes the most courage and is the most terrifying. To heal, you've got to get over fear of being yourself.

John admits he is less than perfect, but this makes him more sympathetic, believable, and persuasive. John's vulnerability is his power. Through his authenticity, others connect deeply with him.

Developing Self-Compassion

Only when leaders accept who they are can they be comfortable in their skin. Then we can have compassion for ourselves and the challenges we face. Only through self-compassion can we have genuine compassion for others and the difficulties they have faced. This requires loving yourself unconditionally.

In *The Poetry of Self Compassion*, poet David Whyte says in knowing your weaknesses and shadow sides, you can accept things you like least about yourself. David says you cannot wall yourself off from the pain of past experiences which you have hidden. If you repress those experiences, you allow them to control you. By confronting your shadow side, you can accept yourself unconditionally, and accept your weaknesses just as you revel in your strengths.

Armed with high levels of self-awareness and self-acceptance, you are prepared to regulate your emotions and your behavior. Emotional outbursts result from someone penetrating things you don't like about yourself and still cannot accept. By accepting yourself, you are no longer vulnerable to these hurts.

Then you are prepared to interact authentically with people in your life—your family, friends, and coworkers, even complete strangers. Freed of wearing a mask, you can focus on pursuing your passions. That leads you to self-actualization, enabling you to fulfill your greatest dreams.

Practice Mindfulness

As the pace of technological change accelerates, leaders face greater pressures and more distractions from an unending barrage of phone calls, calendar appointments, text messages, and emails. Too often, our culture equates busyness with success—glorifying modern execs as on-the-go, tech-enabled, multitasking operators who do everything at warp speed.

In today's frenetic world where we are electronically connected 24/7, we need to have daily practices that enable us to pause and focus on ourselves. You should take at least 20 minutes every day to pause and reflect on your day and your leadership. Mindfulness is an especially valuable way to do this because it increases your tranquility, wisdom, and ability to focus on what is important.

As a mindful leader, you can ask how you can reshape the way you work rather than letting it control you. Mindfulness focuses your attention on your thoughts, emotions, and feelings in the present moment. In so doing, you can take stock of your actions and pressures, and go deeper inside yourself. Meditation is the introspective practice leaders find most effective in focusing their attention and calming themselves. In recent years it has come of age as a mainstream practice.

If you have ever tried to pause for a few minutes and clear your thoughts, you realize how hard it is to separate yourself from the constant whirlwind of activity in your mind. The conscious mind is conditioned to think constantly. You try to focus on your breathing, but you think about the upcoming presentation at work, the conflict with your spouse, or how to get your kids to their soccer games. Meditation is simply acknowledging your thoughts and letting them go.

For 45 years, mindfulness expert Jon Kabat-Zinn has created secular programs in mindfulness-based stress reduction. Jon observes,

> Mindfulness is about our whole beings. When we are all mind, things get rigid. When we are all heart, things get chaotic. Both lead to stress. When the mind and heart work together—the heart leading through empathy, the mind guiding us with focus and attention—we become harmonious human beings.

Neuroscience research shows that a regular mindfulness practice helps rewire the brain, making us calmer, more compassionate, more focused, and less reactive. Leading companies, such as General

Mills, Aetna, BlackRock, and Goldman Sachs, are encouraging employees to establish meditation practices. At Google, Chade-Meng Tan created Search Inside Yourself, a program that teaches 2,000 Googlers per year to meditate. He says, "My breakthrough came when I discovered meditation."

> *This was a moment of insight where everything in my life made sense.*
> *Through meditation I learned the ability to calm my mind and stay in a state*
> *of clarity and calmness. Kindness and compassion are key to my practice. You*
> *cannot be genuinely compassionate toward others if you have no compassion*
> *for yourself.*

Seventh Generation's John Replogle says meditation is key to his leadership: "It grows from a personal practice, but it's key to well-being. If we want people to achieve their fullest potential and be happy and successful at work, we need to create an environment where people can thrive." John personally meditates or does yoga every day. There are other introspective practices that leaders find effective: centering prayer, time in nature, or deep discussions with a loved one. The important thing is having a practice you do daily.

Read More

Chade-Meng Tan, Former "Jolly Good Fellow," Google

Discover how meditation transformed Chade-Meng's life and inspired him to share the practice with thousands of people around the world.

Seek Honest Feedback

Another important skill that leaders need to develop self-awareness is the ability to see themselves as others see them. The Johari window is a framework that leaders use to be fully open, transparent, and authentic with others (Figure 4.3).

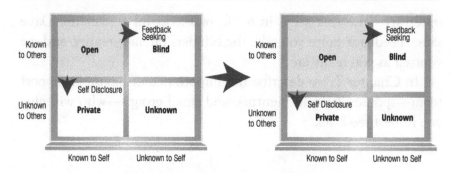

Figure 4.3 The Johari Window

For many of us, the upper left quadrant (*known to ourselves and others*) is far too small. Opening up this quadrant enables us to become more authentic by sharing our hidden areas with other people, describing our life story and difficult times, and exposing our weaknesses. When we do, we are validated by others—not rejected as many fear—which enables us to be ourselves.

Our blind spots in the upper right quadrant (*known to others but unknown to us*) is the most difficult area to address. All of us have traits, habits, and tendencies that others see in us, but we are unable to see in ourselves. The only way to open our blind spots is to get honest feedback from others and take it to heart. Honest feedback is often hard to get, because many people tell leaders what they want to hear. For this reason, leaders should solicit feedback from their peers and subordinates through one-on-one meetings or 360-degree surveys. Taking psychological inventories can be helpful too, such as Myers-Briggs, StrengthsFinder, and Enneagram.

Former Kroger CEO Dave Dillon discovered the value of feedback during college after he lost an important election. His first reaction was to get defensive and think, "I'm better than that guy. Why didn't they choose me?" Following introspection, he realized, "My point of view wasn't relevant. The important one was what others thought." Through feedback, he learned he had traits that needed improvement. As a result, he went on to become president of the student body at the University of Kansas and of his fraternity—the first steps in a life of successful leadership. Dave says, "Feedback helps you take the blinders off, face reality, and see yourself as you really are."

In Chapter 7, we describe the importance of having a support team—spouses, friends, mentors, and small groups—who will give you honest feedback.

Emerging Leader: Davis Smith

"From the time I can remember, I was different," says Davis Smith, the 42-year-old CEO of fast-growing adventure gear company Cotopaxi. Davis lived in the Dominican Republic from age 4 and, as a Mormon, had a different religion from everyone else. When his family moved back to the United States, he says he was very aware of those who were different—because he had been that person.

Growing up around extreme poverty while immersed in a different culture, Davis became more attuned to others. "One of the things I learned was that I am not better or smarter or more ambitious; my life is different simply because of where I was born," he says. "Those experiences shaped my worldview."

Davis gained greater self-awareness as a Mormon missionary. During this time, he says, "Your entire life is focused on other people."

Listening to others and talking about your connection with God, you must be self-aware. That experience plays a huge role in my life. When I'm focused on others, I feel the most fulfillment.

Cotopaxi has grown nearly 100 percent annually since inception as top private equity firms have lobbed in rich offers to invest. But in our interview, Davis wasn't interested in talking about the business's financials; he wanted to talk only about its culture.

Two times a year Cotopaxi employees gather for weeklong summer camp experiences. Davis offers employees 10 percent time to volunteer or be in nature as part of their work hours. The company holds weekly nature zooms, where people walk through forests and share what they're seeing. Employees volunteer together, eat meals together, and strive for balance. Davis himself leaves the office at reasonable hours and spends significant time parenting his four children and volunteering as a lay leader in the Church of Jesus Christ of Latter-day Saints.

While Davis has significant demands on his time, he prioritizes daily prayer and reflection, which he likens to meditation. "I'm constantly reflecting on how I can improve and identifying areas where I need help and guidance." Davis is extremely open about failures in his earlier business ventures, shortcomings at Cotopaxi, and his weaknesses as a leader. "We all know the successes, but when we hear about heartbreaks and challenges from people we admire, it gives us hope."

Through these experiences and practices, Davis cultivates a deeper level of self-awareness and radiates authenticity. He has built trusted partnerships with his team members who are highly engaged in Cotopaxi's mission. He is excited about his company and the ways it is uplifting communities through ethical sustainability while giving a minimum of 1 percent of revenues for grants to humanitarian organizations. "Our purpose here on earth is to discover our talents and use them to help others," he says. "My goal isn't to sell outdoor gear; it's to fight poverty. We exist to do good. We sell the best outdoor gear to fund our impact work, not the other way around."

Bill's Take: Feeling Good in My Skin

For many years, I felt I had to do things perfectly and have all the answers. I lacked confidence to share my weaknesses, fears, and vulnerabilities. Early in my career I worked under a CEO who tried to bully me, triggering my tendency to overreact. I found it more difficult to regulate my emotions and control my fears. To protect myself psychologically, I put on armor.

At Penny's insistence, I attended a 2-day program on transcendental meditation in 1975. At the time I was going nonstop from dawn until dusk, having late dinners and coming home exhausted. It took meditation and honest, critical feedback for me to change. Since then, I have mediated daily, and my life has improved significantly because I feel comfortable in my skin.

Years ago, I learned an important lesson from Buddhist monk Thích Nhất Hạnh, who told me, "The longest journey you will ever take is the 18 inches from your head to your heart." Our hearts are where such essential leadership qualities as compassion and courage reside. Meditation is the best thing to calm myself and disconnect from the 24/7, connected world. Through meditation, I have gained clarity about important issues and developed an inner sense of well-being. Meditation has enabled me to build resilience to deal with difficult times.

The Oracle of Delphi says, "Know thyself," but few of us really do. Developing self-awareness takes reflection and feedback. That means getting rid of the electronics to clear your head and having open, unhurried dialogue with those who know and trust you. Penny's insights and my True North group have been sources of truth during big inflection points in my life. Self-awareness is the key to everything because all positive changes begin with an honest appraisal of who we are, where we are, and why we are here.

Idea in Brief: Develop Self-Awareness

Recap of the Main Idea

- Self-awareness is the most essential determinant of your effectiveness as a leader.
- Developing greater self-awareness begins with real reflection on your life journey, including what your crucibles reveal.
- Leaders build self-awareness through both feedback and introspection on a regular basis.

- Introspection increases your own attunement to the relationship between the stimuli you face and your response, enabling you to *choose* your behavior in the moment between them.

- When compassion is combined with self-awareness, we begin to see self-acceptance, which will move you closer to the full realization of your talent and potential (i.e., self-actualization).

Questions to Ask

1. How comfortable are you with who you are right now?
2. What are your vulnerabilities and shadow sides?
3. Who are your truth tellers?
4. How do you handle displeasing situations or critical feedback from others?
5. Whom do you speak to about complex or sensitive issues?
6. How skillful are you in building lasting relationships?

Practical Suggestions for Your Development

- Ask for informal feedback from someone at least once a day; this could be as simple as a 1–5 rating after each meeting.

- Find a centering practice such as meditating for at least 20 minutes each day.

- Promote vulnerability by making a regular effort to disclose a weakness or development area to a colleague.

- Receive a confidential 360-degree assessment from those around you at least once a year.

5

LIVE YOUR VALUES

The softest pillow is a clear conscience.
—N. R. Murthy, *founder and CEO, Infosys*

Your values are standards of behavior that shape your True North, derived from your beliefs and convictions. Staying centered on those values is not easy because temptations and pressures of the outside world often conspire to pull you away from your True North. Being clear about your values is essential to sustaining your leadership and not getting pulled off course as Rajat Gupta did.

The most challenging test of your leadership comes when you have a great deal to lose by staying true to your values. Upholding your values requires moral courage by taking action for moral reasons despite the adverse consequences. Are there moral issues you would stand up for that could cause you to lose everything you worked for your entire life? For Merck chief executive officer (CEO) Ken Frazier, that answer is yes.

Ken Frazier: Demonstrating Moral Courage

Ken Frazier learned the importance of staying true to your values from his father. "My father was self-taught, read two newspapers daily, and spoke immaculate English," Ken says. "To escape indentured servitude, he was sent north by my grandfather, who was born a slave in South Carolina."

My father was the most influential human being I have ever known. He taught me the most important lesson of my life: "Kenny, what will you do as the grandson of the man who started this narrative of being free and being your own person? You better do what you know is right, and not fixate on what other people think of you." I learned from my father not to go along with the crowd.

At 15, Ken won appointment to West Point but was denied admission for being too young, so he attended Penn State on scholarship. While there, he decided he wanted "to become a great lawyer like Thurgood Marshall, effecting social change." At Harvard Law School, he was acutely aware he wasn't from the same social class as his classmates. He notes wryly, "Lloyd Blankfein and I were among few students who 'were not of the manor born.'"

Upon graduation, Ken joined a law firm with a public service ethos, making partner at age 30. Once again, he found himself crossing social barriers, observing, "I was an African American from the inner city in a firm of lawyers from Philadelphia's upper crust." His legal work included pro bono efforts, such as teaching Black lawyers in South Africa during apartheid. He says, "My proudest moment came from winning freedom for an innocent prisoner who was on Alabama's death row for 20 years."

In Alabama, I was a stranger in a strange land. Entering the courtroom that first day, the bailiff told me, "Down here we don't wear blue suits," which are reminiscent of the Union Army. Next time I wore a gray suit. My client was Bo Cochran, who had been convicted of a crime he never committed. He is one of the greatest people I have ever met because he had no recrimination. In that situation, you are either consumed by bitterness, or rise to a higher state of awareness. I have experienced discrimination and know life is not always fair but feeling victimized gives one a sense of false power. Don't let bitterness control you. That is the opposite of taking responsibility for your life.

Joining Merck in 1992, Ken used his legal skills to help a company creating medicines that save lives. Seeing Ken's potential, Merck CEO Roy Vagelos appointed him head of public affairs after a year. Eventually, Ken became general counsel, where he had to defend Merck against 50,000 lawsuits filed by Vioxx patients after Merck voluntarily withdrew the drug. Plaintiff attorneys saw an opportunity and filed thousands of lawsuits alleging that Merck did sham science. Ken saw this as a test of Merck's values, and he tried the cases individually instead of negotiating a blanket settlement.

> When plaintiffs alleged Merck put profits ahead of safety, did low-quality science, and had questionable integrity, we had to defend Merck science and our values. We lost our first case in rural Texas, as the jury recommended damages of $253 million for one patient. The New York Times wrote, "Merck could find itself bankrupt and can blame it on their lawyer's ineptitude."
>
> We learned from that experience and started winning cases. After eight consecutive wins, the judge told the parties to settle the remaining cases. We eventually did, but not for anything close to the $30 to 50 billion the plaintiffs were seeking, but for $4.85 billion. Most importantly, we defended Merck's mission and values, our science, and our people.

When Ken was elected CEO, he immediately reaffirmed Merck's mission: "To discover, develop, and provide innovative products and services that save and improve lives around the world." His strategy to fulfill the mission was to develop transformational medicines focused on unmet medical needs. Yet shortly after becoming CEO, shareholders pressured Ken to cut research to achieve his predecessor's earnings guidance. He resisted that pressure, committed to spending a minimum of $8 billion per year on research and development (R&D), and withdrew earnings guidance, triggering a near-term decline in Merck's stock.

His focus on R&D paid off as Merck scientists created breakthrough drugs, such as Januvia for diabetes, vaccine Gardasil, and Keytruda for cancer. Ten years later, Keytruda enabled former president Jimmy Carter to heal from brain cancer and will become the best-selling drug in history.

Ken faced his greatest values challenge after the 2017 Unite the Right demonstrations in Charlottesville, Virginia. As part of the President's Council on American Manufacturing, he was deeply troubled when former president Donald Trump said there were "very fine people on both sides," creating a moral equivalence between White supremacists and counterprotesters.

On Monday, Ken publicly resigned from the council, stating, "America's leaders must honor our fundamental values by clearly rejecting expressions of hatred, bigotry, and group supremacy." Then the president attacked him on Twitter. In taking a public stand, Ken risked Merck's relationship with the U.S. government, which holds the power to approve and recall its drugs as well as force price cuts.

After Ken's announcement, a remarkable thing occurred. Forty-two CEOs of major American companies joined Ken in resigning from the president's advisory councils, which forced the president to disband them. Never in U.S. history had the business community united so quickly to deliver such a clear message to an American president, thanks to Ken's remarkable moral courage and leadership.

Retiring as CEO in early 2021, Ken is pursuing his calling to service through the OneTen initiative for business to hire one million Black workers in 10 years. He and former American Express CEO Ken Chenault also led the campaign against the Georgia voting laws that make voting more challenging. They believe that without democracy, capitalism cannot survive.

By staying true to his values under pressure, Ken is a role model for other leaders. He never forgets his father's influence, saying "If he were alive today, Dad would say, 'The boy did what he was supposed to do.'"

Values, Principles, and Ethical Boundaries

There is no right set of values. One person may value kindness. Another person may value excellence. Only you can decide what your most deeply held values are. When you do, you will be able to align with people and organizations that share similar values.

When you clearly understand your values, your leadership principles will become clear, because they are your values translated into practice. For example, a value such as "Concern for others" might translate into the leadership principle, "Create cultures where people are respected for their contributions, provided job security, and inspired to fulfill their potential."

After defining your leadership principles, you need to establish ethical boundaries. If moral values inform the positive principles you live by, ethical boundaries set absolute limits on your actions. You will encounter many gray areas in life and work. Where do you draw the line between the actions that are acceptable and those that are not? What lines will you refuse to cross? Let your True North guide your decisions. Developing a clear sense of your True North, values, leadership principles, and ethical boundaries gives you the moral courage to make difficult decisions in complex dilemmas (Figure 5.1).

David Gergen wanted to lead a life consistent with values he learned from his family in Durham, North Carolina. He is the only leader to serve as a senior White House adviser to four U.S. presidents: Republicans Richard Nixon, Gerald Ford, and Ronald Reagan and Democrat Bill Clinton.

True North:
The essence of who you are; your moral compass to judge what is right and wrong, and acting accordingly.

Values:
A person's standards of behaviors; one's judgment of what is important in life.

Leadership Principles:
A set of standards used in leading others, derived from your values. Principles are values translated into action.

Moral Courage:
The courage to take action for moral reasons despite the risk of adverse consequences.

Ethical Boundaries:
The limits placed on your actions, based on your standards of ethical behavior.

Figure 5.1   Defining True North, Values, Leadership Principles, Moral Courage, and Ethical Boundaries

Hired as a 28-year-old White House speechwriter during Nixon's first term, David was at the center of history as it was being made. "When I first arrived, the power, glamour, and status went to my head," he says. Years later, he realized how naive and unprepared he was for the events of the next few years, particularly the Watergate scandal.

As a rising star in the Nixon administration, David recalls, "I was grasping for the brass ring and was as ambitious as everybody else, probably more so." After Nixon's 1972 reelection, he was named head of the president's speechwriting and research team. "It was tempting to fall into the trap of thinking I was important instead of recognizing you're important only because of your position."

When stories about the Watergate cover-up emerged in early 1973, David didn't believe they were true. "We were continuously reassured that neither Nixon nor anyone in the White House had done anything wrong," he explains. "Nixon told us that directly, as did chief of staff Bob Haldeman." As the Watergate scandal became public in 1973 and 1974, several staff members resigned, but David felt he couldn't leave. "My resignation would have been a public statement about President Nixon's integrity, so I stayed and kept hoping against hope he was innocent."

David learned of Nixon's guilt just 2 days before the news broke in August 1974. Even then he didn't feel he could leave, lest he be viewed as a rat leaving the sinking ship, especially after Nixon asked him to write his resignation letter. As he watched Nixon fly away from the White House on *Marine One*, David thought his career in public life was over. He recalls the infamous 1919 Chicago Black Sox World Series team whose players were accused of cheating and banned from baseball for life. "I thought I'd never play again," he says. "Watergate was an epiphany for me, shattering my notion that in a position of power and glamour, you can rise above being challenged. You can't."

Almost immediately, David's phone stopped ringing. "Suddenly, you realize how fast it all comes and goes," he says. During the lonely and depressing days that followed, David was buoyed up by people who stood by him—mostly his old friends from Durham and college classmates. "When you're in trouble and all your defenses get stripped away, you realize what and who really matters," he says. "That's when you turn to your roots and your values."

"Since that searing experience with Watergate," David concludes, "I have always favored transparency." His Watergate experience shaped his assertiveness in advising Presidents Ford, Reagan, and Clinton.

> *I frequently disagree with those I work for, because Watergate's lessons are so vivid in my mind, reminding me to stay true to my values. Nixon did not have a moral compass, and everything went off track.*

As founding director of the Center for Public Leadership at Harvard Kennedy School since 2000, David has inspired and prepared more emerging leaders for public service than anyone else. His breakthrough book, *Hearts Touched by Fire*, calls to the new generation to make this world better by living their values. In the section "Find Your True North," David writes,

> *Emerging leaders must settle upon the values and beliefs that will guide them through life. Through the centuries, leaders have been judged by their character, courage, and capacity. Those remain core values in navigating through today's rough waters.*

Read More
Jon Huntsman, Founder, Huntsman Corporation

Follow Jon's journey as he overcame three major tests of his values, while maintaining his character and integrity along the way.

Organizational Values

Are your moral values aligned with your company's values? It is essential to ask this question before taking a job, but it is difficult to know the differences between the organization's *stated* values and its *actual* values. You only learn that from working in the organization. One way to determine the organization's true values is to look at the character of its leaders and the decisions they make. Do they put the company's values ahead of making money in the short-term?

Narayana (N. R.) Murthy is an entrepreneur who built his company around ethical values. In 1982, N. R. and younger colleagues founded Infosys Technologies and built it into India's leading information technology outsourcing company. Infosys gave N. R. the platform to translate his values into practice. "Our dream was to demonstrate you could run a business in India without corruption and create wealth ethically," he says.

From the outset, N. R. wanted to create India's most respected company but ran into difficulties starting his business while adhering to his values. Because he refused to pay bribes, Infosys had to wait a year to install telephone lines. But he stayed the course. "What drains your energy or enthusiasm is not the fiscal problem, but violating your value system," he says.

Leaders with values and principles are less likely to get bullied or pushed around because they can draw clear lines in the sand. We believe the softest pillow is a clear conscience. I feel fortunate we have never lost sleep because we did something wrong.

Eventually, the demands for bribes ceased. "If you refuse to buckle on the first couple of transactions," he says, "they will go trouble someone else."

Complying with your value system enables people to have high aspirations, self-esteem, confidence in the future, and the enthusiasm to take on difficult tasks. Leaders must "walk the talk" and demonstrate their commitment to the value system. There is a direct correlation between the value system of our company and the success we have had the last 40 years.

While N. R. Murthy started a company based on values, IBM CEO Sam Palmisano shifted the company's culture from "management by objectives" to "leading by values." In doing so, he united IBM's diverse organization. Taking over from Lou Gerstner, Sam did not merely reiterate the values that founder Thomas Watson established. Instead, he initiated a 3-day company-wide workshop in which all employees collaborated in determining what IBM's values should be. In announcing IBM's 2003 Leading by Values initiative, Sam wrote:

> Many people these days have lost faith that business, government, or any other institution can be run with enduring, commonly held beliefs. Maybe people wouldn't feel that way if more people, not just the leaders, declare what they believe in, and take meaningful steps to put their values into practice. These must be genuinely shared values. They can't be imposed top-down.

For Sam, values are key to building a winning culture. During IBM's values jam, he posted, "The old model of the heroic superman is increasingly archaic. Never confuse charisma with leadership. Successful leaders today are part of the global community, building sustainable cultures."

Set Ethical Boundaries

Your ethical boundaries set clear limits on what you will and will not do under pressure or rationalizing marginal decisions. If you establish clear boundaries early in life, your moral compass will kick in when you reach your limits and tell you it is time to pull back, even if the personal sacrifices are significant.

That's what Enron leaders Ken Lay and Jeff Skilling lacked as they veered from deal-making into dishonesty. Ultimately, they made a series of aggressive accounting decisions to inflate short-term profits. A rising stock price rewarded their decisions, but they later paid an enormous price as Enron imploded. Ken Lay died, and Jeff Skilling wound up in prison.

What do the former CEOs of McDonald's, Intel, Hewlett-Packard, Best Buy, and Boeing have in common? Steve Easterbrook, Brian Krzanich, Mark Hurd, Brian Dunn, and Harry Stonecipher all violated their company's values by having inappropriate relationships with company employees. As CEO, each was charged with enforcing the company code of conduct, which expressly banned such behaviors, while they were terminating employees who violated their codes.

Why would these talented leaders knowingly violate company values? There are two explanations: either they thought they could get away with it without anyone knowing, or they were above the rules, given their importance to the company. Neither reason holds water. CEOs know all their actions ultimately become public, so their behavior must be beyond reproach. Their boards of directors had no choice but to use the same standards to their CEOs applied to everyone else. In doing so, they maintained the company's integrity.

Leaders can ascertain whether their actions exceed their ethical boundaries by using the *Wall Street Journal* test. Before proceeding with any action, ask yourself, "How would I feel if this entire situation, including transcripts of my discussions, was printed on the *Journal's* front page?"

If your answers are negative, it is time to rethink your actions. If they are positive, you should feel comfortable proceeding, even if others criticize your actions later. When you operate with integrity, you will be comfortable having the media or anyone else examine your words and actions.

Testing Your Values under Pressure

It is relatively easy to practice your values when things are going well. To understand your values, examine situations when you were tested under pressure. What behaviors do you regret? Were you honest even if it came at great personal cost? Or did you dissemble or stretch the truth?

When you are forced to make values-based decisions with a lot to lose, you learn what is most important in your life. With reflection, you can assess whether your moral values match your actions. With resolve, you can commit to overcoming vulnerabilities that could cause you to stray. You will have many opportunities to realign your values with your True North and live out your values.

Like Ken Frazier, today's leaders face increasing challenges to their values. Should they speak out to defend their values, or remain silent while hiding behind their public relations departments? CEOs and leaders today are public figures, and the media analyzes every word they say—or fail to say. Let's look at how some leaders have addressed such challenges.

Sallie Krawcheck has been called Wall Street's most powerful woman, but more importantly she stands out as a leader who places client's interests ahead of making money, although it cost her job. She says, "The wealth management business is a noble calling because you have the opportunity to help families figure out how to live the life they want."

Sallie has few kind words for the Wall Street culture, though, saying that short-term financial pressures have destroyed the financial industry's focus on its mission. "The financial services industry could have made an enormous difference but got caught up in the short-term game, not its mission to serve clients."

During the 2008 global financial crisis, Sallie was under enormous pressure at Citi. She advocated returning client funds on certain products, bluntly asserting Citi had broken clients' trust by pushing high-risk investments that were mischaracterized as low risk. When Citi CEO Vikram Pandit vehemently disagreed, Sallie had the courage to tell Citi's board of directors, "We must do the right thing for our clients."

> This is going to hurt the quarter, but in the long run we'll have a more valuable company. If we don't do it, clients are going to be angry as they should be, and they're going to leave us. We must have a long-term perspective and do the right thing for our clients.

In taking this position, Sallie was guided by her moral values. The board sided with her, but Pandit fired her days later. She says she knew taking this moral stand would get her fired, but doesn't regret taking controversial positions, saying "My ability to see things differently is why I succeeded."

Today, Sallie runs Ellevest, an investment platform and financial literacy program "built by women, for women" to help close gender wage gaps and support female entrepreneurship. Sallie had the moral courage to put her job on the line to stay true to her values. She paid a high price but has no regrets.

Delta CEO Ed Bastian also paid a price by standing up for his values. Troubled by the shooting massacre in Parkland, Florida, Ed decided to eliminate Delta's discounts for National Rifle Association (NRA) members for its annual conference in 2018. Outraged, Georgia legislators voted to punish Delta, whose headquarters are in Atlanta, by eliminating a $40 million jet-fuel tax break the airline traditionally received.

During this time, Ed came under tremendous pressure from gun-rights activists who called for the public to boycott Delta and conservative news articles that accused him of "treating conservatives differently" and finding their views "deplorable." Despite the backlash, Ed defended his actions, saying, "Delta's values are not for sale." Ed's values prevailed, and later the Georgia legislature came around, voting to retroactively restore Delta's tax break.

Apple CEO Tim Cook has been unwavering in his company's commitment to protect its users' privacy. Apple has access to an enormous reservoir of personal data from its users' phones, iPads, and computers, but Tim says the company won't access it: "We're not going to traffic in your personal life. Privacy to us is a human right, a civil liberty. This current situation is so dire that some well-crafted regulation is necessary."

In 2015, Tim said of Facebook and Google, "Prominent and successful companies built their businesses by lulling their customers into complacency about their personal information. They're gobbling up everything they can learn about you and trying to monetize it. We think that's wrong, and it's not the kind of company Apple wants to be. We could make a ton of money if we monetized our customer. We've elected not to do that."

Asked how he would respond if he were CEO of Facebook, Tim says, "I wouldn't be in that situation."

Emerging Leader: Jonathan Lee Kelly

Jonathan Lee Kelly grew up in Greensboro, North Carolina, in a working-class Black family that lived in an integrated neighborhood. His family, church members, and teachers all played important roles in his development as a leader.

Jonathan graduated from Wake Forest University and later Harvard Business School, where I was his mentor. He has strong values, self-confidence, and an ability to make people feel comfortable. When Jonathan launched his investment holding company, Asymmetric Holdings, he incorporated values imparted by his childhood and early work experiences into three leadership principles for his company.

#1: Work Hard and Do Your Best

Jonathan's parents shaped his strong work ethic. He says, "My parents had an expectation that I do my best. If your best is an A, the expectation is you get the A. If you give your best, then there's nothing else to talk about."

His father worked for a local construction company where he advanced into management before starting his own company. Jonathan recalls his weekends growing up, "We'd get up at 6:00 a.m. and go work construction with my dad, or we had to go move piles of wood, bricks, or cinder blocks. There was this constant emphasis of being engaged. His admonition was 'an idle mind is the devil's workshop.'"

#2: Care for People and Treat Everyone with Respect

Jonathan is creating a culture focused on treating everybody with respect and recognizing dignity in all work. He says,

> When I think about my employees, I think about my mom. When she was pregnant, she was working at Hardee's at 5:00 a.m. making biscuits. I look at our success, our ability to grow and succeed as creating opportunities.

Jonathan's company has a history of diversity and inclusion with women, underrepresented groups, and individuals who self-identify with the LGBTQ+ community finding leadership roles both at and above the store level at levels materially higher than competitors. He says the secret to building this diversity is to create a place where talent can thrive. He shares, "I want my employees 'to be able to create [a better] way of life for themselves and those they care about'; that's the promise of General Management as the greatest profession that Dr. James Cash taught me. I have people working for me who are thriving and have opportunities they never would have had in other organizations."

#3: Demonstrate Ownership and Accountability

When Jonathan first acquired his business, he left dinner to work with the team to close a store. "The next morning, I was at a store and had to grab feces out of the clogged toilet," he says. "If I ask people to do it, I have to do the same thing."

By building a values-centered culture of ownership, Jonathan's team drives results. He hopes their success will be part of a larger picture. "Realizing the promise of the New South is critical to America's competitiveness globally," he says. "I want to be part of that."

Bill's Take: Testing My Values

I have tried to live my life following a strict moral code, but at several key points fidelity to my values was tested under pressure.

As president of the microwave oven division of Litton, it took me a while to realize the corporation made its numbers by creating excess reserves for acquisitions and later booking them as profits as needed to make quarterly targets. When I overheard Litton's CEO tell another GM, "I know you have to do what you have to do to get the business, but if you ever put it in writing again, you're fired," that's when I knew I had to leave.

I joined Honeywell because of the leadership of Ed Spencer, a great global leader who never wavered from his unbending commitment to values and integrity. Serving as president of Honeywell Europe, I learned firsthand how to navigate ethical challenges in Russia, Saudi Arabia, and Nigeria without bending your standards.

My decision to join Medtronic was based, in large part, on the inspiration I felt by its mission and the alignment I felt with its values. Thus, I was shocked to discover that leaders in our international division didn't take these values seriously. When internal audit reports revealed repeated violations of company standards overseas, I decided we had to make significant management changes, including retiring the international head and replacing him with Art Collins.

Art cleaned up the unethical behavior by replacing the heads of Europe, Asia, and Latin America, as well as several other countries, with leaders who were committed to strong values. When Art became my successor, he never deviated from these high standards. During the company's rapid growth phase in the 1990s, Medtronic's values were invaluable in introducing new employees to the company's culture.

As we strive to follow our True North, it is important to acknowledge just how easy it is to get on a slippery slope that pulls us off course. Pressures to perform, rewards for success, and our ingrained fear of failure can cause us to deviate from our moral values. By adhering to our True North, we can live our values as moral leaders.

Idea in Brief: Live Your Values

Recap of the Main Idea

- Your values are standards of behavior that are important to you; they are derived from your beliefs and convictions.
- There is no right set of values; only you can decide what your most deeply held values are.
- Staying true to your values requires moral courage—the courage to act for moral reasons despite the risk of adverse consequences.
- Leadership principles are values translated into action and act as a set of standards you use in leading others.
- Ethical boundaries are limits placed on your actions, based on your standards of ethical behavior.
- Being clear about your values, leadership principles, and ethical boundaries is essential to becoming an authentic leader and following your True North.

Questions to Ask

1. Recall a personal situation in which your values conflicted with each other. How did you resolve this conflict? How pleased were you with the outcome?
2. Recall a situation in which your values were tested under pressure. To what extent did you deviate from your values? What resources did you call upon? What would you do differently if you had to do it all over again?

Practical Suggestions for Your Development

- List the values that are important to your life and your leadership; rank them in order of their importance to you.

- Use the *Wall Street Journal* test to consider whether your actions are ethical by asking, "How would I feel if this was printed on the front page of the *Wall Street Journal?*"

- Evaluate whether your values are aligned with your company's values by looking at the character and decisions of its leaders. Are they willing to put the company's values ahead of short-term profit?

6

FIND YOUR SWEET SPOT

Whatever you do, or dream you can do, begin it.
Boldness has genius, power, and magic in it.
—*Johann Wolfgang von Goethe, German poet*

Your sweet spot is the intersection of your motivations and your strengths. When you are operating in your sweet spot, you feel inspired, energized, and confident that you can do great things. You're fulfilled by your work because you are passionate about it. This creates a powerful flywheel that enables you to be satisfied and successful.

Warren Buffett Found His Sweet Spot

No renowned leader has focused their time and energy around their sweet spot more than Warren Buffett. Through his stewardship of Berkshire Hathaway since 1965, he has created hundreds of billions in value for his shareholders. Yet Warren made the choice to spend time doing what he loved, and delegate the rest—well before his success was assured.

Born in Omaha, Nebraska, Warren made his first stock market investment at age 11. As a teenager, he read Benjamin Graham's seminal book on value investing, *The Intelligent Investor*, and became a believer in Graham's thesis to value stocks based on the company's business fundamentals. Graduating from the University of Nebraska, Warren studied economics at Columbia University under Graham.

Although Warren loves investing, his first full-time job as a stockbroker tortured him because brokers were rewarded for networking and selling, which were not his strengths. Instead of becoming a broker who generated commissions by pushing clients to trade actively, he yearned to analyze financial securities.

If you think that Warren Buffett operating in his sweet spot doesn't apply to you, consider this: Warren left the brokerage business to start his own investing firm, an unusual move in the cautious postwar era. At 26, he was unimpressive, insecure, and unproven. Nobody would have predicted he would become a business titan. He was so afraid of public speaking that he took a Dale Carnegie course. He was rejected by the local country club because people thought his investing firm was a Ponzi scheme.

German poet Johann Wolfgang von Goethe wrote, "Whatever you do, or dream you can do, begin it. Boldness has genius, power, and magic in it." By opening his own firm, Warren could spend time on what he loved: fundamental analysis of financial securities. His early decision to position himself at the intersection of his motivations and his strengths turns out to be the best investment he ever made because he is operating in his *sweet spot*.

Warren's investment philosophy evolved from focusing on cheap stocks to identifying companies with sustainable competitive advantage and high-quality leadership. As his reputation grew, he won access to investments because of his my-word-is-my-bond character and the value of his imprimatur. While he stayed away from investing in tech stocks, more recently his investment in Apple netted his firm a $120 billion gain.

Despite this success, Warren manages to retain his modesty and humility. My MBA student Vitaliy Pereverzev told me about his experience with Warren when he traveled to Omaha with 80 members of his investment club. After lunch at Warren's favorite restaurant, Vitaliy realized he left his camera at Berkshire Hathaway's offices. Rather than sending a member of his staff to get it, Warren offered him a ride in his Lincoln Town Car. Warren immediately offered him some advice: "Vitaliy, you have to do what you love. I do not want to live like a king. I just love to invest."

Intrinsic and Extrinsic Motivations

To deliver high performance, leaders need to sustain high levels of motivation, just as Warren Buffett has done. There are two types of motivations: *extrinsic* and *intrinsic* (Figure 6.1).

Extrinsic motivations—such as getting good grades, winning athletic competitions, or making money—are measured by the external world. Most leaders have had a strong achievement orientation since childhood, as they excelled in school and competed in athletics. After graduating, many young leaders want a job with a prestigious organization. Eventually, their extrinsic motivations take the form of wealth accumulation, power, and prestige.

Although reluctant to admit it, most leaders are motivated by achieving external success. They enjoy the feelings of recognition and status that come with promotions and financial rewards. However, each success often leads to a desire for more money, fame, or power. That's why people with great wealth and power are always comparing themselves with those who have more. Being driven entirely by extrinsic motivations is a dangerous trap that can lead you astray from your True North.

Extrinsic Motivations	Intrinsic Motivations
• Monetary compensation	• Personal growth
• Having power	• Helping others develop
• Having a title	• Satisfaction of doing a good job
• Public recognition	• Finding meaning from efforts
• Social status	• Being true to one's beliefs
• Winning over others	• Making a difference in the world

Figure 6.1 Extrinsic and Intrinsic Motivations

Intrinsic motivations are derived from your deepest inner desires and are closely linked to your life story and your crucible. Examples include personal growth, building your family, helping other people, taking on social causes, creating great products or services, and making a difference in the world.

Because modern society has placed unprecedented attention on visible achievements, extrinsic measures of success cause many leaders to seek the world's acclaim rather than pursuing their inner motivations. The pressure starts early when college graduates compare salaries and evolves as they compare new home purchases. Alan Horn, chair of Walt Disney Studios, describes how he consciously avoided these traps:

> Early in your career, the incremental dollar can change your quality of life because it enables you to buy a better car or bigger house. At some point, the incremental dollar does not change your quality of life; rather, more purchases just increase the complexity of life, not its enjoyment.

Debra Dunn, who spent decades at Hewlett-Packard, advises emerging leaders to beware of getting caught up in social, peer, or parental expectations:

> The path of accumulating material possessions is clearly laid out and easy to measure. If you don't pursue it, people wonder what is wrong with you. The only way to avoid getting caught up in materialism is understanding where you find happiness and fulfillment.

The term *sweet spot* describes your motivated capabilities when your motivations and your strengths align (Figure 6.2). Late Claremont professor Mihaly Csikszentmihalyi, a pioneer in positive psychology, provided us this simple advice about motivation: "Find out what you are good at and what you like to do." In these two dimensions, Csikszentmihalyi cut through the jargon and summed up what our interviewees learned through hundreds of years of experience.

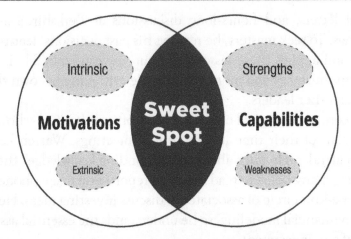

Figure 6.2   Finding Your Sweet Spot

You will be most effective as a leader when you find opportunities that highly motivate you and use your greatest capabilities. One without the other is insufficient. To find these opportunities, you must understand your deepest motivations and be honest with yourself about your capabilities. You won't be successful as a leader by pursuing something you're not good at or by pursuing leadership roles that don't motivate you. When you find a role that meshes your motivations with your capabilities, you will discover the sweet spot that maximizes your effectiveness as a leader.

Keys to Warren Buffett's Success

All of us have some level of extrinsic motivation, which is natural. Extrinsically, Warren enjoys public recognition and being valued. Moreover, he has used his media savvy to raise his profile and gain unique access to deals. However, these motivations don't control him. He cares more about his character and reputation than celebrity and isn't interested in accumulating possessions. He still lives in the Omaha house he bought for $31,500 in 1956, and he eats burgers at Omaha diner Gorat's.

Warren's intrinsic motivations include learning and teaching. He shares his knowledge through frequent media interviews, lengthy annual letters, and hours-long discussions at Berkshire's annual meetings. To seek mastery, he reviews his past decisions, learns from them, and applies these lessons to future investments. He is open about his mistakes and more comfortable critiquing his own thinking than other leaders.

In contrast to typical chief executive officers (CEOs) who spend 60 percent of their time in face-to-face meetings, Warren keeps a blank calendar. He talks about "compounding knowledge" through reserving many hours to read financial reports and make phone calls to a close-knit circle of associates to discuss investing ideas. He does his own financial modeling, so he understands the essential assumptions of any investment.

To emphasize how unusual his time allocation is, in his small office the window blinds are pulled to eliminate distractions, there is no computer (and thus no emails), and stacks of financial reports and newspapers to read. On his desk sit three boxes: Inbox, Outbox, and "Too Hard." Well before he was wealthy, Warren designed his life to spend disproportionate time on his areas of strength.

He also avoids his weaknesses. He quickly left his first career as a stockbroker which required sales and networking skills that he did not have. Often verbally attacked by his mother, he has little interest in fighting with others. If he smells conflict in a deal, he avoids it. He also steers clear of hands-on management. Company leaders are welcome to call him for advice, but he places responsibility for decisions squarely on their shoulders. He has joked publicly that his management style is abdication.

Putting this all together, Warren's *sweet spot* formula has produced stupendous results. Berkshire Hathaway's returns have more than doubled the Standard & Poor's 500 Index for the past 40 years. To put that success in context, Warren has created twice the combined shareholder value of financial giants Goldman Sachs and Morgan Stanley.

The irony of Warren's success is that he sought mastery instead of success. Still to this day, he exudes modesty and remains grounded. His joie de vivre comes from aligning his personal motivation and professional abilities with his company's focus. How many other people still tap dance to work each day at age 92?

A Contrasting Sweet Spot

Like Warren, Mike Bloomberg is an extremely successful businessperson—yet that's where the similarities end. While Warren keeps an open schedule, Mike enjoys being double-booked. While Warren prefers Omaha, Mike hops across the globe. While Warren avoids management, Mike is notoriously hands-on. While Warren works on financial analysis, Mike is the front man.

Their contrasting mutual successes illustrate an important truth: you cannot achieve sustained success by emulating someone else. You must do the hard work of self-discovery to unlock your personal potential. Zeroing in on your sweet spot may take years, as it did for me.

I have known Mike since business school, where he was both brilliant and brash. While I had to work my butt off, Mike was so smart he could skim the material, go out and party, yet offer brilliant insights in class. He recalls the time he was cold-called in class when he hadn't bothered to glance at the case.

> Called out for not being prepared, I suggested to the professor he should first get inputs from several students and then I would summarize and draw conclusions. With that, he dismissed the entire class and told us to come back prepared the next day. When he called on me, I offered a radical solution that he and the rest of the class rejected. Years later, the company did exactly what I suggested and was highly successful.

After graduation, Mike went to work at Salomon Brothers. Fifteen years later, he was a rising star as head of equity trading at Wall Street's hottest firm. When Salomon merged with Phibro, he was ushered into Chair John Gutfreund's office and abruptly fired. Mike was shocked and hurt. "I was 39 years old, terminated from the only full-time job I'd had and the high-pressure life

I loved. Was I sad? You bet, but as usual, I was much too macho to show it."

His firing gave Mike something to prove and freed him to start his own company. He used $4 million from his $10 million termination settlement to create the Bloomberg Terminal. There he found his sweet spot—building his own company. Extrinsically, Mike loves recognition and being at the center of the action. He enjoys the trappings of success, including private planes and multiple homes, but he isn't just about money.

Mike served as mayor of New York City for 12 years, taking a $1 per year salary. At business school, I would have guessed Mike would be the last person to run for office, shaking hands and holding babies, yet he turned out to be the best mayor New York ever had, restoring it to greatness after September 11, 2001.

Direct, practical, and completely unafraid of confrontation, he has taken on tough issues and powerful groups, including liberal teachers' unions and the conservative NRA. When Goldman Sachs cancelled its plans for its new headquarters across the street from 9/11's Ground Zero site due to security concerns, Mike knew he needed an anchor tenant and forced his departments to meet Goldman's needs. Today New York's lower West Side is flourishing thanks to his tenacity.

Mike explains,

To succeed, you need a vision that's affordable, practical, and fills customer needs. Then, go for it. Don't worry about details; don't second-guess your creativity; most importantly, don't strategize too much about the long-term.

Worth an estimated $70 billion, Mike told me, "I intend to give it all away. The best financial planning ends with bouncing the check to the undertaker." True to his word, he is one of the country's three most significant philanthropists, as Bloomberg Philanthropies gives away billions to restore cities, reduce the racial wealth gap, prevent gun violence, and support women's economic development.

Mike knows his strengths and what motivates him and has found his sweet spot to make a unique impact on the world.

Read More

Chuck Schwab, Chairman, The Charles Schwab Corporation

Follow Chuck's journey to his "sweet spot"—learning from dyslexia, drawing on his strengths, and finding a passion for democratizing the financial services industry.

Recalibrate Your Motivations

Emerging leaders are often too eager to get ahead. My friend Kevin Sharer is a talented leader who lost his way midcareer when he grasped for the brass ring before he was prepared. Yet he learned from his painful experience, recalibrated, and found his sweet spot at Amgen, where he had a spectacular 12 years as CEO.

As a submarine officer and McKinsey alum, Kevin's early experiences prepared him for the bare-knuckle intensity of GE. A rising star at GE, he was eager—too eager—to get to the top. By age 40, Kevin ran GE's satellite business, was elected a corporate officer, and was promoted to run the jet engine business. This would be heady stuff for anyone, but especially for someone as ambitious as Kevin. When the headhunters came looking for a new head of marketing for MCI, he seized the opportunity to leapfrog his career.

"The CEO race is wide open," MCI's vice chair assured him. Kevin took the bait. This time, however, things did not go his way. Upon joining the company, Kevin learned the chief operating officer (COO) was in line for the top slot and didn't welcome competition, especially from the young, ambitious GE hotshot.

Kevin wasted no time in developing his strategy to transform MCI and position himself for promotion. Within six weeks, he concluded that the company's geographic marketing organization was improperly structured. "I was at the zenith of my arrogance at that time," Kevin says. "I marched into the chairman's office and proposed restructuring MCI's sales organization." His proposal was threatening to senior executives who had spent their careers building MCI. Lacking telecommunications experience, Kevin faced failure for the first time in his life.

"MCI was a crucible for me," Kevin observes. "I learned that there is a price to be paid for arrogance." He also found out his style did not suit MCI's hypercompetitive culture. "People were personally competitive in a way that was inconsistent with my values," he explains.

> The internal competition was mean-spirited and at your throat. It was eating me up, and I was becoming less effective. If your values aren't consistent with the people you're working with, you shouldn't be there.

Desperate to escape from MCI, Kevin telephoned CEO Jack Welch and asked to return to GE. Upset with the way Kevin bailed out after he had promoted him, Jack said, "Hey, Kevin, forget you ever worked here." Kevin recalls,

> I realized I couldn't just bail out. It was a gut-wrenching 2 years for me. I'm not a good knife fighter, and I was getting outmaneuvered. At first, I went into denial; then I became defeatist and cynical. Without question, it was the toughest time of my life.

Kevin's story illustrates the difficulties that many leaders face. Their egos tempt them into situations that don't play to their strengths and don't inspire them. With self-awareness and insight, they readjust their compass to get back on track of their True North to find opportunities where they are in their sweet spot. Kevin's crucible at MCI was invaluable; it forced him to control his arrogance and recognize there is more to life than just the next promotion. Kevin got caught up in the glamour of being a rising star, but MCI brought him back to reality.

Two years later, Kevin nominated himself to become president of Amgen and was offered the position, under the tutelage of CEO

Gordon Binder. Having learned a painful lesson at MCI about being a know-it-all, Kevin recognized he knew nothing about the bio-technology business. "Had it not been for that chastening experience at MCI, I could easily have blown up at Amgen," he says.

> My last brush with health care had been ninth-grade biology, so I asked one of our scientists to teach me biology. By being patient, I became an insider before I started making changes. I learned the business from the ground up, made calls with sales representatives, and showed my desire to learn.

Kevin patiently understudied Binder for 8 years. This time around, he wasn't seduced by headhunters, telling them being number two at a rapidly growing company like Amgen was "better than anything else on the plate." When Amgen announced Kevin would become CEO, he met individually with the top 150 people in the company to get their insights. "These interviews were the most important thing I did upon becoming CEO. They gave me the mandate to create a shared reality for the company and align around the new vision and strategy for building Amgen for the next decade."

Early on, Kevin knew his intellect, determination, and drive were strengths. Through searing experiences at GE and MCI, he learned about his limiting behaviors that offput others, and that pushing too hard to get ahead could be detrimental. At Amgen, he learned the business before taking charge, listened to his colleagues' wisdom and experience, and was patient in reaching his goal. As a result, he led Amgen for a decade with spectacular success, transforming the company from a two-drug firm to a highly innovative organization that continues to produce breakthrough drugs.

Reflecting on his experience, Kevin says, "We are the mosaic of all of our experiences."

> In retrospect, the MCI experience wasn't all bad. It gave me genuine empathy for other people. I learned the importance of doing what you love, because if you don't, you won't do your best.

Avoid Focus on Extrinsic Motivations

Ignoring external validation from your achievements isn't easy. Ambitious leaders grow so accustomed to successive accomplishments in their early years that they don't pursue their intrinsic motivations. For many authentic leaders it takes a crucible to free them to do what they love rather than seeking external acclaim.

Many leaders we interviewed turned down higher-paying jobs early in their careers to pursue roles they were passionate about. In the end, they came out ahead—in both satisfaction and compensation—because they were successful in doing what they loved. Former *Time, Inc.* CEO Ann Moore had a dozen job offers after business school and took the lowest paying one, with *Time*. "I had student loans hanging over my head, but I took the job because I loved magazines. At the time nobody in my class understood why I made that choice, but at our twenty-fifth reunion they understood completely."

When Dave Cox was CEO of Cowles Media, an MBA student told him, "I get my satisfaction someplace else and just do the business part to make money." Amazed by the comment, Dave raised his eyebrows quizzically, asking,

Why would you spend your time doing work you don't enjoy? These are the best years of your life. You add the greatest value when you connect with your passions.

It is natural to seek the esteem of peers, promotions, and financial rewards that come with success. The danger comes when leaders become so enamored with these external symbols that they can never get enough. At this point, they are at the greatest risk of losing touch with their intrinsic motivations and abandoning things that give them a deeper sense of fulfillment.

If your life's purpose is to accumulate possessions, fame, or power over others, you may discover these rewards are unsatisfying and chasing them will pull you away from your True North. Fame is fleeting—it can be built for many years and then slip through your fingers. Seeking power over others is the ultimate corrupter of the human character.

Many young leaders make the mistake of taking high-salaried jobs to pay off loans or live the high life, even if they have no genuine interest in the work. They erroneously believe they can move on to do the work they love after 10 years. By then, they are so dependent on maintaining expensive lives that they are trapped in jobs they don't like yet perceive they cannot afford to do work they love. That holds people back from pursuing what truly brings them satisfaction.

Many leaders have learned the hard way that external recognition is a fickle lover. When things do not go their way, external sources of gratification quickly disappear. So do superficial friends and acquaintances who are more enamored with their success than they are in supporting them when things go poorly.

Finding Your Sweet Spot

Many emerging leaders still early in their careers haven't yet found their sweet spot. You may be terrific at your first job, but you need to look deeper at whether it motivates you. Do you feel connected to the organization's purpose? Is the industry one you feel proud of? Do you have a boss who is helping you develop? Are you in a job that doesn't play to your strengths? Look for opportunities in your company better suited to your skillset.

When you are operating in your *sweet spot*—in a role where you add distinctive value and are highly motivated (Figure 6.3), you'll develop your skills faster because your work fascinates you. Great people will find your passion attractive and want to join your team. Your success will give you a deeper sense of fulfillment.

Minnesota Commissioner of Department of Human Services (DHS) Jodi Harpstead knows her greatest strength and her motivation is creating breakthrough cultures that achieve amazing results.

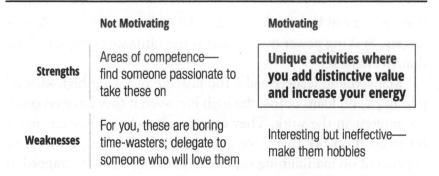

	Not Motivating	Motivating
Strengths	Areas of competence—find someone passionate to take these on	**Unique activities where you add distinctive value and increase your energy**
Weaknesses	For you, these are boring time-wasters; delegate to someone who will love them	Interesting but ineffective—make them hobbies

Figure 6.3 Operating in Your Sweet Spot

She did just that as president of marketing and sales at Medtronic. Then she took a less lucrative position to became CEO of Lutheran Social Services, where she used the same skills to build a highly successful nonprofit organization. Currently, she is turning around an ailing DHS with the same approach to creating a breakthrough culture that provides services to needy people throughout Minnesota. Her career in leading across three sectors shows what can be done when you utilize your strengths and are a highly motivated leader.

Success versus Significance

As we strive to get ahead in our careers, many of us—myself included—strive so hard for success that we fail to ask ourselves: Is our leadership significant? Are we making a positive difference in the lives of others?

In *The Road to Character*, David Brooks challenges us to ask whether we are merely building resumes or leading in ways for which we will be remembered—our eulogy virtues, the kind of person we are, and how we care for others. Resume achievements are easy to measure and give us superficial self-esteem, whereas eulogy virtues are more difficult to gauge. At the end of our lives, our net worth, press clippings, or power we once held pale beside making a significant impact on the lives of others. The former is fleeting, the latter is eternal.

Emerging Leader: Tracy Britt Cool

There is a paradox that leaders who focus on their intrinsic motivations wind up achieving the greatest extrinsic success. Tracy Britt Cool illustrates how this paradox works in practice. She grew up working long hours on her family farm in Kansas. Friends describe her as kind, thoughtful, and honest. In my MBA classroom, she had deep insights in recognizing human dimensions of business challenges.

While still in school, Tracy wrote dozens of letters to notable investors asking to meet with them. One day she received a response from Warren Buffett, who invited her and her investing club to meet with him in Omaha. Thereafter, she continued to correspond with Warren and volunteered to help him on projects.

As Warren got to know Tracy, he sensed her talent and integrity and invited her to join Berkshire. She didn't hesitate, saying yes without asking about her title or compensation—an unusual response in the finance industry. Tracy served as Warren's financial assistant for 5 years, researching investments worth billions, sitting on Kraft Heinz's board, chairing four Berkshire portfolio companies, and organizing dozens of events for Berkshire's CEOs.

The pressure of such a position in your 20s is intense. Tracy's early stumbles were dissected in media articles questioning her competence. Bankers, consultants, and CEOs flattered her, trying to win access to Warren. During this time, Tracy stayed focused and grounded, shunned the spotlight, and learned from her experiences. Meanwhile, she took numerous leadership assessments to build self-awareness of her strengths and weaknesses.

At 30, Tracy became CEO of Berkshire subsidiary Pampered Chef. Warren told her to treat it like a family business she would own for 50 years and make decisions on that basis. For someone who had solely worked as an investment analyst, the shift to operating a company was a significant challenge, as she had to turn around a company in free fall. She succeeded with flying colors—growing revenue from $300 million to $700 million, dramatically increasing profitability, and increasing employee engagement.

In 2020, Tracy left Berkshire Hathaway to form Kanbrick, an investment partnership to acquire and build businesses. Why leave the job working for the world's best investor? She says, "There are companies that we can help take to the next level, but they're too small for Berkshire." She also realizes her strengths lean more toward people and strategy than analyzing securities. Creating her own firm allows her to custom design her role to her strengths and motivations.

Whereas many investment funds think in quarters and plan to exit from the day they invest, Tracy committed to raising a longer-term vehicle, enabling her firm to operate with a time horizon akin to Berkshire's philosophy. Throughout the year Tracy convenes CEOs for free workshops in which she and her partners share their knowledge and ideas about building growing and healthy organizations. The approach gives credibility to Tracy's claim that "we are business builders who happen to invest."

Tracy has positioned herself in her sweet spot as she values learning and personal growth more than money or fame. She knows her strengths as an astute team builder and strategist who partners with strong operational leaders.

Bill's Take: Finding My Sweet Spot at 46

It took me 2 decades in business to find my *sweet spot*. In midcareer, we may find ourselves in situations from which we think we cannot escape. As Dante wrote in *The Divine Comedy*, "In the middle of the road of my life, I awoke in a dark wood, where the true way was wholly lost."

In the mid-1980s I was en route to the top of Honeywell, promoted several times while developing a reputation as "Mr. Fix-It" for turning around Honeywell's troubled businesses. I know how to turn businesses around, but that's not what I love to do.

Driving home one day, I looked in the rearview mirror and saw a miserable person—me. On the surface, I appeared to be confident and successful, but inside I was deeply unhappy. I realized I wasn't passionate about Honeywell's businesses, nor was my job playing to my strengths. I had all the trappings of success, but my life lacked the significance I yearned for. Worse yet, I was losing sight of my True North—more concerned about becoming CEO than making a positive impact on the world. I faced the reality that Honeywell was changing me more than I was changing it, and I didn't like the changes in myself.

Over the years, I had turned down three opportunities to join Medtronic, which was then a fledgling medical device company. It finally dawned on me that I was so caught up in my drive to run a major corporation that I was in danger of losing my soul. In the process, I realized I had sold Medtronic short and maybe myself as well.

In moving to Medtronic, I joined an organization whose mission to "alleviate pain, restore health, and extend life" was extremely inspiring, and I felt fully aligned with Medtronic's values. My job gave me the opportunity to build an organization in a role which used all my strengths.

At age 46, I finally found my sweet spot.

Idea in Brief: Find Your Sweet Spot

Recap of the Main Idea

- Extrinsic motivations, such as getting good grades or making money, are measured by the external world.
- Intrinsic motivations are derived from your deepest inner desires, not the world's adulation. Examples of intrinsic motivations include personal growth, helping others, taking on social causes, creating great products or services, and making a difference in the world.
- When you combine your motivations with a role that utilizes your strengths, you are operating in your *sweet spot*.

Questions to Ask

1. What are your extrinsic motivations? Which of them might become too dominant?

2. If money or success didn't matter, what would you choose as your vocation?

3. What are your intrinsic motivations? How do you ensure you are prioritizing them?

4. Recall and then list one or more instances in which your extrinsic motivations conflicted with your intrinsic motivations. What did you do?

5. What are your greatest capabilities? How does your work and life use them?

Practical Suggestions for Your Development

To accelerate the discovery of your strengths and your intrinsic motivations:

- Take personality tests like Enneagram, StrengthsFinder, and Myers-Briggs, which provide deeper insights into your natural way of being. Tests such as Hogan, DISC, and Caliper make distinctions around the suitability of your personality traits to different roles, such as sales or operations.

- Inventory your effectiveness by activity. Rate it on two dimensions: first, how effective are you at the activity; second, how much do you enjoy it?

- Use this inventory to create a set of unique activities that fully use your strengths and energize you. Each week, evaluate your calendar and determine what proportion of your time you spent on these unique activities.

7

LEAD AN INTEGRATED LIFE

The world will shape you if you let it. To live the life
you desire, you must make conscious choices.
—John Donahoe, CEO, Nike

The most frequent question emerging leaders ask is, "Can I have
a great career *and* a great family life?" Increasing job pressures,
time demands, and the complexities of two-career partnerships
make this integration more challenging than ever. Young leaders
have seen many in their parents' generation sacrifice their families for their careers and have lived through the pain of broken
marriages and estranged relationships. They are committed to
living differently.

If you find yourself getting too caught up in your work, ask yourself, who are better leaders: 80-hours-per-week executives who live
for work and subordinate everything to their career, or leaders who
work hard 50–60 hours per week but balance their work with the
needs of their families? Which leader would you want to work for?

Paradoxically, people who live for work are less effective
than well-balanced leaders who integrate work into their lives.
One-dimensional, work-obsessed leaders struggle to relate to others,
develop perspective, and stay grounded. In contrast, leaders who
cultivate an integrated life commit to invest time in all aspects
of their lives: family, work, community, friends, and personal time
(Figure 7.1).

As the frequency of communication has intensified, the pace of
business has increased. There is never enough time to do everything
because the world around you makes ever greater demands on your
time. Nobody achieves a perfect balance between all aspects of life.

Figure 7.1   Integrating Your Life

Inevitably, you will have to make trade-offs. How you do so will determine how fulfilling your life is.

John Donahoe: Living an Integrated Life

Nike chief executive officer (CEO) John Donahoe is a very busy leader with a two-career marriage and four children who has been able to integrate all aspects of his life.

On a tranquil Boston evening in 1983, John was enjoying dinner with his fiancée, Eileen. John had an excellent reputation at consulting firm Bain. His eyes lit up as he talked about his career prospects. As dinner continued, Eileen voiced concern about the toll John's career could take on his life. She worried that the long hours, constant travel, and stress might limit his ability to have close relationships. Then she asked him pointedly, "Is that really what you want in life?" John answered adamantly, "No!" and wrote on the back of a bank receipt, "I will not live the life of a management consultant."

Rising through the ranks to become Bain's worldwide managing director, John worked hard at leading an integrated life. "My ultimate goal is to have an impact in business, as well as be the kind of father, husband, friend, and human being I want to be. The human side is the highest goal and ultimate challenge."

> Leading a satisfying life is a quest worth taking. I believe integrating my life has enabled me to be a more effective leader. The struggle is constant, as the trade-offs and choices don't get any easier as you get older. My personal and professional lives are not a zero-sum trade-off. Having a strong personal life has made the difference.
>
> The world can shape you if you let it. To have a sense of yourself as you live, you must make conscious choices. Sometimes the choices are really hard, and you make a lot of mistakes.

During John's first year at business school, Eileen went into labor with their first child on the eve of finals. When he asked himself what was more important, the birth of his child or his grades, the answer was obvious. Having achieved in every academic environment, he had to let go of his desire to get top grades. "In a strange way, I had an excuse for not doing well and accepted the fact that I wasn't going to get straight As," he says. As finals approached, John spent more time with Eileen and felt oddly relaxed.

To his surprise, he earned the highest grades possible that quarter. "It was only because I had a bit of perspective. I certainly wasn't the smartest person," he says. "I remember watching the inefficiency that kicked in when people stressed out." That experience convinced him that a strong personal life could be an ally in achieving professional success.

A few years later, John faced another difficult choice. After graduating from law school, Eileen received an offer to clerk for a federal judge, a job requiring her to be at work by 7:30 a.m., so John had to take their two kids to school every day. Because his job required extensive travel, he told his boss, Tom Tierney, he had to quit. Tom just laughed and said, "We can work around this." He reassigned John to a local client, enabling him to take his kids to school before arriving at the client site. John explains,

> My client responded positively as he appreciated my commitment and contributions even more. I didn't have the courage to think about it that way before. There's an inclination to put on a tough exterior to give the impression that you have everything under control.

John's experience challenged the conventional wisdom of how to succeed in high-intensity professional services firms. The more John integrated his life and embraced his humanity, the more effective he became as a leader. "That was my best year of client work. Our client understood, and I became more relaxed," he recalls. By showing his team and clients his vulnerabilities, John discovered his teams performed better and his client relationships strengthened.

After 6 years as head of Bain's San Francisco office, John was burned out by his fast-paced life and wanted to spend more time with his two oldest sons, so he handed off his work to colleagues and took a 3-month sabbatical. "It was an opportunity to bring our family closer together," he explains.

First the family went to Europe, then John took separate week-long trips with his wife and each of his four children. He returned to Bain reenergized. A year later, he was named worldwide managing director, succeeding Tierney, just as the economy was plummeting and the health of one of his children tested him as never before. "This was the hardest thing I've ever dealt with."

> My family, friends, coaches, and colleagues were unbelievably helpful. Real life forced me to bring a sense of authenticity and vulnerability to the workplace, because life humbles you.

Sharing his personal situation helped him connect with his partners, so they could rally during the downturn. "I had faith in our people," he says. He believes he was effective precisely because he was able to integrate his personal and professional lives during stressful circumstances.

> Because so much emotional energy was going to my family, I didn't take the downturn personally. As a result, I was more effective as a leader. My legacy to Bain partners will be the way I led us through the downturn.

After concluding his leadership of Bain, John became CEO of eBay, succeeding Meg Whitman and transforming the company into a vibrant competitor in the high-tech world. In 2015, he retired from eBay after completing the successful spin-off of PayPal.

Once again, John took a sabbatical. At age 55, he started with a 10-day silent Buddhist retreat and then began a "wisdom tour" to meet with 50 people who could offer perspective on his next chapter. He observes, "One of my mentors told me, 'Do not lose sight of your gifts.'"

> God gave me certain gifts, and my job is to utilize them in service to others. That animates me inside and makes me happy because I've learned that all the success and wealth and fame in the world cannot make me happy.

The Donahoes have successfully weathered challenging stages of their lives and dual careers as they strive for an authentic life together. Eileen served as Ambassador to United Nations Human Rights Council in Geneva under President Barack Obama, and John is currently in his fourth CEO role as head of Nike after building ServiceNow for 3 years.

Despite his highly demanding job, John prioritizes daily meditation and exercise and cherishes his support team. "I've embraced a lot of help," he says. "I've had the same therapist for 30 years. I have spiritual advisors and business mentors, whom I call often for guidance. I can't imagine performing today without help."

John and Eileen's partnership serves as an excellent example of how to intentionally build an integrated life and how rewarding it can be. Although 40 years have passed since their conversation that night in Boston, Eileen has not forgotten the signed bank receipt. "I keep it inside my purse and have brought it out many times over the years," she says.

Setting Ground Rules

Most of us want to have a successful career *and* a rewarding relationship and family life. The problem comes when you get into the habit of sacrificing yourself and your family for the company. Years later, you may find yourself in a career trap you can't withdraw from because your living expenses are so high you can't afford to quit. My advice is to establish clear ground rules for your work-life integration and stick to them, rather than doing whatever it takes to get ahead.

When I was at Litton, my boss owned an expensive home in Beverly Hills and belonged to exclusive country clubs, yet he called regularly to say how much he hated his job. One day I asked, "If it's that bad, why don't you quit?" Instantly he replied, "With all my expenses, I can't afford to." A few years later, he died of lung cancer from smoking to relieve his stress.

To achieve work-life integration, it is essential to set clear boundaries between work and home life. If you do so, you will be pleasantly surprised about where life will lead you. After all, the alternative is to earn a lot of money and not have the time to share it with your family, or to become estranged from your spouse and children because you neglected them.

Integrated leaders find life more fulfilling and develop healthier organizations. They radiate authenticity because they are the same person at home and work. They delegate well and empower others because they cannot cram it all in themselves. They make more thoughtful decisions because they have perspective and trusted support teams. They bring positive energy because they are recharged and rested. In the long run, they achieve better results.

Your Support Team

Leaders don't succeed on their own. The loneliness of leadership has been well documented, but remedies have not. Everyone has insecurities; some are just more open about them than others. Even the most outwardly assured executives need support and appreciation. Authentic leaders build close relationships with people who will counsel them in times of uncertainty, support them in times of difficulty, and celebrate success with them.

Essentially, leaders facing personal or professional turmoil face two choices: wear a mask and try to fix the problems themselves or reveal their innermost thoughts and feelings to those closest to them so they can help. Many leaders choose to wear a mask even with their spouses, advisers, leadership teams, and friends. Without confidants to provide perspective in crisis, it is easy to lose your way. That is risky, because crises are times when you need your support team the most.

Leaders need a multifaceted support structure that includes:

- Your spouse or partner
- Your mentors and/or coach
- Your support group
- Your friends and community

Your support team provides affirmation, advice, perspective, suggestions for course corrections, and love. During their most difficult times, leaders find comfort in being with people they trust so they can be open and vulnerable. During low points, they cherish friends who value them for *who* they are, not *what* they are.

Your leadership journey is likely to take many unexpected turns. Life is full of challenging situations, including ethical dilemmas, midcourse career changes or burnout, interpersonal challenges, marriage and family issues, failures, and loneliness.

That's when you need your support team, which will help you stay on track, especially when outside forces pressure you to deviate. It is important to build these relationships long before there is a crisis in your life. Shared experiences and vulnerability create the trust and confidence you need in times of uncertainty. Leaders must give as much to their relationships as they receive so that mutually beneficial relationships can develop. Developing these relationships now may be one of the most important ways to prevent crises from occurring and stay on the course of your True North.

Your Spouse or Partner

Your spouse or partner is the most valuable member of your support team—the person who knows you intimately and with whom you can share your fears, uncertainties, and vulnerabilities. When you do so, you will find your partner will give you deep insights, candid advice, and loving support when you need it most.

Too many people get into autopilot with their partner. After a failed marriage, successful investor Peter Graham told us that he realized he needed to establish rhythms that would help him cherish his spouse. They do weekly dates and a quarterly retreat to foster connection. Even if the retreat is just a half day at a coffee shop, finding the space to check in at a deeper level is essential to maintaining a strong partnership.

Mentors and Coaches

Most authentic leaders have mentors who help them develop the skills to become better leaders and the confidence to lead authentically. The best mentoring interactions spark mutual learning, exploration of similar values, and shared enjoyment. Mentoring is a two-way street in which both people learn a great deal from each other, and the bilateral connection sustains it.

As a young entrepreneur, Howard Schultz realized he needed someone with whom he could share his fears and vulnerabilities. When Starbucks had only 11 stores, Howard heard Warren Bennis lecture on leadership and thought, "Here is someone I can learn from."

> Whom do you talk to when you're afraid to demonstrate vulnerability and insecurity to others? You need advice from someone who has been there before. I asked Warren for his help, calling frequently. He taught me that vulnerability is a strength. Demonstrating your values, emotions, and sensitivities empowers others, as no one is impervious to having doubts.

Warren was an amazing mentor for me as I started writing *Authentic Leadership* in 2003 and then *True North* in 2007. He never wrote or edited my work, but his wisdom on key points was invaluable.

As Zach reflects on his close mentors, he observes, "Many emerging leaders want a magical mentor who shares advice that helps solve their problems." That model is rarely sustainable because it's a one-way model. The people you want to mentor you are busy and don't have a lot of excess time. They might have lunch with you once a year, but you cannot build a deep relationship that way. To know someone well you need to spend consistent time together where they come to know you deeply. Zach speaks about how our relationship grew:

> When I first met Bill in 2009, he wanted to learn how to use social media to connect with my generation of emerging leaders. Over time, our discussions broadened, and I shared research and made suggestions about his writing. As we worked together, Bill shared advice and perspectives on my strengths and my business, challenging me by asking deep questions.
>
> A decade later, we have spent hundreds of hours together which has shaped me in so many ways. Were it not for his challenges, I would have taken a position at a consulting firm out of graduate school instead of having the courage to start Three Ships. My life would be totally different.

Since leaving Medtronic in 2001, I have spent much of my time mentoring emerging leaders, as I feel you are the great hope to positively impact the world through leading authentically. While teaching MBAs, I spend 3 hours a day talking with future leaders in my office. This has enabled me to walk in their shoes, appreciate what's important to them, understand their work lives, and see how they are struggling to live integrated lives. These relationships inspire me and provide deep insights for this book.

In the past, hiring a coach was seen as remedial. Today, it is a developmental step in becoming the best leader you can be. Many CEOs and executives have recently hired coaches to help them become more effective leaders. The dean of CEO coaches is Marshall Goldsmith, who has coached Best Buy's Hubert Joly, Ford's Alan Mulally, Mayo's John Noseworthy, and many others. A good coach can help you see your blind spots and find ways to address your shortcomings without taking away your strengths.

True North Groups

Having a support group that convenes regularly for deep dialogue helps you stay on track of your True North. In 1975, my late friend Doug Baker and I formed a group of six men committed to meet weekly on Wednesday mornings from 7:15 a.m. to 8:30 a.m. to discuss important issues in our lives. Doug and I later wrote a book about this experience called *True North Groups*.

Each week, one member initiates the discussion with a thoughtful set of questions or readings that focuses on challenges we are facing. In a sense, we are a personal board of advisers for each other. This group was invaluable to me when I was going through the process of changing jobs from Honeywell to Medtronic. Our group is still going strong after 45 years.

Penny and I have a couples' group that meets monthly and has traveled the world together on hiking trips and visits to the Holy Lands. When Penny was diagnosed with breast cancer in 1996, the group was present to support her through her surgery and healing process.

Over time, both groups have helped our members deal with difficult dilemmas and provided support through their most challenging times. At times, these groups function as a nurturer, a grounding rod, a truth teller, and a mirror. At other times, the group functions as a challenger or an inspirer.

Friends and Community

Having close friends is essential to living a fulfilling life. While it is wonderful to make new friends, it is most important to stay in touch with long-term friends from school and early work experiences, especially if you are living in different parts of the world.

In addition, being part of a community and doing community service grounds you in your life and leadership and provides support in difficult times. In Minneapolis we learned just how important our community is during the COVID-19 pandemic and the aftermath of George Floyd's murder. As you advance in leadership, it is important that you stay in touch with diverse people who expose you to new ideas, challenges, and perspectives.

Navigating Challenges with Your Support Team

Facing dual crises in his personal life and at work, Piper Jaffray CEO Tad Piper learned just how essential his support team was in navigating difficult challenges. At age 36, Tad was appointed chief executive of his family's financial services firm. He felt he had little time for intimate groups because of his hectic life. He notes, "If you told me 20 years ago I would be part of three groups that talk about feelings and God, I would have said, 'Thank you, but I don't do groups.'"

Many of us find excuses—I'm too busy, the payoff isn't clear, I'll do it next year—to avoid building the types of relationships these groups engender. For Tad, the realization that he needed greater support came after he underwent treatment for chemical dependency. "In treatment, my family told me about how my chemical use was affecting them," he explains. "It was horrible."

Afterward, he joined Alcoholics Anonymous (AA). He notes, "My AA group is invaluable."

We are hardworking people trying to stay sober, lead good lives, and be open, honest, and vulnerable. We talk about our chemical dependency in a disciplined way as we go through the 12 steps. I feel blessed to be surrounded by people who are thinking about these kinds of issues and doing something, not just talking about them.

With the help of this group as well as his couples' group and Bible study group, Tad rebounded. He credits all three groups with transforming his relationships and his life. "Most of us don't find the balance we so desperately seek," he says. "It is incredibly valuable to be reinforced by others who are wrestling with similar issues and actually doing something about them."

When Tad faced a monumental financial and legal crisis in his business, he drew on the reservoir of these deep relationships for strength. He began by sharing his emotions in a long, tearful conversation with his wife and then shared the pressures with his closest friends. "Our friendships weren't based on whether I succeeded or failed on this problem," he says. Acknowledging to these close confidants that the situation was out of his control brought him a sense of relief. With their support, he faced his fears and finally accepted his situation.

Tad says his experience with chemical dependency taught him how to ask for help and be vulnerable, which allowed him to connect deeply with his team. He turned a crisis that could have killed his company into a professional triumph.

Managing Dual Careers

One of the greatest challenges couples face today is managing dual careers, particularly while raising families. Can both people achieve their career ambitions, or does one person's career take precedence? Will their children grow up healthy or feel neglected? During

COVID-19, many leaders found their lives were more manageable while working from home. Will that last in the postpandemic era?

As the following stories illustrate, you can make dual careers work if both you and your partner are flexible, in constant communication, and steadfast in establishing boundaries on work and home life.

Anne Mulcahy and her husband, Joe, are both Xerox veterans who made significant trade-offs in managing their dual careers. Anne says, "I work hard at my career, but my family is the most important thing in my life. I love Xerox, but it is not even on the same scale as my family." She and Joe decided one of them would be at home with their kids every night. They also agreed they would not move; instead they commuted, even when their jobs required traveling great distances. Anne says, "To be CEO of Xerox never having moved is quite extraordinary, but it's doable. At Xerox, we expect people to put their families first. Unacceptable trade-offs should not be part of work."

Ulta Beauty CEO Mary Dillon and her husband, Terry, both came from large families and wanted to have a large family of their own, but weren't sure how they would manage that with two careers. Mary explains how they made it work: "It became clear early on that it made sense for my career to take the lead. I had a career in business that I loved and was starting to really take off. Terry was a biochemist, and while he liked the field, he wasn't as devoted to his career as I was."

> After our first child was born, I created Quaker Oats' first job-sharing program with another female executive. We both worked three days a week and had two days at home, while running a P&L and managing a team. After our second child, I was up for a promotion that would have required that I go back to full-time. That is when we made the decision for Terry to retire, and it worked so well that we had two more kids after that.

Phil and Annika McCrea have constantly made trade-offs throughout their marriage while raising three children. Phil made the difficult decision to plunge ahead with starting a company as they were starting their family, while Annika built her consulting practice. Living in San Francisco, Phil was exhausted from traveling coast-to-coast virtually every week to meet with his pharmaceutical customers, so they made the difficult decision to relocate to New Jersey after Annika persuaded her firm to transfer her. For the last decade they have maintained dual CEO careers, Annika at Bonvent Holdings and Phil at ClearPoint. In 2015, they moved their family to Sweden so their children could learn Annika's Swedish culture. Their story illustrates the challenges of dual-career families, but also that it can be done with mutual flexibility.

As young professionals achieve greater success in their careers, their salaries increase, but so do the demands on their time. Many people choose to use their extra income on a more luxurious car or nicer vacations. A better expenditure may be to spend money on support systems—nannies, home maintenance providers, house cleaners, cooks, or lawn care services—that allow you to prioritize the important people in your life.

Healthcare technology entrepreneur Ben Lundin found himself deeply engaged with his work. Yet at home, the drudgery of picking up toys and cleaning for an hour each evening became monotonous. He worked out a weekly arrangement where his nanny would stay late and clean up while he went on a date with his wife, Julia. Buying quality time together offers a higher return for Ben than anything else he could do with the money.

Create Well-Being in Mind, Body, and Spirit

Do you have a sense of well-being in your life? Well-being exists when you feel harmony, serenity, and a sense of fulfillment in your mind, body, and spirit.

The COVID-19 pandemic caused people to ask hard questions about their well-being at work and in their lives. For many, the pandemic has raised the question, "Why do I work? Is it worth it?"

It also triggered the Great Resignation, when millions left their jobs because they found little meaning in their work.

Many people find working from home so satisfying and productive that they are refusing to return to their office on a regular basis. In contrast, others are eager to get back as they are starved for the human interactions and communities. Regardless, employers report high levels of stress, burnout, and mental health needs in their workforce.

Long after COVID-19 abates, the psychological impact of the pandemic will be with us. People want to find harmony in their lives as well as fulfillment. No longer are they willing to sacrifice their lives for their work. The solution is found in nurturing yourself in all aspects of your life: mental, physical, and spiritual.

Develop Mental Acuity

Think of your mental development as a "T": in the early stages of your career, you are learning a great deal and going deep into your field of expertise. As you progress in leadership roles, it is essential to broaden your perspective by being well-informed about a wide range of subjects inside and outside the company. You need to develop what Microsoft's Satya Nadella terms a worldview, a clear vision of where the world is going and how your organization fits in. Doing this well requires a great deal of reading, both about current events and world history.

In taking on greater leadership roles, your job inevitably involves more stress, which can cause you to lose perspective and cloud your decision-making. That's when you need to take a pause—personal time to reflect. As Chapter 4 describes, some people practice meditation or yoga to center themselves and relieve anxiety. Others find solace in prayer. Some people release tension by working out at the end of a long workday. Still others find relief through laughing with friends, listening to music, reading, or going to movies.

It's not important what you do, so long as you establish routines to relieve your stress and think clearly about life, work, and personal issues.

Don't abandon these routines when you're facing an especially busy period, because that is when you need your stress reduction techniques most of all.

Take Care of Your Body

To be most effective through all the challenges you will face, you need to treat your body as an athlete would—exercising regularly, pacing yourself throughout the day, and observing healthy eating and drinking habits. In the past, many leaders relaxed with heavy meals and several drinks. As a result, they gained weight and lost mental acuity.

New research is demonstrating the benefits of a full night of sleep and limited alcohol on your physical health and sense of well-being. No longer can leaders sustain sleeping only five or six hours per night. You need seven to eight hours of sleep for your body to recharge and your mind to reset.

Exercise must be an essential part of your day; it too often gets squeezed out unless you protect the time. Having survived a bout with cancer, J.P. Morgan's Jamie Dimon exercises four times a week despite his busy schedule and avoids black tie and sports events to prioritize eating right, sleep, and family time. Your leadership journey is a long one, and you will have the resilience and stamina to navigate it successfully only if you take good care of your body.

Nurture Your Spirit

The most personal area of our leadership development is understanding our purpose in the world. Nurturing your spirit requires asking profound questions such as, "Why am I here?" and "What is the meaning and purpose of my life?" For most of us, it is hard to address these deep questions by ourselves. That's why we need trusted people in our lives whom we can be fully open with as we share our deepest dilemmas, ask questions, and discuss different points of view. As I have learned over many years, having a close group of friends outside your work, as well as a True North Group, are invaluable.

Many leaders have an active religious or spiritual practice to engage these issues. Some seek the answers through a process of introspection. Others explore them through discussions with close confidants. To ignore these important issues means that you are at risk of being trapped by external expectations rather than seeking what is authentic to you.

Leading an authentic life requires openness to all that life has to offer and a willingness to go with the flow of life. It is important to seek this richness early in life when you are in a formative stage and open to the breadth of your experiences. You will be surprised at the way early experiences open new avenues of exploration, lead you to interesting people, and shape your thinking about your professional life as well as your personal life. At the end of the day, you will be able to tell your grandchildren that you had the cour-age to dive into life, experience its joys and sorrows, and savor each day as a blessing.

The Flexible Workplace

In this postpandemic era, COVID-19 is having long-lasting effects on people's attitudes about why and where they work. People are more concerned about their well-being than ever before, as they should be. In March 2020, most companies hoped that after a 2-week quarantine, life would return to normal. Two years later, the psy-chological impact on people is being felt even as the virus fades.

During the interlude, habits changed as people embraced the benefits of avoiding long commutes and spending more time with family, while others were stressed by back-to-back Zoom meetings that were largely transactional with few opportunities to build rela-tionships. While office workers could have more flexibility, people in manufacturing, research, health care, and service industries must be in the workplace, which creates cultural disparities.

While norms have changed, human nature has not. It remains challenging to develop deep relationships entirely remotely. Many people miss the collegiality of their workplace, opportunities for informal interactions, collaboration, creativity and mentoring, and the sense of belonging that comes from healthy workplaces.

Looking ahead, key to bridging these differences is workplace flexibility. The standard 8:30 a.m. to 5:00 p.m. workday is gone. Organizations need to create hybrid workplaces, with some people in the office while others are remote yet still creating a sense of belonging for everyone. Or they may revert to select days of everyone being in the office with the remainder being flexible.

Each organization is different and will tailor its workplace to the nature of its business and its people. As leaders, you will face the challenge of making this new environment effective, while ensuring that you use your leadership to ensure the well-being of all your employees.

Emerging Leader: Martha Goldberg Aronson

Martha Goldberg Aronson started her career at Medtronic and quickly developed a reputation as a high-potential leader. She joined the company's acquisitions group and was chosen two years later as a Medtronic Fellow to attend graduate business school. After rejoining Medtronic as a product manager, she was promoted to general manager of its rapidly growing Urology and Gynecology business.

One day, she was home alone with her 3-year-old and 5-week-old sons when the phone rang. Medtronic's head of human resources asked her, "What would you think about an international assignment?" Martha recalls, "I hemmed and hawed and told her this wasn't the best day to talk about a move." Martha was skeptical about whether an international move was right for her career or her personal life. Being far from the support of her parents and siblings with a toddler and a baby was not part of her game plan. She worried about the impact on her husband's career and was hesitant to walk away from the dynamic team she had built in her business.

When she discussed the European opportunity with her husband, Dan, his immediate reaction was, "Let's go," although it meant a break in his career. Realizing this was a unique opportunity to live and work overseas and give her young children exposure to another culture, she accepted the job. Martha flourished in the European environment, as she grew from daily exposure to the wide range of cultures. She took a risk when an opportunity arose, and embraced leading in a complex geographic environment without knowing the next step in her career.

After three years in Europe, Martha became pregnant with her third child and felt that she needed to be closer to her family in Minnesota. Her husband was also eager to resume his career. She called Medtronic CEO Art Collins, who immediately offered her the position as head of investor relations. Just a year later, she was promoted to head of human resources.

Eager to return to a line position, Martha became national sales manager for Hill-Rom based in Chicago, a position that required constant travel. Unhappy with being away from her family, Martha reconsidered her move, and accepted a position at Minnesota-based Ecolab as executive vice president and president of its $500 million global healthcare business.

Martha's motivation to take on significant challenges in stretch roles comes from her passion for helping others, which she tries to instill in her children as well. She recalls, "The other day I told my son, 'I'm going away on business, but I'll only be gone one night.'" He told her she could stay longer if it meant that she could help more people.

More recently, Martha left Ecolab and transformed her career yet again to focus on board service. These days she is chair of the board of Beta Bionics, past chair of the Guthrie Theater, and a board member of Cardiovascular Systems and CONMED Corporation.

All leaders face difficult questions about work-life integration, but Martha's story offers some essential lessons. Her European role proved to be a formative experience for her career and her family. However, too many sacrifices for your career may be a signal your life is out of balance. You must remain mindful of what you and your family can handle, then put boundaries around your work decisions, or you may find that work takes over your life—and then you will not be effective in either domain.

Bill's Take: Knocking Down Artificial Walls

From the time I was a teenager, I was committed to leading a great organization and having a great family life. When Penny and I were dating, we talked about how we could support both our careers and still have plenty of time for our family. Before our children were born, finding a balance was easy.

The birth of our sons, Jeff and Jon, changed everything. Penny was working as a consulting psychologist just as my travel was heating up. My absences put pressure on Penny to raise the boys *and* get her work done. I tried to do my full share of the child rearing but cannot say I succeeded. As hard as I tried, Penny wound up with a greater share of the burden.

Can you imagine yourself trying to be a strong, mature leader at work, impervious to the pressures? A rising leader in your community? A laid-back person at home? Practicing a private spiritual life? That's what I was doing in my early 30s. To cope with these different roles, I created internal compartments for them and behaved according to the expectations in each environment. Anyone who knew me well saw I was anything but authentic.

Then Penny and I went on a life-changing spiritual retreat. The sharing of love we experienced deeply moved us, but I also saw clearly how I was compartmentalizing my life. I did not have the courage to share who I really was with people in these different environments, especially my superiors at work.

After the weekend, I decided to knock down these artificial walls and decompartmentalize my life—committing to be the same person at home, at work, in the community, and in church. Penny was my reality check, challenging me when I got too busy. Still, it took several years before I felt fully comfortable letting people see who I truly was.

In the late 1980s, high stress at Honeywell carried over into my home life. I was traveling almost constantly, unhappy in my work, and began turning to activities outside the company for fulfillment, such as coaching youth soccer. Meanwhile, I was in denial about how the stress was affecting my family and me. It was a good thing Penny confronted me about my behavior and the stress it put on her. In retrospect, it took pain at work and at home for me to face up to changing directions in my career and focus on what is important in life.

Idea in Brief: Lead an Integrated Life

Recap of the Main Idea

- Nobody achieves a perfect balance between all aspects of life. How you make trade-offs between your career, family, friends, community, and personal life reflects your values and determines how fulfilling you find your life.

- Think about integration in terms of bringing the major parts of your lives together.

- Integrated leaders establish clear ground rules to balance the different parts of their lives, relieve stress, and think clearly about personal and professional issues.

Questions to Ask

1. What do you do to ensure that you stay grounded professionally?

2. In what ways do your family life, personal life, friendships, and community life add to or detract from your professional life?

3. What is the most difficult trade-off between various aspects of your life that you have made in the past? What would you do differently in the future?

4. How do you measure success in your life? What is your personal scorecard? What long-term achievements would you like to realize in your life?

5. Make a list of the most important relationships in your life. Why are these people important to you? How do you look to them for support?

6. Do you have a personal support group? If so, what is its value and meaning to you and your leadership?

Practical Suggestions for Your Development

- Reflect on the time you're allocating to each part of your life and consider whether you're allocating time to the areas where you're most fulfilled.

- Prioritize finding time for yourself by establishing consistent routines such as meditation, yoga, exercise, or spending time with friends.

- Gain perspective by seeking out ways to get involved in your community through charity events or volunteer opportunities.

- Build a personal support team through small groups and/or mentorship; ensure these are two-way relationships by helping others as well.

- Create a personal scorecard for how you measure success in your life; review the scorecard and grade yourself on it regularly.

Part Three

Lead People

Part I looked inward as you explored your life journey and development as an authentic leader. In Part II, we used a compass to capture the idea of True North and bring together the practices of cultivating self-awareness, developing values, finding your sweet spot, and integrating your life. These practices help you stay grounded and serve as essential preparation for making the journey from *I* to *We*, or from self-centeredness to other-centeredness.

In Part III, the focus shifts outward. As a well-developed leader, how will you apply your energies to meeting the needs of society? The real measure of your effectiveness as a leader is your ability to use your True North to lead a group of people in solving challenging problems that truly impact the world.

By shifting your focus from yourself to others, you make the transformation from *I* to *We* (Chapter 8). Fundamentally, this is about adopting a servant leadership approach.

Then you are prepared to discern your personal purpose, what we call North Star, in leading others. When you bring your North Star into alignment with your organization's purpose, you unleash tremendous passion (Chapter 9).

Having this clarity enables you to COACH your teammates instead of using traditional top-down managerial techniques. To bring this idea to life, we propose a framework of Caring, Organizing, Aligning, Challenging, and Helping (Chapter 10).

8

I TO *WE*

> The best way to find yourself is to lose
> yourself in the service of others.
> —*Mahatma Gandhi*

We now tackle the greatest challenge of your journey: the transformation from *I* to *We*. In your early years, you are measured primarily for your individual contributions. Thus, the most difficult transition for emerging leaders is recognizing that leadership is not about them—it's about serving others and bringing out their best. *We* leaders are servant leaders.

I first encountered the notion of servant leadership in 1966 when I invited Robert Greenleaf to share his views with a Harvard seminar I was leading. As he wrote in his 1970 essay, "The Servant as Leader,"

> The servant leader is servant first. One wants to serve first; then one aspires to lead. This is sharply different from one who is leader first, perhaps because of the need to assuage an unusual power drive or to acquire material possessions.
>
> A servant leader focuses primarily on the growth and well-being of people and their communities. The servant leader shares power, puts the needs of others first, and helps people develop and perform as highly as possible.

Nelson Mandela: Seeking Reconciliation

While spending 27 years in prison for a political crime he didn't commit, Nelson Mandela endured many different forms of pain: hard labor, racist taunts, and extreme illness. Because of his efforts, he saved South Africa from civil war and inspired leaders all over the world.

On February 11, 1990, he walked out of his prison cell on Robben Island, a free man for the first time since 1963. He described the scene:

> As I walked toward the prison gate, I raised my right fist and there was a roar from the crowd. I had not been able to do that for 27 years. It gave me a surge of strength and joy.

That evening, Nelson spoke to a large crowd at the Grand Parade in Cape Town. His carefully chosen remarks set forth his plan for South Africa's future:

> I stand here before you not as a prophet but as a humble servant of you, the people. Your tireless and heroic sacrifices have made it possible for me to be here today. I therefore place the remaining years of my life in your hands.

In those few words, Nelson declared that his purpose was to be a servant leader for all South Africans. Despite his many years in prison, he harbored no bitterness. He wanted democracy for all, not just Black South Africans. In his book, *Long Walk to Freedom*, Nelson Mandela elaborates,

> I knew people expected me to harbor anger toward Whites. But I had none. I wanted South Africa to see that I loved even my enemies while I hated the system that turned us against one another.
>
> We did not want to destroy the country before we freed it, and to drive the Whites away would devastate the nation. Whites are fellow South Africans. We must do everything we can to persuade our White compatriots that a new, nonracial South Africa will be a better place for all.

Nelson Mandela did not start as such a servant leader; he learned to be one through years of reflection. When the Afrikaners took power in South Africa in 1948 and created apartheid, he became a founding member of the Youth League of the African National Congress (ANC), aligning with young leaders that included Walter Sisulu, Oliver Tambo, and Thabo Mbeki. Eventually, the Youth League took over the ANC.

In the 1950s, Nelson was repeatedly arrested for sedition. Later, he joined the South African Communist Party and founded a militant group to sabotage the Afrikaners' apartheid government. He frequently organized anti-apartheid boycotts and demonstrations that erupted in violence.

In 1956, the Afrikaner government arrested him for high treason in causing violence. He endured the 4-year treason trial and was declared not guilty. That didn't satisfy the Afrikaner government, which arrested him for political crimes in 1962. During the ensuing Rivonia trial, he gave his most important speech, defending the ANC's actions and laying the groundwork for South African democracy 3 decades later. He concluded his 3-hour oration, saying:

> I have dedicated my life to this struggle of the African people. I have fought against White domination, and I have fought against Black domination. I have cherished the ideal of a democratic and free society in which all persons will live together in harmony and with equal opportunities. It is an ideal for which I hope to live and to see realized, but an ideal for which I am prepared to die.

The speech was to no avail. On June 12, 1964, Nelson Mandela was sentenced to life imprisonment. During his long years in prison, Nelson went from a young rebel to a transformative leader who realized his greater purpose was to serve his nation by saving it from civil war and reuniting *all* the people of his country. He reframed his leadership purpose from the *I* of leading Black South Africans to becoming a servant of all South Africans who could reconcile Blacks and Whites to create the new South Africa, centered on social justice and opportunity for all.

If ever someone had a right to be bitter toward his captors and the injustice done to him, it was Nelson Mandela. How then could he honor the prison guards who looked after him and forgive the judge who sentenced him? How was he able to negotiate with the leader of a minority government that repeatedly ordered his people beaten and killed to stay in power? When he was elected president, how was he able to cast aside calls for revenge and offer reconciliation to his oppressors?

To know the answers to these questions, one would have to walk in Nelson Mandela's shoes or look into his soul. When I met privately with him in 2004, I was moved by his serenity. He was passionate and calm, focused entirely on his mission of reconciliation from racial injustice. As a servant leader, Nelson Mandela rose above discrimination, injustice, and hatred. His leadership transformation inspires us to serve and lead others in greater callings.

Hero's Journey to Leader's Journey

As we enter the world of work, most of us envision ourselves in the image of a hero who can change the world for the better. This is a perfectly natural embarkation point for leaders. After all, so much of our early success in life depends upon our individual efforts, from the grades we earn in school to our performance in individual sports to our initial work assignments. Admissions offices and employers assess us based on these achievements. But as time moves forward, it is imperative to grow past this narrative.

PPG executive Jaime Irick explains the *I* to *We* transformation:

> *You must realize that it's not about you—your ability to do well on a standardized test or be a phenomenal analyst or consultant. When you become a leader, your challenge is to inspire others, develop them, and create change through them. If you want to be a leader, you've got to flip that switch and understand that it's about serving the folks on your team. The sooner people realize it, the faster they will become leaders.*

When we are promoted from individual roles to leadership, we believe we are recognized for our ability to get others to follow us.

If we think leadership is just about getting others to follow us and do our bidding as we climb the organization ladder, we will alienate those whom we need as teammates.

While people succeeded in the past by pushing others aside to get ahead, our colleagues today won't tolerate that kind of behavior. A *New York Times* headline blared, "No more working for jerks"; Stanford Professor Bob Sutton wrote *The No Asshole Rule*; and financial services firm Baird has even codified "the no asshole rule" in its training and terminated employees for violating it.

Unfortunately, most organizations tolerate people with these bad behaviors, thinking they cannot get along without their performance. That is a myth. These *I* managers create a lot of destruction in their wake, have high turnover in their organizations, and never empower their teams to perform. As I learned from many of my mentees, people don't leave companies—they leave bad managers. I know that from personal experience as I had two jerks as bosses, which accelerated my departures.

On our journey to be authentic leaders, we must discard the myth that leadership means having legions of supporters follow us as we ascend to the pinnacles of power. In place of this myth, we realize that leadership is serving others and empowering them to achieve their dreams. This transformation from *I* to *We* is the most important step in your development as a leader.

Only when leaders stop focusing on their personal needs and begin to see themselves as serving others are they able to develop other leaders. They feel less competitive with talented peers and subordinates and are more open to other points of view, enabling them to make better decisions. They overcome their need to control everything and learn that people are more interested in working with them. A light bulb turns on as they recognize the unlimited potential of empowered leaders working together toward a shared purpose. An empowered team unleashes much greater energy than a directed team because people can do the work to fulfill a purpose, not to meet the boss's objective.

I Leaders	We Leaders
Attain power and position	Serve others
Self-interest drives decision-making	Purpose drives decision-making
"I can do it on my own"	"It takes a team with complementary strengths"
Pacesetter: "I'll be out front; follow me"	Empowering: "Work together to fulfill mission"
Ask for compliance with rules	Seek alignment through values
Arrogance	Humility
Directs others	Coaches and mentors others
Focus on near-term results	Focus on serving customers and employees
Fire in their eye: extreme conviction	Inspiring and uplifting
Developing loyal followers	Empowering people to lead
Credits themselves	Credits the team

Figure 8.1   *I* versus *We* Leaders

Figure 8.1 captures distinct differences between *I* leaders and *We* leaders.

Making the journey from *I* to *We* is not easy. It not only requires a mental rethinking of your leadership but also necessitates changes in behavior to focus on others rather than yourself. A fulfilling life is about serving something or someone greater than ourselves—a worthy cause, an organization important to you, your family, or a friend in need. In my experience, that's the best way to know your life matters.

See Yourself as Others See You

One of the hardest things for leaders to do is to see themselves as others see them. When they receive critical feedback, their initial response is often defensive—challenging the validity of the criticism or the critics themselves. If they can process the criticism objectively, however, constructive feedback can trigger a fundamental reappraisal of their leadership and propel them on the journey from *I* to *We*.

That's what Doug Baker Jr. learned as he was rising through the ranks of Ecolab. At 34, Doug saw himself as a fast-rising star, moving rapidly from one leadership role to the next. "I had become arrogant and was pushing my own agenda," he says. Then he got results from a 360-degree feedback survey in which his colleagues told him all this. "I got a major dose of criticism I didn't expect."

> *As part of this process, I went away for five days with a dozen strangers from different companies and shared my feedback with them. Since I had been so understanding in this session, I expected people to say, "How could your team possibly say you were ego-driven?" Instead, I got the same critical assessment from this new group.*
>
> *It was as if someone flashed a mirror in front of me at my absolute worst. What I saw was horrifying, but also a great lesson. After that, I did a lot of soul-searching about what kind of leader I was going to be. I talked to everyone on my Ecolab team about what I had learned, telling them, "Let's have a conversation. I need your help."*

Doug Baker Jr.'s critical feedback about being an *I* leader came just in time. On the verge of becoming overly self-confident and thinking leadership was about his success, the criticism brought him back down to earth. It enabled him to realize his role as a leader was to unite the people in his organization around a common purpose. Several years later, Doug was named chief executive officer (CEO) of Ecolab at age 45, where he built the company into a global leader for 16 years and accomplished remarkable things as a leader in his community as well.

We leaders should consider inverting the organizational chart from having the CEO on top to putting the frontline workers at the top. In that case, everyone in leadership can envision their roles as supporting frontline workers in serving customers instead of trying to control them.

Finally, *We* leaders make judgments about where to add value. Zach's colleague Aarti Sura, chief people officer of Three Ships, coaches him, "This area doesn't need you to lean in. It's okay if it's not done exactly your way." When leaders step back, they create opportunities for their teammates to step up.

Learn How to Delegate

As CEO of the American Red Cross, Gail McGovern has never forgotten struggling with leadership upon her first promotion to the role of telecommunications manager. "Within 1 month, I went from being the best programmer to the worst supervisor in Pennsylvania Bell," she says.

> It's unbelievable how bad I was. I didn't know how to delegate. When somebody had a question about their work, I'd pick it up and do it. My group was not accomplishing anything because I was on the critical path of everything. My boss saw we were imploding, so he did an amazing thing: he gave me every new project that came in. It was unreal. At 4:30 p.m., my team would leave, and I'd be working day and night trying to dig through this stuff.
>
> Finally, I couldn't take it any longer. I went to his office, stamped my foot like a 5-year-old, and said, "It's not fair. I have the work of 10 people." He said calmly, "Look out there. You have 10 people. Put them to work." It was such a startling revelation. I said sheepishly, "I get it."

Gail learned an essential lesson. Her value as a leader was not measured in how much she accomplished. It was measured in the output of her team and those they influenced.

Share Power

Steve Jobs struggled with sharing power in his career. As founder of Apple, Steve was teamed with CEO John Scully, who was recruited from PepsiCo. He not only competed with John but also intentionally undermined engineering teams competing with his beloved Macintosh. That forced the Apple board to fire him from the company he founded because he was so disruptive in pursuing his own agenda.

In his Stanford commencement address, he reflected on the experience:

> *Getting fired from Apple was the best thing that ever happened to me. The heaviness of being successful was replaced by the lightness of being a beginner again, less sure about everything. It freed me to enter one of the most creative periods of my life. During the next 5 years, I started a company named NeXT, another company named Pixar, and fell in love with an amazing woman who would become my wife.*

When Apple bought NeXT, Steve returned to Apple. During his time away, he realized he didn't have to do everything himself and that his greatest gift was inspiring innovative people to create great products. At Pixar, he worked with two of the world's best innovation leaders, Ed Catmull and John Lasseter, and learned the benefits of nurturing great teams. When Steve passed away from cancer in 2011, he left Apple in an extremely strong competitive position. His hand-picked successor, Tim Cook, has built Apple into the world's most valuable company.

Life is about serving something or someone greater than ourselves—that's the way to know that your life matters. Becoming a servant leader propels you on the *I* to *We* journey.

Read More
John Mackey, Founder, Whole Foods

Follow John's journey as he transformed from an outspoken lone ranger to a co-CEO who demonstrates mutual respect and welcomes constructive feedback.

Emerging Leader: Anjali Sud

Anjali Sud grew up in Flint, Michigan, in a traditional Indian immigrant family where she was raised to pursue the American dream. "My parents helped me see that one of the ways I could have an impact on the world was through business, because business can have a real impact on the community." Anjali's father is a doctor and entrepreneur who instilled in her a passion for lifting others up: "Even though he was saving lives, what he found most fulfilling was creating livelihood through economic opportunity and jobs for people."

At 30, Anjali joined IAC's video platform, Vimeo, as director of marketing. Three years later, Anjali was promoted to CEO, and four years after that, the company went public with a market valuation of $5 billion—a stunning rise.

Before Anjali became CEO, the company was pursuing a different strategy as a consumer media company. Anjali sensed that Vimeo was missing a better path, so she approached the interim CEO and pitched him on pivoting the business from a consumer viewing destination to a software company for business customers, saying, "It's not as sexy and it's not media, but it's a huge, untapped market. I have a personal conviction that there's something here." Anjali was given a small team to test the thesis. The new strategy quickly got traction—revenue began accelerating and customer satisfaction scores skyrocketed.

One Friday, the interim CEO called Anjali into his office and asked what her plan would be if the company shut down the consumer business and gave her all the company's resources. "I wasn't prepared for the question, but I had an answer," she says. The following Monday, the IAC board appointed her CEO.

Anjali credits building strong relationships as the chief reason for her successful rise to CEO, because they gave her credibility and momentum throughout the organization.

> The greatest strength I have is building good relationships. I've always believed that if you support your colleagues and give credit where it's due, that will ultimately help you effect change.

Within a week of her appointment to CEO, Anjali laid out a new mission, vision, values, and strategy for Vimeo. "I knew I had to inspire the team to be passionate about something totally different. The vision was Creators First. Instead of focusing on the viewer as we had previously, we care about the creator and their success. And we broadened the definition of 'creator'—it was no longer just the filmmaker or video pro, but every business in the world."

Anjali gained buy-in from her team on the new strategy by being transparent with them about the problems the company was facing and collaborating with experts across the business—always with the goal of helping *them* be successful. "People saw that I was respecting their roles and not trying to take something away from them but genuinely wanting to do what was right for the business so we could all succeed together, which really helped."

For leaders like Anjali, the *I* to *We* transition isn't an easy one. She admits she can still struggle with delegation:

> *One of the hardest transitions for me was going from being a doer to an enabler. As a leader, you get to a point where you realize, I'm not the expert—my job now is to set a vision and then empower other people to do their best work and be the expert.*

Ultimately, Anjali sees her *I* to *We* journey as a badge of honor:

> *Now a decision gets made and I think, "Wait a minute, nobody checked with me on that. I can't believe everyone's just moving." Initially, I questioned whether that meant I was doing my job well. Now I recognize that if that's happening, I'm absolutely doing my job!*

Bill's Take: My Long Journey from *I* to *We*

Early in my career I thought I had great visions and innovative ideas, so I tried to sell people on them, rebutting their concerns and not really listening to their feedback. I was aggressive and willing to take risks and couldn't understand why people weren't willing to get on board. Quite often, I overpowered them by signaling people what

I wanted to do, and they went along, however reluctantly. I had not yet adopted the adage, "People support what they help create."

It took lots of feedback from people I respected before I realized I needed to listen much better to people's ideas, understand their concerns, and bring them together as a group to make decisions. At first, I didn't trust they would come to the conclusions I thought were right. As I matured and gained confidence in my leadership, I became a better listener and learned to trust my teammates. I realized that when I gave people space to develop their own ideas, we generated better ideas and greater commitment to the eventual plan.

For me, it was a long journey from *I* to *We*.

Idea in Brief: *I* to *We*

Recap of the Main Idea

- *We* leaders are servant leaders, focusing primarily on the growth and well-being of people and the communities to which they belong.

- When leaders make the transition from *I* to *We*, they move from thinking that leadership is about them and their personal needs to seeing themselves as serving others by bringing out the best in them.

- The journey from *I* to *We* is difficult because leaders are used to being measured for their individual contributions like good grades or promotions. *We* leaders are measured on the success of their teams.

Questions to Ask

1. Have you made the transformation from *I* to *We*? If so, what experience(s) triggered this transformation for you?

2. If you have not yet made this transformation, what do you need to let go of for a transformation like this to occur?

Practical Suggestions for Your Development

- Ask your team to conduct a 360-degree survey on your leadership, with specific questions on how well you empower, inspire, and grow individuals.

- Create a personal leadership development plan based on the feedback; share the plan with your team and ask for their help in measuring your progress.

- Meet with each of your team members to discuss their strengths, weaknesses, and motivations. Consider how you can help them apply their strengths and improve their weaknesses. How can you use their motivations to help them reach their full potential?

9

YOUR NORTH STAR

Work takes on new meaning when you feel you're
pointed in the right direction. Otherwise, it's just
a job. And life is too short for that.
—*Tim Cook, CEO, Apple*

Your North Star is the purpose of your leadership. You may search for many years until you find your North Star, and an organization where your purpose is in sync with its purpose.

First, you need to discover your True North, which reveals *who you are*, and develop yourself as we discussed in Part II. This process includes "rubbing up against the world" to understand the challenges you will face and be able to make thoughtful choices about where to devote yourself and your leadership.

Then your compass will point the way to your North Star, a constant light in the sky that reveals your purpose. In turn, your North Star unlocks your passion and energy and draws people to you as a leader. If you find alignment between your personal purpose and your organization's purpose, it becomes the motivating force of your leadership that binds people together toward common goals.

Hubert Joly: Finding His North Star

From an early age, French-born Hubert Joly achieved at a prodigious pace. He built a reputation at McKinsey as the smartest guy in the room and made partner by age 30, a signal achievement. He went on to lead EDS France and then turned around Vivendi's video games division.

Leaving Vivendi to become chief executive officer (CEO) of Carlson-Wagonlit Travel (CWT), Hubert thought he was leading effectively, until his head of human resources showed him an organization chart with his name in every box. He says, "I thought I had all the answers, so I tended to look at others as obstacles rather than valuable partners. I focused on their imperfections and kept trying to solve problems for them."

Despite his success, Hubert recognized something was missing. He explains, "In my mid-40s, I felt I reached the top of my first mountain."

> That mountaintop felt desolate. The idea of success I had been chasing turned out to be hollow, and I felt disillusioned and empty. I was also struggling in my marriage. I needed to step back and spend time looking into my soul to find a better direction for my life.

Hubert embarked on a 2-year spiritual journey with a monk as spiritual director, undertaking the spiritual exercises of Ignatius de Loyola, founder of the Jesuit order. During this process, he realized that work is a noble calling to serve others and an expression of love. He quotes the poet Kahlil Gibran, who wrote, "Work is love made visible." He adds, "Work must be guided by the pursuit of a noble purpose with people at its center."

That process enabled Hubert to discover his North Star: "*To make a positive difference for people around me and then to use the platform I have to make a positive difference in the world.*" Hubert's North Star is evergreen—it works for him as long as his purpose is congruent with his organization's purpose.

A year later, Hubert moved to America as CEO of Carlson Companies, CWT's parent company. In 2012, after a successful 5 years at Carlson's helm, he took on the challenge of turning around a flailing Best Buy, where the board had fired the CEO and was battling the founder, who wanted to use private equity funds to take over the company.

In his first week at Best Buy, Hubert didn't go to the corporate headquarters but instead worked in its St. Cloud, Minnesota, store. Describing his experience, he observes,

> *Wearing khaki pants and the iconic Best Buy blue shirt with a "CEO in Training" tag, I spent my first days listening, asking questions, visiting every department, and observing sales associates interacting with customers. What I learned then, I could never have fathomed poring over spreadsheets or sitting in meeting rooms with other executives at headquarters.*

That experience enabled Hubert to learn just what was wrong with Best Buy and to formulate his turnaround plan. He eschewed the classic formula of closing stores, terminating tens of thousands of people, and squeezing suppliers. Instead, he inspired Best Buy's employees to engage in its "Renew Blue" turnaround strategy by increasing revenues and margins and partnering with suppliers, including Samsung, Apple, Microsoft, and Amazon. By 2016, when the turnaround was complete, he worked with his team to craft the company's new growth strategy and mission: *"To enrich customers' lives through technology."*

He explains, "The heart of business is pursuing a noble purpose by putting people at the center and creating an environment where you can unleash human magic." He defines noble purpose at the intersection of four circles:

1. What the world needs
2. What you are good at
3. How you can make a positive difference in the world
4. How you can make money

Hubert warns against making profits your organization's purpose, explaining that "profits are the outcome, not the goal." He also cautions that leaders should avoid purpose statements that are too abstract or too glossy, instead grounding them in true customer needs and demonstrated abilities to achieve competitive advantage.

Hubert notes that "companies are not soulless entities, but human organizations made up of individuals working together in pursuit of a goal to produce value for all stakeholders."

> To unleash human magic, everyone must feel at home, fully valued for who they are, with the space and freedom to be themselves and bring their best selves to work. When a company's noble purpose aligns with employees' individual search for meaning, it can unleash human magic that results in irrational performance.

After leading the spectacular turnaround of Best Buy and the dramatic growth phase that followed, Hubert embarked on the next phase of his leadership journey by becoming a professor at Harvard Business School, where he works with MBAs and executives to imbed his ideas on leadership, noble purpose, and creating human magic (see Hubert's career lifeline in Figure 9.1).

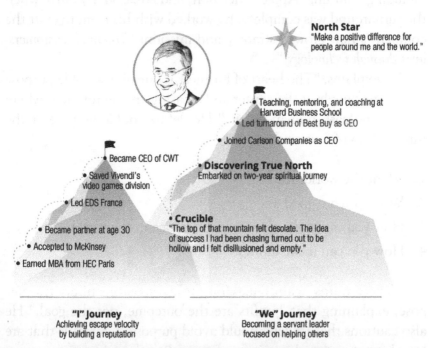

North Star
"Make a positive difference for people around me and the world."

• Teaching, mentoring, and coaching at Harvard Business School
• Led turnaround of Best Buy as CEO
• Joined Carlson Companies as CEO

• Became CEO of CWT

• Discovering True North
Embarked on two-year spiritual journey

• Saved Vivendi's video games division

• Led EDS France

• Crucible
"The top of that mountain felt desolate. The idea of success I had been chasing turned out to be hollow and I felt disillusioned and empty."

• Became partner at age 30
• Accepted to McKinsey
• Earned MBA from HEC Paris

"I" Journey
Achieving escape velocity by building a reputation

"We" Journey
Becoming a servant leader focused on helping others

Figure 9.1   Hubert Joly's Career Lifeline

Pursuing Your North Star

Your North Star emanates from your life story and crucibles. By understanding the meaning of key events in your life and reframing them, you can determine your leadership purpose. Defining your personal purpose is not as easy as it sounds. You cannot do so in the abstract; it takes a combination of introspection and real-world experience to determine where you want to devote your energies.

For some leaders, a transformative event in their lives inspires them and lights the way to their purpose. Other leaders like Hubert have several leadership experiences before discovering their purpose. When we asked emerging leaders about their North Star, many expressed discomfort with the types of organizations they led: "I'm just a banker," or "I lead a marketing company." When we reframed the question by asking what they wanted written on their tombstones, their personal purposes became clearer:

- "Building community and relationships."
- "Using my leadership to help level the playing field for minorities."
- "Developing people and teams to solve interesting, meaningful problems."

Each of these statements is more specific than "make the world better" yet not so narrow that it precludes serving in different positions or types of organizations.

For many of us, we spend our 20s and 30s building skills and establishing our identities. As the priest Richard Rohr says, "We must create our container before we can transcend it." While some may find their North Star at a young age, it is far more common to discover it in the mid-30s through the 40s.

Identifying your purpose frees you to apply yourself fully to it. If you're starting an organization, its purpose should align with your North Star. On the other hand, if you work in an organization that already has a purpose, you should seek congruence between your North Star and the organization's purpose.

Eager to get ahead, young leaders often focus on promotions and titles. When Avon's executive vice president Andrea Jung was passed over for CEO at age 39, her board member Ann Moore, then CEO of *Time, Inc.*, gave her invaluable advice to "follow your compass and not your clock." Setting a timetable for your desired goal will lead you astray; instead, following your compass will show you the way to your North Star.

In Andrea's case, she stayed at Avon and 2 years later was named CEO, a position she held for a dozen years. By the time she became CEO, her North Star was clear: *the empowerment of women*. She comments, "There is purpose in my work: enabling women to be self-empowered, learn to run their own businesses, and achieve economic means to provide education. At the end of the day, that trumps all things."

Saving Lives

Roy Vagelos discovered his North Star as CEO of Merck, where he carried out founder George Merck's passion for discovering life-saving drugs for 2 decades. Roy had been an academic medical researcher for 19 years when he was asked to become dean of two prestigious medical schools, the Universities of Chicago and Pennsylvania. "I was horrified about becoming a dean, because you don't teach or do research; you just shuffle papers and push people around," he explains. Then he got an offer to lead Merck's research.

> I could use my knowledge of biochemistry to discover new drugs, I could impact human health far beyond what I could as a practicing doctor, and I could change the technology of drug discovery. I never thought of myself as a leader but asked myself instead if I was contributing something to the world.

Roy demonstrated his North Star—*to impact human health in the broadest sense*—with his leadership in eliminating the African disease known as river blindness with the drug Mectizan. When market projections indicated Africans could not afford it, Roy took the courageous course of completing the drug's development and distributing it for free throughout Africa until all river blindness was eradicated. He explained, "Here's a drug that can prevent blindness in 18 million people. That single decision put Merck in a position where we could recruit anybody we wanted for the next decade."

During the 1980s and early 1990s, Merck had the most productive record in producing life-saving new drugs of any pharmaceutical company, in large part because of the inspiration Merck's researchers drew from Roy's passion and sense of purpose. Not surprisingly, Merck's shareholder value increased 10 times in 10 years. Now in his 90s, Roy is still going strong. As chair of biotechnology firm Regeneron for the past 25 years, he has guided the creation of numerous revolutionary drugs using monoclonal antibodies and a 4,300 percent increase in shareholder value.

It is hard to find a more noble purpose than the one Roy Vagelos pursued. His leadership is an inspiration to us all. He concludes, "Given a choice of working just to make a living, or benefiting the people of the world, the majority of people will choose the latter."

Read More
Steve Rothschild, Founder, Twin Cities RISE!

Discover how Steve found happiness and fulfillment by shifting from building a business to building lives—leaving his job at General Mills to found an organization that helps the underprivileged.

Align Your Organization around Purpose

As an emerging leader, your most important task is to bring people together to pursue a shared purpose that inspires them. The company's purpose should emanate from the roots of the organization—its founder's intent and the reason it was created in the first place. No organization illustrates the commitment to purpose more vividly than Johnson & Johnson (J&J) and its credo.

J&J's credo was written in 1943 by General Robert Wood Johnson, who was from the company's founding family and chair from 1932 to 1963. The credo articulates the company's responsibilities to its stakeholders, starting with its customers ("patients, doctors and nurses, to mothers and fathers and all others who use our products and services"), followed by its employees, communities, and stockholders.

The credo has been the guiding light of every J&J CEO since Johnson, most notably Jim Burke. In 1982 and again in 1986, Jim was under tremendous pressure when a terrorist laced Tylenol capsules with cyanide, killing several people. Following the charge of the credo, Jim decided to remove all Tylenol from retail shelves, warehouses, and factories until the source of the cyanide was determined. His decision cost J&J a lot of money but has inspired J&J leaders for the past three decades and greatly enhanced the company's reputation among its customers.

Today the J&J credo dominates the lobby at its corporate headquarters. Executive chair Alex Gorsky refers to it regularly in making difficult decisions, such as launching its COVID-19 vaccine. Meanwhile, J&J has increased its shareholder value by more than 2,300 percent since 1982.

It is certainly easier to create a sense of purpose when your company is saving lives like J&J, but can every business have a purpose? Kroger may not save lives, but former CEO Dave Dillon passionately makes the case that serving the public in a service-oriented grocery operation is a dignified, proud profession.

> All human beings want to find meaning in their lives. Our objective is to give them that meaning. We have opportunities to make customers' lives better by making them feel good about the world around them because someone was friendly to them.
>
> Little touches of human kindness can literally change their day. If I deliver that human kindness, I wind up feeling better about myself as well. At the end of our careers, we can look back and say, "I was part of something special."

All too often leaders overlooked the roles of frontline workers in making the company's purpose real, as Dave has done. After all, the frontline workers have the greatest contact with customers in all service businesses and thus are the greatest determinants of customer satisfaction. During the early stages of COVID-19, they were the ones risking their lives to provide essential services to customers while the rest of us were protected behind Zoom screens.

Pursuing a Transformational Purpose

Kees Kruythoff is one of the boldest and most passionate leaders I know when it comes to his purpose and the impact he can have on society. After retiring from Unilever in 2020, Kees founded the LiveKindly Collective to transform the global food system through plant-based foods. "Our reliance on animal products is destroying the earth," he says, "but it doesn't have to be this way. We can give consumers plant-based products that taste like conventional meat but made with sustainable ingredients."

As CEO of Unilever North America, Kees was a passionate advocate for Unilever's mission of sustainability—its corporate purpose. Kees says, "The Unilever sustainable living plan is about how business can be a force for good to have a positive impact on society." When Unilever CEO Paul Polman asked me to become Kees' coach, I enjoyed helping him build on his enormous enthusiasm, drive, passion, and ability to inspire others, while working with him to slow down and smooth off some rough edges.

In 2019, he was deeply disappointed when the board shared that Polman's successor would be his highly respected colleague, Alan Jope. Kees took a 6-month sabbatical to contemplate what lay ahead. It was then he discovered a way he could continue pursuing his North Star of sustainability. He reflects, "My biggest passion, expertise, and what the world needs most all came together in being part of the global transformation from an animal-based to a plant-based system. This is the world's biggest hunger and what it needs most."

Kees continues, "We're blessed with this generation of Gen X, Millennials, and Gen Z, who are leading the plant-based foods revolution."

My teenage daughters ask me, "Dad, why do we ever eat animals?" This generation demands transparency and trust in authentic leaders and insists that business is a force for good. Every company must ask why their business exists and whether it serves society.

Now business leaders are realizing that purpose, relevance, and therefore growth are inextricably linked. For the first time, financial markets recognize that investors will pay a premium for companies that have the environmental, social, and governance at their core.

Kees recognized that the next step of his journey must be about the joy of business as a force for good by creating networks around the world with people whose values are aligned to have a positive impact on society. Kees says, "As I turn 50, I am keen to do another 50 years putting my experience and expertise at service to society. I believe in personal growth, being curious, reinventing yourself, and making conscious choices."

Making Purpose Real

When you know your North Star and feel aligned with your organization's purpose, how do you translate your purpose into action? Purpose without action is meaningless, so your task as a leader is to translate it into tangible reality.

A Spear-in-the-Chest Moment

John Replogle realized that at age 35 in a striking moment.

He yearned to be of service to the world. As an idealistic college student, his peers elected him as student body president at Dartmouth. Later, he used his intellect, teambuilding, and persuasiveness to climb the corporate ladder, first as a consultant at Boston Consulting Group and then at spirits company Diageo, where he became president of Guinness Beer at age 35.

While Guinness's positive essence was communion, John witnessed the other side through his brother's struggle with alcoholism. "One Saturday, in my car with my kids, I looked in the rearview mirror and had my 'spear-in-the-chest' moment. I realized my work and my purpose in life were incompatible. My purpose is to inspire people to take great care of people and planet. As much as I loved Guinness, I wasn't building a future for my kids or caring for people or the planet."

> I asked myself a fundamental question: Now that I have security and comfort and can feed my kids, what am I doing for my self-realization and making the world a better place? My personal mission hadn't manifested in my work. Finally, I said, "I'm not congruent. My two worlds don't support each other."

For John, this moment launched a metamorphosis. He explains, "My prior stage had been about learning skill and competencies."

> I was more focused on professional development than on pursuing my purpose. I asked myself, "Whom do I have an impact on in work and the world around me? Where do I want to fly?"

John left Guinness to join Unilever as head of its beauty line, moving closer to a purpose he believed in. Three years later, he joined Burt's Bees in his first CEO role. Burt's Bees gave John the platform to use purpose as a differentiator for the business. In one dramatic event, his team secretly collected all the trash discarded at the office for two weeks and stacked it at the entrance to a company picnic. In an instant, everyone understood the company's efforts to cut packaging waste through its supply chain. After selling Burt's Bees to Clorox, John became CEO of Seventh Generation with ecofriendly products made from plant-based ingredients.

Between these career transitions, John took periods of "intentional pause" during which he connected with friends and mentors, did volunteer work, and engaged with coaches to ensure he was intentional about his path. He explains, "If you want to find your North Star, start with your personal purpose, then understand your business's purpose, and find the points of intersection so they work together."

Banking with Heart

Tim Welsh's realization came when he was 50. Born in an orphanage and adopted by a Catholic family, Tim realized "my adoption was the only thing that mattered."

> *That was the moment when it became clear God was looking after me in a deeply profound way. That realization has shaped my life since then. I'm among the luckiest people because I've had one mother who loved me so much, she gave me up, and two parents who took me in. When you've been loved that profoundly, your purpose is clear: you're going to be loving to everyone else.*

Tim comes across as so caring, thoughtful, and committed to his purpose and values that when you first meet him you would be excused for thinking that he's a priest or a teacher, but he is vice chair of the nation's fifth largest bank, U.S. Bank.

After graduating from business school, Tim joined McKinsey, where he was inspired by 85-year-old founder Marvin Bower and his clarity of purpose of helping people. Tim adds, "Our purpose should be about serving someone else. The minute we confuse ourselves that our purpose is about us, and we should be rewarded financially, bad things happen. The times I have fallen short are when I forgot that."

> *For example, I lost focus on my purpose when I applied for two roles at McKinsey and got neither of them, because I was focused on me and my promotions. I went on to lead global learning programs at McKinsey for 10 years.*

I blossomed and had the greatest satisfaction of my career because I focused on other people.

In his early 50s, Tim made the bold move to U.S. Bank because he was attracted to its mission: "We invest our hearts and minds to power human potential." He says, "I went there because the bank's purpose aligned with mine."

My personal purpose is to help as many people as I can. With several million clients, I realized I can make a big difference in the lives of millions of people. Our values call for us to put people first, value diversity, and innovate to stay a step ahead. I would only work at a place where the purpose and values aligned with mine, so I can be who I am.

When COVID-19 hit in early 2020, Tim came up with a creative solution. Recognizing that the bank's clients were hurting and stuck at home, as were his employees, he launched an outreach program in which all employees called their clients, not looking for business but simply asking them how they were doing. They said, "Hi, it's Tim from U.S. Bank. It's a tough time, and I want to check in and make sure you're okay. If you need any help or have financial needs, I'm here to help you."

From April to June 2020, bank employees made 1.4 million calls to clients simply offering help. Tim says, "People were shocked. When was the last time you got a call like that from a bank?" As in-person meetings became feasible again in 2021, Tim got his teammates to proactively reach out to clients, scheduling two million appointments, compared with only 50,000 in 2019.

He notes, "All this is rooted in our purpose of helping clients."

We're seeing the highest levels of customer satisfaction ever. On our Friday calls, our bankers share their heartfelt stories and satisfaction in doing something good for someone else. As bankers, we are in a position to empower people to live lives they want to live and enable their businesses to grow. In addition, our foundation gives $150 million per year to the communities we serve. Banks cannot thrive unless the community thrives.

Tim Welsh is the model of a modern banker, who is more focused on serving his clients' needs than on making money, but the virtuous circle he has created has enabled U.S. Bank to perform extremely well.

From Making Money to Improving Lives

Unlike other leaders in this chapter, Omar Ishrak found his North Star not in a moment of great revelation but rather through a lifelong process of introspection. Omar traveled a long way from his home in Bangladesh to become the highly successful CEO of Medtronic. Yet throughout his life and career he has remained true to his life story, his faith and values, and his commitment to using his gifts to make the world a better place.

I asked Omar why so many South Asian immigrants have reached the top of major American companies like Microsoft, Google, Mastercard, Medtronic, and Adobe. His answer: Indians focus on technical education, rigorous thinking, humility, desire to help others, and being satisfied with what you have. He explains, "For immigrants, there is a culture here of wanting to win. America offers opportunity. If you come here and work hard, it doesn't matter what color you are or what language you speak, you will be rewarded."

Omar learned those characteristics from his family growing up in Pakistan and Bangladesh. Shortly before his 18th birthday, Omar moved to London to complete his A level exams. He then entered King's College London, eventually gaining his PhD in E.E. "Doing that was one of the best decisions I ever made," Omar says. "It taught me reasoning, the linkage between theoretical, computational, and empirical approaches and essentially how to think differently."

Omar's thesis was in ultrasound, which became a lifelong passion and led him to focus his purpose on improving people's lives and restoring their health. His ultrasound expertise took him to California, where he worked for Philips and Diasonics, and eventually went to GE. Omar went from thinking "engineering is all I could ever do to wanting to run a company." At GE, he spent 16 years leading its imaging and medical equipment business. He observes, "GE struggled with mission. There was no real consistent corporate mission; financials were always the main priority."

When the opportunity came along to become CEO of Medtronic in 2011 and restore the company's flagging growth, Omar saw his purpose aligned with Medtronic's mission, "To alleviate pain, restore health, and extend life." The day Medtronic announced his appointment, Jack Welch called me, saying, "Bill, you got a good man. He is the finest innovator in all of GE."

Throughout his decade at the helm of Medtronic, Omar was a passionate advocate for the mission, using it to inspire employees, develop the company's innovation strategies, and build the company's growth culture. Omar saw his purpose at Medtronic not just as making money but expanding the number of people restored to full health by Medtronic products. Initially, he focused on expanding Medtronic's reach in emerging markets like China, India, and Latin America. Then he focused Medtronic's research and innovation by addressing unmet medical needs with breakthrough solutions. He explains,

> I am proudest that Medtronic today restores two patients to full health every second, compared with every five to seven seconds when I joined. We created entirely new solutions for challenging diseases with technology for leadless pacemakers, closed loop diabetes treatment, thrombectomy, stroke reduction, clot removal, and blood pressure reduction.

Since retiring, Omar is using his deep understanding of technology and wisdom to help others. As chair of Intel, he is guiding the company through a turnaround. He serves on the boards of

Amgen, Cargill, and Cleveland Clinic and contributes his time to helping people in Bangladesh and nonprofits like Children's HeartLink, which helps children around the world with genetic cardiac disease.

Across these endeavors, Omar still faithfully follows his North Star, concluding, "I want to do something where I can see the difference in people's lives by using humanity and technology. That's what I find most satisfying."

Taking Faith to the Streets

Jim Wallis is a purpose-driven leader who is using his faith to address social justice issues. In 1971, he founded Sojourners to pursue his mission, as he became one of America's leading religious figures. Jim believes purpose has little meaning unless it is translated into action:

> My vocation is for faith to hit the streets in our work, neighborhoods, nation, and the world. If it's not a driving force in your life, it won't be sustained. At Georgetown, I ask students, "How does your faith hit the streets?" If religion doesn't ever change things on the street, it has little impact.

Jim grew up in a White neighborhood of Detroit. As a teenager, he was troubled by the disparities he saw in Black Detroit just a few blocks away, concluding, "Something is terribly wrong with my city and my country. I went into the city to find answers."

> Becoming friends with young Black guys as a janitor at Detroit Edison changed everything. Back at my church an elder told me, "Jim, Christianity has nothing to do with racism; that is political, and our faith is personal." I left my church that night as a teenager. The issue of race was consuming me in mind and heart. I said, "If the Christian faith has nothing to do with racism, then I want nothing to do with Christianity."

While studying at Michigan State, Jim was deeply involved in civil rights and antiwar movements and arrested 20 times in nonviolent civil disobedience. He says, "As a radical student activist, I could put 10,000 people on the streets in two hours." In 1970, when tensions over the Vietnam War brought emotions to a boil, he led the student strike that temporarily shut down Michigan State. Ironically, 44 years later his alma mater awarded him an honorary degree for his unwavering commitment to social justice.

Jim had a conversion during college from studying Matthew's Gospel and a passage in Chapter 25: "Inasmuch as you have done it to one of the least of these my people, you have done it to me." He explains,

> Here is the Son of God saying, "I'll know how much you love me by how you treat them." Them is the marginal, vulnerable, poor, and oppressed. How we treat the poorest and most vulnerable is the real test of our faith. My life's purpose has been figuring out the public meaning of faith.

Jim founded Sojourners in the early 1970s as a faith-based social organization with the mission of "Putting faith into action for social justice." For the past 40 years, he has vigorously pursued that mission, never wavering in his commitment to help the oppressed in society.

He makes a sharp distinction between climbing the career ladder and pursuing your vocation, explaining, "Career is climbing the ladder of success. Vocation is discerning your gifts and your calling, your North Star."

> Your vocation is where the world's crying needs intersect with your gifts. Rather than looking for opportunities to ascend, ask what you're called to be. The difference between career and vocation is central to your leadership— what you're doing every day in your work and relationships. When people ask how to find their North Star, I say, "Trust your questions and follow where they lead."

True to his calling, Jim has taken his work to the streets of South Africa, inmates at Sing Sing Correctional Facility, and the poorest residents of inner-city Washington, D.C., never ceasing in his efforts to help society's underprivileged. Upon retiring from Sojourners in 2021, Jim is chair of Georgetown University's Center on Faith and Justice, still pointing to his North Star in a new role focused on deepening the role of faith in civic life.

Emerging Leader: Rye Barcott

Rye Barcott has made 21 trips in 21 years to help people in Kibera, Africa's largest slum. More than 300,000 people live there in abject poverty in an area the size of Central Park on the outskirts of Nairobi, Kenya. Rye still chairs the board of CFK, which he formed with a Kenyan nurse and a Kenyan youth leader while he was an undergraduate at the University of North Carolina. CFK has become a leading non-governmental organization working with youth in African settlements. *Time* magazine and the Gates Foundation have recognized it as a "Hero of Global Health."

When Rye was 13, his parents took him on a family trip to Africa. He says, "In Nairobi, kids were open and friendly, though the conditions were so toxic my throat burned raw from the dust and fumes. Kids my age were just as smart as I was with big dreams and goals but lived in squalor and had few opportunities for a better life."

While in college, Rye studied Swahili and returned to Kenya to understand Kibera's ethnic violence. Renting a small shack, he caught malaria. "Curled in the fetal position, my stomach heaved, and my head ached so badly I wondered if whatever was inside my body might kill me."

A local woman named Tabitha helped nurse Rye back to health at no cost. In appreciation, he gave Tabitha $26, which she used as seed capital to start a vegetable-selling business. When Rye returned a year later, she had converted her shack into a small medical clinic. He says, "Tabitha showed me the secret of service. It forces you to think less about your problems, as helping others helps yourself." Today Tabitha's medical facilities treat more than 40,000 patients a year and produce important public health research.

Rye carried through his North Star of *being a bridge to disparate groups* from Kibera to his service in the Marines, where he led diverse teams of Americans in combat in Iraq and helped communities rebuild on peacekeeping missions in Bosnia and the Horn of Africa.

Back in Charlotte, North Carolina, Rye launched Double Time in the solar industry with partner Dan McCready. "We did the *True North* exercises and asked ourselves: What does success look like? What other goals do we have in our lives? What type of world do we wish to leave for our children?" Rye recalls,

> *Starting a business is all-consuming. I had three months of savings and two kids. We believed financial success could give us freedom to go back to public service in the future. We enjoyed working together and believed deeply in advancing the solar industry.*

Then Rye formed the cross-partisan effort, With Honor, to reduce polarization and dysfunction in Congress by electing veterans who pledge to serve with integrity, civility, and the courage to work across bitter partisan divides. With Honor aligns closely with Rye's North Star. "Veterans can cross partisan chasms because of our shared experience serving in war," he says. "We cannot remain this polarized and expect our children to inherit a better world."

Leader and North Star	Organization	Organization's Mission	Congruence with North Star
John Replogle Inspire positive change for people and the planet	GUINNESS	Craft distinctive beer of the most outstanding quality fueled by a spirit of innovation	
	Unilever	Make sustainable living commonplace	
	BURT'S BEES	Reconnect people to the wisdom, power, and beauty of nature	
	seventh generation	Transform the world into a healthy, sustainable and equitable place for the next seven generations	
	ONE BETTER ventures	Partner with exceptional entrepreneurs to unlock potential and build an inspired community to do well and good	
Rye Barcott Be a bridge to separate and disparate groups	CFK CAROLINA for KIBERA	Develop local leaders, catalyze positive change, and alleviate poverty in the informal settlement of Kibera in Nairobi, Kenya	
	MARINES	Protect our Nation and advance its ideals	
	DUKE ENERGY	Make people's lives better by providing gas and electric services in a sustainable way: affordable, reliable, and clean	
		Create compelling returns while strengthening communities, building a smarter economy, and advancing energy independence in North Carolina	
	WITH HONOR	Promoting and advancing principled veteran leadership to reduce polarization	
Omar Ishrak Make a difference in people's lives by using humanity and technology	PHILIPS Healthcare	Improve people's health and well-being through meaningful innovation	
	GE Healthcare	Help clinicians provide the best patient care possible	
	Medtronic	Alleviate pain, restore health, and extend life	

Figure 9.2   How Leaders Align Their North Star and Their Work

Bill's Take: Aligning My Work and North Star

From the time I was a boy, I yearned to make my life meaningful by having a positive impact on the world. As far back as high school and college, I tried to build organizations committed to making the world a better place for everyone, but it took lots of experiences before I recognized my North Star all along had been *developing authentic leaders.*

At Medtronic I finally found the place—or it had found me—that offered everything I wanted: values, passion, and the opportunity to help people suffering from chronic disease. The Medtronic mission to restore people to full health inspired me from the moment founder Earl Bakken described it.

In the middle of my career, I had the good fortune to find congruence between Medtronic's mission and my North Star. Yet in growing Medtronic rapidly with increasing complexity in our technology, business units, and geographical areas, we faced an enormous challenge to develop enough authentic leaders who were mission-driven, values-centered, and up to the challenges.

My 13 years at Medtronic were the best professional experience of my life. I embraced the Medtronic mission and followed my North Star to develop authentic leaders who in turn empowered and inspired our 26,000 employees. Two decades after retiring, I have great satisfaction seeing the organization thrive under extraordinary leaders like Omar Ishrak and now Geoff Martha.

While teaching at Harvard Business School since 2004, I have continued to follow my North Star of helping leaders develop. Instead of focusing on a single company, I have the privilege of working with many authentic leaders from all walks of life.

My focus has broadened through writing books, giving speeches and making media appearances, working with CEOs, and mentoring leaders at all career stages. My purpose has not changed—only the venue. At my stage of life, I no longer strive for my own accomplishments but take great satisfaction from the achievements of others.

Idea in Brief: Your North Star

Recap of the Main Idea

- Your True North compass points you toward your North Star, your leadership purpose.
- Your North Star will guide your purposeful leadership to an organization where you can align with your organization's mission.
- Then you need to align your people's personal purpose with your organization's mission and translate that mission into reality.

Questions to Ask

1. Recall your early life story and use it to identify sources of your passions that are close to your heart. By reframing your life story, can you discern your passions more clearly?
2. In what ways do your passions lead you to your North Star, the purpose of your leadership?
3. What is the long-term purpose of your leadership? For the near term, what is your purpose in leading? In what ways does the purpose of your leadership relate to the rest of your life?

Practical Suggestions for Your Development

- Write down your True North and show how it points to your North Star.
- Examine your current organization's mission and discern how it aligns with your North Star.
- Make a list of specific actions you can take to translate your organization's mission into reality.

10

THE LEADER AS COACH

> The most important thing in leadership is truly caring.
> The best leaders care about people they lead, and
> people know when caring is genuine.
> —*Dean Smith, University of North Carolina*
> *Basketball Coach*

Those who make the *I* to *We* transformation connect authentically with their team because they have their best interests at heart. People follow leaders who understand them and are invested in their success. When such leaders point their teams toward a clear purpose, they ignite a new energy: "We can change the world for the better!" These principles are key to your leadership, but a final quality—*coaching*—is required to unlock your team's full potential.

The time is overdue for rethinking leaders not as managers but as coaches. Although in recent years many leaders have hired external coaches, shouldn't your leader be your coach, not your manager or supervisor?

The concept of the leader as coach contrasts with decades of literature describing the leader as manager. My colleague John Kotter articulated the difference between leaders and managers in his book *A Force for Change*. Yet even today, business leadership is still not fully accepted as an academic discipline. Many business schools prefer to teach traditional managerial techniques of exerting power over subordinates, directing them, delegating work, and evaluating their performance via quantitative metrics.

In contrast, *coaching* is the process of fully engaging a team and bringing out the best qualities and skillsets of each member. The best coaches are deeply engaged and care about each team member, even in very large organizations. The coach and the team share a common definition of success and are measured by the same score-card. They have a unified desire to win, yet everyone respects the different roles of the coach and team members.

Just as great athletes seek the best coaches, the best people want to work for leaders who are actively helping them to perform at their best. The coaching leader relies far less on positional power and more on trust, empathy, mentoring, and feedback. Those who work with great coaches rarely describe the experience as easy, because these coaches are extremely demanding and hold their teammates to high standards with full accountability. As a result, they lead their teams to greater heights than anyone believed possible.

Engaged Leaders Coach Their Team

There are legions of legendary sports coaches, and many like Vince Lombardi and John Wooden have written business books. Yet perhaps the most successful sports-to-business crossover is the late Bill Campbell. He had a mixed record as Columbia University football coach but truly thrived as coach to the founders of Silicon Valley, including Apple's Steve Jobs, Intuit's Scott Cook, Amazon's Jeff Bezos, and Google's Larry Page. Another Bill Campbell mentee, Eric Schmidt—Google's chief executive officer (CEO) during the company's hypergrowth period—wrote a book about Bill called *Trillion Dollar Coach*. The title estimated the value created by the leaders Bill coached.

How did Bill make such a mark? He turned the idea of hierarchy on its head, saying, "Your title makes you a manager; your people make you a leader." Bill had tremendous respect and love for his people. His manifesto proclaimed, "People are the foundation of any company's success. The primary job of each leader is to help people be effective in their job and grow and develop through support, respect, and trust."

Care

Understand the individual's strengths, weaknesses, and motivations.

Organize

Get people playing as a team in their individual sweet spots.

Align

Unite people around a common purpose that inspires them.

Challenge

Summon each person's best work; create audacious goals.

Help

Work with your team to solve problems and celebrate successes.

Figure 10.1   The Leader as Coach

To describe what it takes to be a great coach, we have developed the acronym COACH. As a leader, you need to Care for people, Organize and Align them, Challenge, and Help them (Figure 10.1).

Mary Barra: Coaching Changes Culture

General Motors (GM) CEO Mary Barra is the pied piper of the new generation of coaching leaders. Mary's leadership sharply diverges from GM's 50 years of top-down financial managers who occupied the CEO chair, such as Rick Wagoner, who eventually led the company into bankruptcy with his short-term focus. In contrast, Mary cares deeply about GM's 155,000 employees, as she aligns them around GM's Triple Zero purpose of "zero emissions, zero accidents, zero congestion" and challenges them to produce top quality, safe vehicles.

Named CEO in 2014, Mary's whole life prepared her for the challenging role of transforming GM. Starting as an 18-year-old co-op student at Kettering University, she has worked at GM for 41 years, including jobs as factory inspector, design engineer, plant manager, and head of human resources. She explains, "While my friends worked at fast-food restaurants, I applied engineering skills in GM assembly plants. That experience was invaluable, giving me an early understanding of the auto business."

No sooner was she named CEO than she was confronted with her first major crisis: Cobalt ignition switch failures causing 124 deaths and 275 injuries. To investigate, she hired former U.S. attorney Anton Valukas. His report revealed GM routinely sent accident reports to its legal department rather than the quality and design teams that needed to fix the underlying issues.

The report declared the root cause was incompetence, describing GM as mired in a bureaucracy that lacked accountability and transparency. "Reading the Valukas report was one of the saddest times of my career," Mary says. "Most frightening was that the report said everything everyone's always criticized us about. It was a gut punch. As the report said, 'No single person owned any decision.'"

Less than 3 months into her role as CEO, Mary was called before Congress to testify about this problem. She acknowledged GM's problems were much deeper than ignition switches, stating bluntly that GM's entire culture had to be transformed. "The Valukas report is extremely thorough, brutally tough, and deeply troubling," she told Congress.

> It paints a picture of an organization that failed to handle a complex safety problem in a responsible way. There is no way to minimize the seriousness of what Mr. Valukas uncovered. Two weeks ago, I addressed the entire global workforce about the report. I told our team bluntly that the series of questionable actions uncovered is inexcusable.

Mary used the ignition switch crisis to create a burning platform to transform GM's culture from a slow-moving bureaucracy that looked inward and denied its problems to a customer-focused, transparent culture that owned its challenges. She committed to establish a new industry standard for quality and safety, recalling 30 million vehicles her first year and creating Speak Up for Safety to reward employees for transparency. "I never want to put this behind us," she says.

> I want to put this painful experience permanently in our collective memories. We've got to create the climate where people can speak up, without fear in the organization, and express different points of view. This requires building a diverse team.

To change GM's moribund culture, Mary transformed the entire leadership team, promoting Mark Reuss to president and filling her executive committee with GM veterans and outside hires who brought fresh perspectives. She sets high standards of behavior for her team and empowers them to meet these standards with full accountability. She frequently meets with employees in factories to see if cultural changes are taking hold and offers to help whenever possible. "If we want to change this elusive culture, it requires changing behaviors because that defines the culture," she says.

> Not that I want to be described as mean, but the company is too nice. To be truly great, your team must have diversity of thought and be willing to collaborate constructively. I've become much more impatient about how we do things and how quickly we do things.

In establishing GM's purpose and strategy, Mary has been bold. In 2017, she announced a new mission: "Our goal is to deliver world-class customer experiences at every touchpoint and do so on a foundation of trust and transparency." In 2021, she committed GM to produce only electric vehicles by 2035.

Mary Barra is the epitome of the new coaching leader. She *cares* about her leaders and employees and connects with them to understand their perspectives and motivations. Having started on GM's factory floor, she is able to build strong relationships and trust with her team. In sharp contrast to the top-down, hierarchical culture that ruled GM for 50 years, she *organizes* her leaders as an integrated team, putting leaders in their sweet spot and empowering them to lead their teams on behalf of the whole enterprise.

In articulating GM's new mission, vision, and leadership behaviors, Mary *aligns* her mammoth organization around common goals but does not flinch in *challenging* people with audacious goals around quality, safety, and electrical vehicles to raise GM's sights. Meanwhile, she expects peak performance from her team, while *helping* them meet challenges and solve problems.

Mary's new approach to leadership was recognized by her CEO peers when the Business Roundtable named her its first female chair in 2021. There she advocates for the multistakeholder approach that focuses first on customers and employees.

Care: Build Understanding and Trust

The capacity to develop close and enduring relationships through care with empathy and candor is essential to building trust. If you do not deeply understand people and care about them, you cannot help them unlock their full potential.

Caring relationships are marked by intimacy and informality. Intimacy requires people to be open, vulnerable, and willing to admit mistakes. Frequently, the best discussions and creative ideas come from informal interaction, rather than back-to-back meetings around conference tables. Spending time together outside the office—taking walks, meeting for coffee, having social dinners, or doing fun activities—develops comfort and trust that leads to more candid conversations. Through these discussions, people understand each other's truths and become thought partners.

When their caring is real, leaders can answer this checklist affirmatively:

☐ I understand my teammate's career objectives and how their current role helps them develop.

☐ I understand each person's intrinsic and extrinsic motivations, as well as their challenges.

☐ I have deep one-on-one meetings that go beyond superficial discussions.

☐ We have natural and free-flowing interaction and are comfortable with each other, including moments of "common humanity."

☐ I know my colleagues' family members and understand their lives outside work.

People demand more personal relationships with their leaders before they will invest themselves fully in their jobs. They insist on having access to their leaders, knowing that it is in the openness and the depth of the relationship with the leader that trust and commitment are built. Because Mary Barra cares about her employees, she realizes from them a deeper commitment to their work and greater loyalty to the company.

Real relationships create empathy—the ability to walk in someone else's shoes. Empathy builds rapport, in which team members feel psychologically safe and believe their leader has their back. Only with empathy are leaders able to draw the highest level of engagement from colleagues from different cultures and empower them to achieve exceptional performance. This requires humility and the capability to engage people personally rather than judging them.

The care factor ultimately creates trust, which Stephen M. R. Covey asserts has quantifiable impact for organizations. When trust is low, there is a measurable "trust tax" that slows down decision-making and increases cost throughout the organization. When trust is high, speed is fast and alignment comes easily.

Embrace Servant Leadership

Former Carlson CEO Marilyn Carlson Nelson dramatically transformed the company founded by her father, Curtis Carlson, who was a consummate salesman and a demanding boss. Rejoining the company after her children were grown, Marilyn accompanied her father to an MBA presentation about their research into Carlson's corporate culture.

When she asked how students saw Carlson, no one dared answer. Finally, one student said, "Carlson is perceived as a sweatshop that doesn't care about people. Our professors don't recommend we work for Carlson." Marilyn was stunned. "That meeting lit a fire under me," she says. She realized she needed to shift Carlson's culture away from her father's top-down, autocratic style.

Marilyn decided to reinvent Carlson as a company that cared for customers by creating the most caring environment for its employees. She shifted away from focus on financial capital toward acquiring and cultivating human capital, as she emphasized caring across the business:

> I looked for people with "a servant's heart." Servant leadership is an important driver of the culture we want to create. Satisfied employees create satisfied customers. In the service business, customers understand very quickly whether you legitimately care about serving them.

Recognizing that changing culture would take tremendous work, Marilyn traveled tirelessly to meet with employees and customers around the world. "We can build relationships only if employees are affirmed and empowered, have clarity of direction, and understand the company's mission," she says. "We cannot just teach restaurant employees to put a meal on the table. They have to customize the experience, depending on whether customers want privacy or an evening of fun."

Marilyn elevated care with her team and across the entire company through her actions and her presence. Her transformation of Carlson to a collaborative culture is a remarkable example of how leaders transform organizations by caring about the people they serve.

Organize: Get People Playing as a Team

As a coaching leader, your second task is to understand the strengths and weaknesses of each team member, along with their motivations. Then you can organize individuals into a cohesive team where all members operate in sweet spots that play to their strengths, compensate for their weaknesses, and motivate them to peak performance. Nothing is more destructive to a team than having someone play outside their sweet spot. Such a situation hurts the individual's confidence, slows the team down, and ultimately prevents the organization from fulfilling its purpose.

How do leaders create a culture where everyone is in their sweet spot, playing together for the greater good of the team? Coaching leaders engage regularly with their team members while observing their leadership. For example, a board chair might attend the CEO's strategy offsite to both add value to the executive team *and* see the CEO in action. Similarly, leaders could join salespeople making customer calls to understand customer needs and wants.

As a leader, are you working side by side with your team members? Do you model appropriate behaviors and provide constructive feedback? Do you know enough about their world and context to make useful suggestions? This is sitting sidesaddle to learn, make suggestions, and encourage them rather than judging them from a distance.

In addition to such firsthand observations, you need data so you can trust but verify your teammates' inputs. Look at leading indicators like employee surveys and customer inputs to predict how your team is doing, as financial performance provides only after-the-fact historical information, which may be too late to act on.

Building an empowered team begins with your daily behavior. You cannot preach empowerment and then behave in a hierarchical manner, or you lose credibility with their colleagues. Nor can you reward or even tolerate power-driven subordinates who behave like jerks or play politics.

Bring the Team Together to Deliver Great Results

In 2006, Alan Mulally arrived at Ford as its new CEO, wearing a sport coat and slacks—attire quite distinct from Ford's buttoned-up executives. He was escorted up to his enormous office where 30 aides greeted him, offering to take his coat and pour his coffee. Within a month, they were all gone, replaced by a single assistant he brought from Boeing.

Walking into the enormous office Henry Ford II once occupied, Alan gazed out the panoramic windows at the Rouge Plant, the automobile industry's most famous factory. Telling an aide he would like to walk through the plant and meet employees, he was told "our executives don't talk directly to factory employees." With that, he insisted on going there immediately.

Alan's initial meetings convinced him that Ford's problems were far deeper than the staggering $12.7 billion in losses projected for the year, the largest in Ford's history. Yet nobody on Alan's executive team was willing to acknowledge its problems. An intuitive leader, Alan understood he was facing a broken culture requiring a massive overhaul.

Realizing decisive action was required to give Ford a cushion against further problems and economic downturns, Alan borrowed $23.5 billion, leveraging Ford's entire balance sheet and the iconic Ford oval as collateral. Alan's strategy to meet customer needs was a new lineup of superior cars and trucks while insisting Ford's factory costs in its unionized U.S. facilities were equivalent to nonunion factories in the South. Meanwhile, he narrowed the company's brands to Ford and Lincoln by spinning off luxury brands like Jaguar and Land Rover.

These strategic moves were accompanied by a less heralded but equally important process: Alan's weekly business performance review (BPR). Alan believed that bringing his senior team together each week for a full day of in-depth, fact-based reviews of Ford's business could transform the culture. During BPR meetings, he dove into details several levels deeper than any senior executive had done previously and expected candid appraisals. He used a green, yellow, and red color-coding system to assess the status of key projects. Given the depth of the company's problems, he was puzzled when every project was coded green.

Despite the gravity of the crisis, Alan did not jump and scream in these meetings. His style was low-key and down-to-earth. As follow-ups, he wrote notes with smiley faces, engaged in casual conversations, popped into meetings unannounced, and often offered hugs. Many of Ford's executives underestimated him at first, describing him as "corny."

By his fifth BPR, Alan confronted his team about the dichotomy between billions of losses and their consistent reports of positive progress. "Is there anything that's not going well here?" he asked. Nobody responded. The following week, America's president Mark Fields signaled a red indication that a key new vehicle launch had to be held up. Mark's colleagues thought he would be fired, but instead Alan clapped, saying, "Mark, that is great visibility. Who will help Mark?" He echoed encouragement throughout his conversations: "You have a problem. You are not the problem."

Alan made few personnel changes upon assuming the CEO position. Rather, he changed the culture by coaching each leader to get them immersed in the details of the business and working like a team to improve performance.

Turnarounds such as Ford's do not occur by accident. They require each team member to give their best. Alan's weekly BPR enabled him to organize his executives and get them to play as one team. He never asked more of team members than he was willing to give himself. He has a unique ability to combine genuine caring for his people with closed-loop accountability for their results.

Align: Unite People around a Common Vision

The coaching leader's most challenging task is to align employees with the company's mission and vision and inspire them to take on bold goals to make the mission real. This is much more difficult than setting financial goals that do not impact or inspire most employees.

The leader's job is to make the mission and vision come to life and to use them in determining strategy, setting goals, and making decisions. In this way they become an incredibly powerful way to bring all employees together with common language and unified objectives. A mission and vision that are nothing more than a poster on the wall have no meaning and may even invoke cynicism among employees.

At Medtronic's Mission and Medallion Ceremony, all new employees receive medallions with the mission engraved on it. This brings home that all employees—whether they work in facilities, research and development (R&D) labs, or sales—must contribute to its mission of "alleviating pain, restoring health, and extending life."

Purpose That Transcends Profit

Named one of the world's best CEOs by *Barron's*, Jim Whitehurst led the open-source software company Red Hat through tremendous growth. During his tenure, revenue increased eightfold, the company's stock grew 10 times, and Red Hat was named a Best Place to Work by Glassdoor, with many employees even tattooing the logo on themselves. Looking for greater innovation, IBM acquired the company in 2019 for $34 billion.

Prior to joining Red Hat, Jim was chief operating officer (COO) of Delta Air Lines, where he was known as "the guy with spreadsheets." At Delta, he ran a company that operated in a highly regulated industry with little strategic flexibility, so he managed by the numbers.

Upon joining Red Hat, Jim realized the context was different from his previous jobs. "I had no idea how cloud computing will unfold," he says. "The pace of change is so rapid that companies used to a major innovation every decade now need one every year.

As the formula for value creation changes, the nature of leadership also must change."

Given the uncertainty and pace of change, Jim chose to align his team around Red Hat's purpose: "If people just work for a paycheck, they won't go the extra mile, but if they believe in a purpose that transcends profit, they will give all they have."

> At Red Hat, we built in intrinsic motivations—the open-source mission, the importance of transparency and openness, and freedom of our intellectual property. People work nights and weekends and think about it in the shower because they believe in the purpose. They're not just doing what they need to do to get by; they're doing what they think makes the organization successful.

As CEO, Jim went to great lengths to make the purpose clear. He says,

> Red Hat's new hires go through more of a cultural indoctrination than new hire orientation. Senior people talk about the importance of culture and history, and our place in the world. People come out of those sessions saying, "I understand the history of Red Hat and why open source is so important, but I still don't have my cell phone or computer."

To emphasize purpose and the shared context, Jim adopted an open management system that empowered teams to innovate:

> The management system needs to be consistent with the leadership behaviors. Budgets are less important than creating space for people to experiment and try new things to invent new products. We experiment, try things, kill some, and invest in others. When change is so fast, you don't have clear endpoints, but you build greater resilience in the organization.

Jim shares his philosophy with frequent and informal communications. "Every Friday, I record a short video—very casual, often in a T-shirt." He might share depressing news like a layoff or inspiring news such as a customer innovation. With video and social media, leaders' opportunities to engage their team and align them around the organization's purpose are better than ever.

Challenge: Summon People's Best

Anson Dorrance, who coached soccer player Mia Hamm and has won 21 NCAA women's soccer championships, creates a weekly stack ranking of every single player that he posts publicly. He calls the exercise "competitive cauldron," as he rates each player on a list of factors such as their speed. On his team, players know where they stand and what they need to do to improve.

Great coaches like Anson add the greatest value by challenging their players. Watching game tapes, creating weekly team ratings, or having one-on-one feedback meetings are ways of challenging people to step up to peak performance. Ask yourself: Have I stretched my team members? Have I challenged someone who is delivering less than their full potential? Have I pushed players outside their comfort zones? Challenging people not only engages them in improving their performance but also helps them develop as leaders. Matt Christensen, who played basketball under Mike Krzyzewski at Duke, says, "Coach K. was in my face every practice to help me get better."

Middle managers frequently characterize such challenging, engaged leaders as micromanagers, but that misses the importance of challenging them by getting deeply involved in the details to help their teams perform.

Engaging with Your Team

When he led biopharmaceutical company Amgen, Kevin Sharer challenged team members to bring out their best. As a young Navy officer, Kevin delivered great results, but his captain told him he risked losing his people due to his intensity. Kevin acknowledges this was integral to his management style: "When I go into my submarine mode, I go very deep into a problem and think I can solve it myself. That's when I risk closing down debate."

As Kevin matured, he learned to identify when to manage more tightly and more loosely. Earlier in his career, Kevin worked for Jack Welch, who modeled how to rapidly shift between levels, or even engage several levels at once. He says, "Most CEOs tend to gravitate toward the altitude where they're most comfortable. Unfortunately, they get in trouble because they get stuck at a particular altitude. You must adapt to the business needs and the team's readiness to operate autonomously."

> At the highest altitude, you're asking big questions: What is our mission and strategy? Do people understand and believe in these aims? At the lowest altitude, you're looking at on-the-ground operations: Did we make that sale? What was the yield on the last factory lot? In between, you ask questions like: Should we invest in a biotechnology company with a promising new drug?

At Amgen, Kevin asked his leadership team to commit to leadership behaviors. To bring them to life, he articulated specific examples of behaviors he expected, such as:

- Provides honest and constructive feedback
- Establishes high performance standards, uses measurable goals to track progress, and continually raises the bar on performance
- Conducts reality-based, results-focused operating reviews and drives quick corrective actions

Kevin modeled these behaviors himself and then used them to assess the company's top 100 people. He grew more comfortable over time with what he calls tough love: "The tricky balance for leaders is to know when to push and when to empathize." As CEO, this approach helped Kevin build an exceptional and stable management team that grew revenues from $3 billion to $15 billion.

Help: Solve Problems and Celebrate Success

Many leaders believe their job is to create the organization's strategy, structure, and processes and then delegate the work to be done while remaining aloof from the people doing the work. *Wrong!* Today you cannot succeed sitting behind a desk in your office; you must be personally engaged with your team where they work.

Coaching leaders help their subordinates figure out the best path to achieving their objectives. Jack Welch was challenging and hard on people, yet those very challenges let people know that he was committed to their success. If something was off track, he dug in to help the leaders course correct through a special set of working sessions he called deep dives. Jack's curiosity and rapid-fire questions enabled him to develop a point of view. Known for his candor and aggressiveness, he also looked for opportunities to celebrate success.

Stephen Hawking once remarked, "Half the battle is just showing up." Many leaders get so busy with meetings they don't take the time to be with people and help them. They say they're too busy to attend award ceremonies, company picnics, sales meetings, or trade shows. Nor do they walk around offices, factories, labs, and field sales and service locations. Showing up at important events or engaging on the frontlines means a great deal to people and enables them to take leaders off their pedestals and see them as real human beings. Celebration is an essential part of helping by rewarding good behaviors and motivating. Coaching leaders will frequently say both "thank you" and "well done!"

Leaders can help their colleagues by counseling them, offering suggestions, or assisting them in making vital contacts. For example, as CEO of Merck, Roy Vagelos regularly ate in the company cafeteria, where he asked people about their work and their challenges. He took notes about the conversations and thought about specific problems for a few days before calling employees back with his ideas.

Imagine how Merck researchers must have felt when they picked up the phone to hear Roy getting back to them with help. "I'd call them up and say, 'That's a tough problem, but here are a couple things you might try,'" Roy says. "People love to have their leader involved. They feel you want to be part of the solution." These interactions reinforced the importance of the researchers' work and had a multiplier effect upon employees.

Often the most helpful thing a leader can do is genuinely *listen*. Active listening is one of leaders' most important abilities, because people sense they are genuinely interested in them. Warren Bennis was a world-class listener, who patiently listened to your ideas and then contributed astute observations that came from a deep well of wisdom and experience. We feel respected when others believe they can learn from us or ask for our advice.

In *Eyewitness to Power*, David Gergen writes, "The heart of leadership is the leader's relationship with followers. People will entrust their hopes and dreams to another person only if they think the leader is a reliable vessel." Authentic leaders establish trusting relationships with people throughout their organizations, with long lasting rewards. In today's world where remote work is far more prevalent, the stakes are higher than ever for an intentional approach to fully engaging everyone. To bring out the best from their teams, authentic leaders must COACH them to success.

Coaching at the Right Altitude

Leadership requires adapting to the context at hand. When do you engage deeply as Kevin Sharer does? When do you only provide context and give people freedom as Jim Whitehurst did to stimulate innovation? First, you should determine the context, throttling your involvement up or down depending on the circumstances. For example, Jim engaged more deeply on safety issues at Delta but managed Red Hat's innovation portfolio with a light touch.

When you understand the context and the readiness of each person, you can select the right level of involvement. Aetna CEO Ron Williams uses management dashboards and personal observations to decide where to focus his time. He says the best leaders have "their head in the clouds and their feet on the street and use their observation powers to know when to be where."

Judgments about your involvement depend upon your assessment of the effectiveness, capability, and experience of your team. Being deeply involved makes sense if the organization is in a crisis or team members are inexperienced. Being less involved makes sense when your team is on track and its members are experienced. Overall, engaged leadership is most effective.

The "Levels of Involvement" framework in Figure 10.2 enables you to decide how to engage your team.

"Too Little Involvement"	Engaged Leadership	"Too Much Involvement"
• Few opportunities to course correct	• Working with teammates on common goals	• Frequency and specificity of feedback erodes sense of ownership
• Few insights into the work prevents concrete and actionable feedback	• Feedback is tailored to each team member's maturity	• Team members lose their initiative
• Leading this way has high failure rates, as you add little value	• Coaching style adapts to get the best from each team member	• Leaders lack perspective because they are so involved in details of execution

Figure 10.2　Levels of Involvement

Your Leadership Style

The topic of your leadership style is saved for last because your style is *the outward manifestation of your authentic leadership*. Style without authenticity makes you a persona, which most people see right through.

Many organizations work hard to get young leaders to embrace the company's normative leadership style by sending them to training programs to bring their styles into line. Therein lies the risk: Will you have to compromise who you are to succeed in the organization? If you do, you will feel like an imposter, trying to be something you are not. All the leaders profiled in this chapter have unique styles that work effectively for them, but you cannot succeed by emulating their styles—you just need to be yourself.

Having a range of styles that enables you to be flexible for the situation is important for your leadership. You need to adapt your leadership style to the capabilities of your teammates and their readiness to accept greater responsibility. For example, if your teammates need clear direction, they may not be ready to handle full delegation. Conversely, creative or independent thinkers will not respond positively to a directive style.

In leading, it is important to understand the situation, as well as the performance imperative, and be flexible in your style to maximize your effectiveness. Once you understand the context, you can adjust your communication and leadership style to get results yet retain your authenticity.

Emerging Leader: Robert Reffkin

Robert Reffkin has grown into a coaching leader as CEO of Compass, a real estate technology company he cofounded in 2012 and took public in 2021. His mantra? "Nobody succeeds alone."

Robert's focus starts with caring for his team—he prioritizes writing handwritten thank-you notes and personally calling new employees to welcome them to the company. He says:

> The more you can take time to develop genuine, authentic relationships, the more you're going to be able to realize your dreams because you can take big risks and know that there's a network of people there to cheer you on.

Robert organizes his team based on advice from his mentor who told him, "Stop trying to make your weaknesses a strength. Minimize your weaknesses and maximize your strengths."

> No one is good at everything, but everyone is great at something. Take the time to identify your strengths and those of each member of your team and then look for every possible way to leverage those strengths.

As Compass grew, Robert collaborated with team members to align them around an aspirational mission statement. He encourages his team to align around tactical visions daily as well by asking, "What does success look like?" at the outset of each new project. He says, "Simply answering that question enables everyone to imagine the same goal."

One of the ways Robert illustrates the challenge principle is through direct, honest feedback.

> The most important lesson I've learned in my life is that feedback is a gift. My relationships with many of my mentors deepened because I started asking them for tough, candid feedback. Then I'd take their advice, apply it in my life, and let them know how it had helped me.

Finally, Robert helps his teams win by sharing concrete advice to improve their performance. His book *No One Succeeds Alone* brims with practical advice on topics such as, "Help people you know be successful at something." He is deeply vulnerable, cataloging his many failures and setbacks. When Robert's team members face adversity, they feel comfortable discussing it with him.

Bill's Take: Applying the COACH Framework

Joining Medtronic in 1989, my first task was to care about the company's mission and values, our leaders, frontline employees, and customers. To learn the business, I adopted a 30–30–30–10 model: 30 percent of my time with customers, 30 percent with employees, 30 percent with executives, and 10 percent with our board and external stakeholders.

New to medicine, I learned how our products worked through the eyes of our physicians and their patients. During my Medtronic years, I witnessed over 700 live procedures. I spent time talking with Medtronic engineers and scientists in their labs and touring factories. On global visits we followed a 1-hour rule, spending only 1 hour reviewing the business and then meeting with customers.

Through these learning experiences, I realized we needed to organize as a global matrix of strategic business units and geographic teams rather than the functional organization Medtronic had. That put decision-making at the point of impact rather than corporate headquarters. We also needed to get people in their sweet spots, moving them to their best positions and recruiting leaders to fill gaps.

Next, we enabled our executives to function as a team of Medtronic enterprise leaders, not separate executives running their own teams. We formed an executive committee and an operating committee to build teamwork, address challenges, and make decisions. The Medtronic Mission enabled us to align our leaders worldwide with a common purpose and behaviors. By focusing on our external purpose of serving patients, we minimized the internal politics that existed before I joined.

I love to challenge people to perform their best. These challenges produced great results, but some people resented being challenged as we raised the bar on performance to meet patients' needs. To help people solve problems came naturally. Some people called this micromanagement, but as they saw results, they recognized that deep engagement in the business worked to everyone's benefit.

In the years since leaving Medtronic, I have mentored many people on leading as coaches—not directors or bosses—which has helped them become more effective leaders. Based on these experiences, I am a firm believer in the leader as coach model.

Idea in Brief: The Leader as Coach

Recap of the Main Idea

- The acronym COACH can be used as a guide for leaders to coach their teams to achieving the very best:
  - *Care*: Build understanding and trust.
  - *Organize*: Get people playing as a team.
  - *Align*: Unite people around a common vision.
  - *Challenge*: Summon people's best.
  - *Help*: Engage with your teams in solving problems.
- The coaching leader relies less on positional power and more on collaboration, trust, empathy, mentoring, and feedback.
- To bring out the best from teammates, authentic leaders COACH them to succeed through strong relationships, providing constructive feedback on their work, and establishing stretch goals.

Questions to Ask

1. Describe an example from your past where you have been effective in inspiring other leaders around a common purpose and shared values.
2. How effective are you at empowering others to step up and lead? What are you doing to improve your effectiveness?
3. Recall a situation in which you faced a conflict between empowering other people and reaching your performance goals.

    a. How did you resolve the conflict?

    b. Did you give preference to reaching your goals or to your relationships?

4. Would you act differently in the future when facing a conflict between relationships and performance?

Practical Suggestions for Your Development

- Rate yourself on the five dimensions of COACH.
- Ask at least two members of your team to rate you on these dimensions.
- Assess the depth of your professional relationships using the five-question checklist on page 204.
- Spend time observing another leader in action. What did you learn? Were you able to provide constructive feedback?
- Ask your colleagues if they know your organization's purpose. Engage in dialogue with your team to ensure everyone is aligned.

Part Four

Navigate Today's Challenges

Parts I, II, and III laid out the structure of authentic leadership. In Part IV, we address special topics of pressing interest: building inclusive organizations, leading through crisis, and moral leadership.

Chapter 11 on inclusive leadership claims that diversity is necessary but insufficient. Too many organizations focus on diversity and equity goals without doing the difficult work to build radically inclusive cultures. We profile a number of diverse leaders—many of whom want to be known more for their character (who they are) and their results (what they achieve) than their demographics (how they were born). We also address the accountability necessary to achieve equality in the workplace.

Chapter 12 addresses the constant stream of crises in the last 20 years and offers 7 practical steps leaders can take:

1. Face reality, starting with yourself.
2. Dig deep for the root cause.
3. Engage with frontline teams.
4. Never waste a good crisis.
5. Get ready for the long haul.
6. In the spotlight, follow your True North.
7. Go on offense, with a focus on winning now.

Finally, Chapter 13 is a call to exemplify moral leadership, the sum of all the concepts we discuss in the *Emerging Leader Edition of True North*. We profile a series of leaders who have recast their work—from making blue jeans to making software—in explicitly moral terms. At the end of our lives, we will be asked how we have treated those we love and left the world around us.

11

INCLUSIVE LEADERSHIP

A diverse mix of voices leads to better discussions,
decisions, and outcomes for everyone.
—*Sundar Pichai, CEO, Google*

The protests of 2020 ripped apart any illusion that America had made peace with its history of racial injustice. Everyone who watched the video of George Floyd's murder witnessed a disturbing, vivid view of police brutality. Our nation erupted—not just because of this incident, but because of so many similar tragedies. As one Black friend told me, "I'm just done."

From my home in Minneapolis, I could hear helicopters overhead and smell acrid smoke from the riots that damaged more than 1,300 buildings across our city. I prayed, sought out dialogue, and joined the Sunday protests. In the aftermath of the civil unrest, people were angry and impatient. They wanted palpable change quickly, and leaders faced unprecedented demands to share their organizations' plans for racial equity.

Reflection is not enough. We must act intentionally to promote inclusion of Black, Indigenous, and people of color (BIPOC), women, immigrants, and lesbian, gay, bisexual, transgender, and queer (LGBTQ+) people. As leaders, it is our responsibility to participate in building a more just society, ensuring opportunity is widely distributed, and bending the arch of history toward justice with our action.

Having diversity in our organizations is necessary but not sufficient. We need to create inclusive organizations where everyone feels a sense of belonging. That is the only way everyone can feel fulfilled and perform to the best of their ability. Those who have

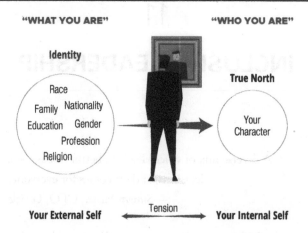

Figure 11.1   What You Are vs. Who You Are

experienced the wounds of noninclusive organizations firsthand want to be accepted for *who they are*, not what they are (Figure 11.1).

Ursula Burns: Where You Are Is Not Who You Are

Former Xerox chief executive officer (CEO) Ursula Burns grew up in a one-bedroom tenement apartment in New York, raised with her two siblings by a single, Panamanian immigrant mother. She says, "My personality was formed by my mother, my siblings, and my community. New York is a tough place. You have to speak up and be gritty, or you will be run over. I had no aspiration to run a major company, but I had clear direction from my mother to be successful."

Ursula's mother was the most powerful force in her life, working at two minimum wage jobs to support her family, living off food stamps, and wearing clothes from thrift shops. When her children left the house, she watched them with opera glasses to ensure their safety.

Ursula never let being a Black woman or growing up in poverty hold her back. She calls her notoriety as the first Black female CEO of a *Fortune 500* company "a ridiculous way to make history."

Why was it so amazing for a Black woman to lead a multibillion-dollar company? I'd gone to two good schools, earned my master's in engineering, spent 28 years at Xerox and did most of the major jobs, so this shouldn't be shocking. The only differences between me and other CEOs were my gender and my race. I earned the position: I wasn't plucked from a circus sideshow.

An outspoken advocate for diversity and inclusion in all organizations, Ursula isn't one to withhold her opinions, saying, "I have always been blunt."

It stimulates discussion and saves time. We all need to be brusquer and risk disagreeing with each other, so we get through problems fast without having to mince words. Being overly polite is such a waste of time. Xerox once suffered from terminal niceness, and we failed to say what we meant, and people sometimes supported each other's mediocrity.

Earlier in her career, Ursula's outspokenness got her in trouble. When a White male asked Xerox's vice chair why the company was so focused on diversity, Ursula chided the executive publicly for displaying a lack of passion and principles, leading to an unfriendly exchange. When he asked her to meet in his office, Ursula thought she would be fired, but instead he merely reprimanded her for being so outspoken and intemperate.

That interaction led to a strong mentoring relationship and an offer to be his assistant. At first, Ursula was incredulous at moving into a position she thought was beneath her, but she now describes it as the most important she's ever held because it enabled her to understand the company's inner workings. Ursula eventually became vice president of global manufacturing, where she teamed with CEO Anne Mulcahy to turn the company around in the face of impending bankruptcy.

Anne and Ursula cut $2 billion in costs and reduced the workforce by 38,000 people. As the turnaround took hold, they formed a powerful team with Anne focusing on customers as "Ms. Outside" and Ursula on internal operations as "Ms. Inside." When Anne announced her retirement in 2009, Ursula was the obvious choice to become CEO.

Throughout her leadership journey, Ursula has prioritized diversity and inclusion as foundational to a company's success, saying, "You can have a little less money, but you can't have a little less diversity or less ethics and be a successful, future-ready company." In 2020, she launched the Board Diversity Action Alliance, whose mission is to increase diverse representation on corporate boards and promote accountability measures on corporate diversity, equity, and inclusion. Ursula believes that companies can improve board diversity by rethinking board member criteria which has been a barrier to minorities, such as the requirement that a board member has had CEO experience.

> In corporate America, the playing field and rules are defined by White men. They say, "We have nobody who fits this game I specifically designed for me except for people who look like me." Well, surprise, surprise.

Ursula is also encouraging companies to set specific goals and track progress on their efforts to increase diversity, noting that she could not have attended college without the affirmative action programs of the 1970s.

> Numbers really do help. If you are one or two of 50, you're a freak show. That can also be advantageous. For 10 years at Xerox, I was the only Black woman in the room. If I raised my hand, I was always called on, because you couldn't miss me. We must get to where that's not an anomaly.

Ursula says she has achieved the American dream, believing it's very much alive, despite the challenges the country faces. While she's disappointed by the lack of diversity in business's top ranks, she is hopeful that the police murder of George Floyd and COVID-19 pandemic are bringing about fundamental shifts on racial and gender equality, encouraging people to have open conversations with people from different perspectives. "We are all learning how to have conversations that are not divisive," she says.

CEOs like Ursula Burns do not want to be defined by diversity; they just want the opportunity to lead their organizations. To ensure an inclusive culture, organizations must have diversity of all types at all levels in their ranks, starting with the board of directors and senior executives.

George Floyd's Murder Ripped the Bandage Off

In the days following George Floyd's murder and subsequent protests, I called a dozen of my Black friends to check in on how they were feeling, and I was shocked at their stories of discrimination—things that I had never experienced as a White man. These conversations were a wake-up call that systemic discrimination is still very much alive in America and many White people are blind to the injustices happening every day. George Floyd's killing ripped off the bandage of America's idealistic façade that had been masking the depth of racism and the plight of Black people and other minorities.

U.S. Bank vice chair Tim Welsh, who lives just a few miles from where George Floyd was killed, was also deeply shaken by the tragedy. "After George Floyd's murder, I felt like a failure," says Tim.

> I've invested 25 years in this community trying to create a more equitable, just society, but I was ignorant about how much racism exists. On my weekly town hall, I shared my feelings about what happened and completely broke down on the phone with 1,000 leaders who manage 26,000 people.

In response, U.S. Bank created the Alliance of Alliances with corporations and community leaders, especially Black leaders. Tim notes, "Instead of White leaders proposing solutions to the Black community, we flipped it to provide financial and human support for solutions originating in the Black community." Leaders are recognizing that they must promote change from the inside rather than impose it from the outside for it to be effective.

Read More

Bob Ryan, Former Sr. VP & CFO, Medtronic

Bob's resume as a corporate director and Fortune 500 CFO sparkles. Yet he found the most meaning in his work to preserve the funeral home that later held George Floyd's memorial service.

Diversity Is Necessary but Not Sufficient

Wells Fargo CEO Charles Scharf came under fire recently when he said diverse candidates just weren't available. What nonsense! If you cannot find diverse candidates, recruit more broadly or look deeper in your organization. Make stretch promotions of younger diverse leaders and support them with coaching and development. Your organization will perform better when the senior team has diverse perspectives.

Since George Floyd's murder, many companies are intensifying their focus on diversity, equity, and inclusion (DEI) through ambitious diversity programs to improve their numbers. The numbers show some improvement—in 2020, women held 27 percent of *Fortune 500* corporate board seats compared with 20 percent in 2016. The share of Black directors rose from 4.5 percent in 2019 to 7.4 percent 2 years later, but there is still a long way to go.

To increase diversity, some companies have mandated that at least one diverse candidate be included in a hiring pool. University of Colorado's research demonstrates the likelihood of hiring a diverse candidate increases dramatically when you have more than one on the slate. "With at least two women or minorities in the finalist pool, the odds of hiring a woman are 79 times greater, and 194 times greater for minorities," the research shows.

Many organizations have learned diversity is necessary but insufficient because people from diverse backgrounds move on if they do not feel fully included. Herschel Herndon, chief diversity officer for Thrivent Financial, says:

> To create a sustainable impact, people must feel fully included, valued, and appreciated. We must be very clear about our destination—our True North—and get everyone aligned. We must create a fully inclusive environment where everyone can perform their best. To achieve that, every individual must feel they have a stake in the outcome.

For 17 years I served on Goldman Sachs' board, working with three CEOs who were committed to diversity. Each year, human resources presented statistics on diversity, but no women or BIPOC leaders ever made it near the top in line roles. While lots of talented diverse leaders were hired, many left because they didn't feel fully included in the culture. When he became CEO, David Solomon promoted two dozen highly talented female and Black leaders in his first year. For example, Stephanie Cohen as global co-head of consumer and wealth management, one of Goldman's four sectors. Rather than talking about diversity, David took bold action and made an immediate impact.

All too often organizations delegate DEI to their human resource organizations rather than CEOs taking the lead. There is no easy answer to building inclusive organizations, but we recommend five things: create a culture of acceptance, provide opportunities, foster belonging, build diverse community, and rigorously track results.

Create a Culture of Acceptance

The media often features Land O'Lakes' Beth Ford as the first openly gay female CEO of a *Fortune 500* company, but that's not how she sees herself. "When I represent our business, I show up as CEO, not the gay CEO, not the female CEO. If that causes anyone discomfort, that's not my issue," she says.

Beth is from a working-class Catholic family in Sioux Falls, Iowa. Her father was a truck driver and used car salesman, and her mother was a nurse whose resilience and optimism had a profound influence on her life. Beth notes, "Although we were financially challenged, my mother talked about our responsibility to give back, help our community, and feel blessed for what we have." Her first jobs included detasseling corn and working as a night cashier and toilet cleaner.

Beth's strong work ethic led her to be selected by a board of 28 men as the best person for the CEO role. She explains, "Whether I am a female or gay wasn't part of the discussion. I'm not here to make a statement but to fulfill my responsibilities as CEO. My journey has taken me to this moment as CEO to do the most meaningful work of my career."

Beth believes that knowing who you are and being authentic leads people to do their best work and deliver superior results. She explains, "Everyone benefits when we bring our authentic selves to all aspects of our lives, including work."

> You do your best work when you show up as your authentic self and you feel you're in a safe environment. In times when I didn't feel I fit in, like meeting with the president in the Oval Office, I follow my mother's advice to "stand up straight, walk in, be the best version of myself I can be, and get comfortable being uncomfortable."

Beth explains that thousands of people have connected with her to talk about leading an authentic life, including parents of gay children. Beth's role takes her to rural areas that are deeply conservative. On one of those trips, she introduced herself to a big man standing near her, who started crying and said, "My son is gay. I'm just so proud of you, so grateful for your courage." She says, "I held him and told him his son was fortunate to have such a caring father."

She concludes, "It's not enough to say we have a diverse management team. It is essential that everyone feel included, accepted, and listened to. When you care about enabling someone else's success, it isn't just virtuous, you'll feel better about your own career."

All of us have hidden differences that we are reluctant, even ashamed, to reveal to those closest to us. What closet are you hiding in? Wouldn't you feel better if you could reveal your secrets to others? Opening your hidden areas is essential to accepting ourselves and finding acceptance from others.

Read More
Lord John Browne, Former CEO, BP

John became the first chief executive of a Fortune 500 company to publicly acknowledge he is gay. He talks about how his fear of not being accepted kept him in the closet for too many years.

Provide Opportunities

There are so many talented people from diverse backgrounds that sometimes we just need to open the door and let them walk through. Hmong refugee MayKao Hang is a leader who was given such opportunities. Now she is using her platform to help underprivileged people reach their full potential as well.

MayKao's family escaped Communist soldiers during the Southeast Asian war and lived amid a colony of quarantined lepers. "My life was saved by the lepers who sheltered and protected us," she says. Years later, two churchwomen resettled the Hang family to Milwaukee and then they moved to St. Paul. There, MayKao grew up in poverty. Speaking only Hmong, she learned English and became her family's translator.

MayKao reflects on her intense childhood: "I faced displacement, war, poverty, mental health and trauma, and learning how to navigate across cultures." Yet from this extreme adversity she learned three lessons—never look down on anyone; there's something to learn from everyone; and don't let circumstances define who you can become.

Brown University awarded MayKao a full scholarship, although she still had to work two jobs to pay for room and board. At 24, she began community organizing to help battered women and children at the Wilder Foundation. One disturbing case haunted her—the Public Housing Authority ignored 17 calls from a woman who then killed her children and tried to kill herself. MayKao says, "She thought it was better for all of them to die than to keep living. Nobody should ever get to that point in our society. At that point I found my life's purpose."

MayKao continued her service even while raising four children and earning a doctorate. When Wilder's president retired, he nominated her for the job. She initially turned him down because she didn't feel qualified. Then, she says, "I asked myself, 'Why can't I say yes to these things? I can't let someone else write my story.'" MayKao put her imprint on the organization by evolving it from programs to emphasizing connection and community:

> We had to be more relevant by focusing on the most vulnerable and disenfranchised in the community. I call this "no handouts without a hand up." To be the go-to place where everybody was coming for research, knowledge and leadership required complete transformation. We developed holistic mental health services and whole family aging and also assisted with doubling the number of certified community behavioral health clinics in both rural and urban areas.

When St. Thomas president Julie Sullivan asked MayKao to become founding dean of its College of Health, in her typically modest way, she laughed and said, "I've never been in academia. I don't even know what deans do." She seized the opportunity and is integrating programs in social work, counseling psychology, and an array of other health and exercise majors across the college while launching a new nursing school to focus on whole person health—mind, body, spirit, and community. "All my life I've heard calls for help and go where I am needed," she says.

Read More
Michele Hooper, President & CEO, The Directors' Council

Learn how Michele's early experiences facing discrimination provided the impetus for her mission to open up opportunities for others.

Foster Belonging

Raheem Beyah, dean of Georgia Tech's College of Engineering, is an inclusive leader helping people from underprivileged socioeconomic backgrounds develop their full potential. He grew up with a single mother in a small apartment and later a house in an economically depressed area of Atlanta. At age 8, Raheem had a physical altercation with his father for abusing his mother, telling him to get out of the house. "You've got to leave Mom alone." Then he told his mom, "You've got to divorce this guy."

After she did so, Raheem became the man of the house, riding public transit to school and cooking his own meals, while his mother worked three jobs and lived off credit cards. When his mother's weight caused health problems, he used his meager savings to buy her a treadmill because it wasn't safe to walk in their neighborhood.

For Raheem, belonging is an essential element of diversity and inclusion. As a Tech faculty member, he always felt completely welcome and included. He notes that isn't true at many institutions, as Black and Hispanic faculty often feel isolated because no one will collaborate with them. He credits Tech's senior leadership, especially the last three presidents, saying that's why Tech's six colleges have three Black deans and three female deans.

Raheem acknowledges Tech's former deans of engineering Gary May and Steve McLaughlin as his mentors who provided him with leadership opportunities. His big break came when he was appointed interim chair of Electrical and Computer Engineering. Initially, he strongly considered turning the position down. "I lacked confidence and felt like an imposter. Steve saw qualities in me I didn't see in myself and took big risks on a young professor in his 30s." With his wife's encouragement, he eventually accepted the challenge.

Years later, when Steve asked Raheem to become dean of engineering, he saw the opportunity to have greater impact.

> In taking this role, my mission is to change lives. My decisions are focused on bringing along people who have been left behind. The challenges transcend race; a lot is socioeconomic. Overnight, I went from being more aligned with the wait staff to head of an enormous department. As shocking as that was, it enables me to appreciate both worlds and be a bridge between them.

Noting that his job requires enabling Tech's engineering college to excel in research and faculty development, grow its endowment, and improve its rankings, he concludes, "These things give me the infrastructure to create the social change I'm committed to, but they aren't the end goal."

> I'm focused on bringing along folks who have been left behind. Access is critical for rural and urban kids in Georgia who have the potential but haven't had the opportunities. That's my mission and what excites me. Every decision I make ultimately leads back to that purpose. I belong here and want to give others the opportunity to belong as well. I want my tombstone to say not that he grew the endowment, but that he built bridges for others.

Build Inclusive Communities

To understand diverse people, we need to live and work together, yet most of our communities are highly segregated. Marnita Schroedl shows how to change that. She has created communities that foster empathy and understanding, inspired by her early life experiences with exclusion, rejection, racism, sexual abuse, and constant discrimination.

As she explains poignantly, "I never belonged anywhere."

My biological family thought I was White until my melanin came in at seven months. Because of the stigma in 1962 of having a Black child in a White family, my biological grandmother insisted I be placed in foster care. I was in three homes before I was two and a half. I grew up as the only Black person in a little all White town in the Pacific Northwest with a conservative German/ Irish Catholic family. The town had the largest population of KKK West of the Mississippi.

From the day I came to that town until the day I left, my foster family and I were terrorized or shunned. Isolation, rejection, and violence were constant presences, reverberating throughout my primary school years. I was not encouraged, valued, or invested in. When I asked my high school counselor about applying to colleges, she said, "Nobody will want you, you're a n*****." I was in the top 1 percent of the U.S. on my SAT with 3.75 GPA but no college would want me because of my skin color. I believed her. I dropped out of high school and attempted suicide instead.

Marnita turned these crucibles of rejection and blatant discrimination into her calling. She says, "Nobody should feel alone or unwelcome. Nobody." Following the Rodney King trials, she used her gift of cooking to host dining table conversations in Los Angeles as opportunities for healing and reconciliation because "my White friends wouldn't talk to my Black friends."

That experience inspired Marnita's Table, which brings together diverse people to share meals while they talk candidly about the unique challenges their communities are facing. Marnita's Table uses "Intentional Social Interaction," a replicable model that is being adopted all over the world, to exemplify American poet Edwin Markham's quatrain:

He drew a circle that shut me out-
Heretic, rebel, a thing to flout.
But love and I had the wit to win:
We drew a circle and took him In!

Marnita says, "To address the lack of access and opportunity, we provide seats at the table for everyone. Sharing power and valuing differences requires practice. Eventually, this becomes a community practice." Marnita's Table has five foundational principles: research and reflection, authentic welcome, element of choice, sharing power, and fun. How might you incorporate these principles into your interactions with others?

Marnita believes sharing food is central as a universally shared experience, explaining, "Humans are like gardens: we are building communities that must be cultivated."

Read More

Tim Cook, CEO, Apple

Learn how stories of others struggling with their sexual orientation encouraged Tim to publicly address his own sexuality and rise above adversity and bigotry by following his own path.

Measure for Accountability

In recent years, companies have begun to publish detailed statistics on diversity, equity, and inclusion. J.P. Morgan and Merck are exemplars of providing transparency into their DEI efforts with reports breaking down the racial and gender makeup of employees across different roles and by lateral movement or promotions.

J.P. Morgan's Workforce Composition Disclosure report shows the ratios of gender and racial composition across the board of directors, operating committee, executive team, and down to the internship class. The company breaks out the percentages of these classes promoted to vice president or above.

In its report, Merck provides a similar breakout of underrepresented ethnic groups and female representation by job category and promotions, with data that goes back to 2016. This report also shows data on post-program retention, lateral moves, and the track record of those who participate in Merck's Women's Leadership and Diverse Leader Programs to help underrepresented employees develop advanced leadership capabilities.

In addition to quantitative measures of diversity and equity, companies should use surveys to measure whether employees feel accepted, believe they belong, and are part of a community at work. In building a more inclusive environment, companies must be transparent about all DEI data if true progress is to be made. While the numbers are not always flattering, measuring these metrics builds trust with stakeholders and holds the organization accountable for progress.

Senior leaders can also engage small groups and individuals informally. Surveys show trends, but they don't provide the inside story. Ask questions such as: "What is holding us back from creating a more inclusive culture? Where did we do well and where can we improve?" Then be prepared to listen deeply.

"You can't fail on earnings growth or product launches and keep your job," says Mellody Hobson, co-CEO and president of Ariel Investments, "but when it comes to diversity, you can say you're just working on it with no consequences." Mellody runs an $18 billion global firm whose leadership is 69 percent minority and women leaders. She's the only Black female chairing a *Fortune 500* board—Starbucks—which she calls "crazy."

Mellody champions measuring diversity and incentivizing results. "Any company that's not truly focused on diversity with measurable outcomes is committing corporate suicide," she says. "It's not a question of if they will die—but when." She says diverse groups with different viewpoints make better decisions. "If you have hard problems to solve, diverse groups get better outcomes."

Yet the progress on increasing diversity in corporate America has been heartbreakingly slow—particularly in Silicon Valley, which Mellody calls "Mad Men without ashtrays, a throwback to 1950." Mellody suggests it starts with transparency, saying, "You have got to report progress every year. You want to show success, want to win, want to improve. This requires transparency and making the results public."

Mellody recommends that boards make diversity a factor in compensation, noting, "Incentives are everything in corporate America. If diversity is the strategic imperative, it must be directly linked to executive incentive compensation."

Emerging Leader Profile: Murisiku Raifu

For hundreds of years, America has been a land of hopes and dreams for people seeking better futures. As a boy, Murisiku ("Muri") Raifu wanted to become a physician to help solve problems with medical care in Ghana. Now he is using his education and skills to transform health care in Africa.

Muri grew up in Ghana with immigrants from all over Africa, and his polyglot neighborhood helped him become fluent in many languages. Muri was the first in his family to attend school. Wanting to continue his studies in America, he chose schools from *Peterson's Guide* and handwrote 30 letters to leading North American secondary schools seeking a scholarship.

When he won it, his trip to America was anything but easy. Muri's mother sold her jewelry to buy him a one-way ticket to John F. Kennedy Airport in New York. "I arrived in America as a 15-year-old with $173 in my pocket, a small clothes bag, and a whole lot of dreams," he says. Not knowing where to go, he eventually got in a taxi and told the driver to take him to the Bronx, where he had someone's name.

With the benefit of scholarships, Muri went to Amherst College and University of Minnesota Medical School, followed by 7 years at the University of California–Los Angeles's (UCLA) neurosurgery residency. To practice neurosurgery, he chose New York–Presbyterian Hospital in Queens, New York, but faced a crucible when he was told, "You should see only Black patients." He explains,

These people tried to take away my agency—which is understanding your True North and why you do what you do. Of course, I want to help Black

patients and give them respect and dignity, but I am here to help any patient. My guiding principle is to heal you with the dignity and treatment you deserve, whether you're the richest person in the world or the poorest. I didn't come this far to be limited in manifesting my full potential by accepting these restrictions.

As a result, Muri took a sabbatical and went to Harvard Kennedy School to get his master's degree in public administration. Upon graduation, he returned to California to restart his practice and launch a tech company called Talamus Health. He explains, "I see myself as a pluripotential who can do much more than surgery and create something beautiful. Our end goal is to change people's lives."

Currently operating in Nigeria, Ghana, South Africa, and Zimbabwe, Talamus is creating a marketplace to give people better access to health care. Using mobile phones, people can book clinic appointments, get lab results, read doctors, notes, order drugs, pay medical bills, and access their medical records. Muri sees an opportunity to transform the entire African system, making it more democratized, enabling everyone to get the care they need when they need it.

Murisiku's story is an example of what highly motivated people can do when given the opportunity while overcoming barriers of immigration and discrimination to fulfill their dreams.

Bill's Take: Time to Act against Discrimination

Interviewing leaders from diverse backgrounds for this chapter was humbling. I was struck by the incredible hardships these leaders overcame to achieve great things and by their passion to provide similar opportunities for others. While their parents had little material wealth, they had enormous impact on their values and purpose. They were deeply committed to give their children opportunities and insistent they use those opportunities to help others.

All these leaders overcame prejudice based on their race, gender, sexual identity, or national origin, but they moved past bias to achieve their goals. Their life stories give them the drive to accomplish great things because they overcame significant challenges. They also give them compassion and desire to ensure others aren't limited by prejudice.

I have never faced discrimination like these leaders have, but I get angry whenever others discriminate against people. As a naive 18-year-old, I was shocked by the discrimination I encountered in the South and then proud when Georgia Tech became the first public school in the South to integrate peacefully. Atlanta and Georgia Tech have made amazing progress since then in becoming more inclusive.

In the corporate world, I have advocated for opening the doors for talented women, BIPOC, immigrants, and LGBTQ+ leaders, and confronted discrimination whenever I encountered it. When White males grouse about the lack of diverse talent, and question whether organizations "are willing to reduce performance," I say, "Nonsense!"

To reach their full potential, diverse leaders need allies to remove barriers, eliminate discrimination, advocate for them, and mentor and guide them, just as older leaders opened doors for me. White males can create opportunities for people who have historically been discriminated against, overtly or subconsciously, and build inclusive organizations where everyone is accepted for *who* they are, not what they are.

To sustain success, as leaders we not only need diverse voices at the decision-making table, but we must also build cultures of inclusion and belonging for everyone.

Idea in Brief: Inclusive Leadership

Recap of the Main Idea

- Diversity and inclusion are essential characteristics for every organization, but diversity alone is not sufficient. Leaders need to ensure everyone feels fully included so they can perform their best.

- To create an inclusive culture, leaders must foster cultures built around a sense of belonging, where everyone feels accepted for who they are, regardless of their gender, race, religion, national origin, or sexual identity.
- The key to inclusive organizations is ensuring everyone is accepted for *who* they are, not what they are.

Questions to Ask

1. Do you have unconscious bias? In what ways are you inclined to make assumptions about others based on cultural stereotypes?
2. How are you interacting with team members in ways that makes them comfortable through inclusive language and open, honest dialogue?
3. What are your goals for creating an inclusive workplace? How can you track these goals and measure progress over time?

Practical Suggestions for Your Development

- Hold town hall–style meetings or facilitate small-group discussions where everyone has an opportunity to speak up and be heard.
- Enroll in diversity and inclusion training and sponsor attendance for your team; share educational content on diversity initiatives.
- Proactively recruit people from diverse backgrounds through outreach, as well as partnering with organizations representing diverse groups.
- Model inclusive language by avoiding sociallycharged or gendered terms.
- Hold yourself and your team accountable for change; set *transparent* goals and track progress against them over time to ensure you're moving the needle.
- Create space among leaders to discuss inclusive leadership and your strategies to achieve it.

12

LEADING IN CRISIS

> Never let a good crisis go to waste.
> —*Winston Churchill, prime minister,*
> *United Kingdom*

In the past 2 decades, we have careened from one crisis to the next. The new century started full of optimism but quickly turned tragic when New York's World Trade Center twin towers were toppled by al-Qaeda on September 11, 2001.

Shortly thereafter, companies like Enron, WorldCom, Tyco, and others melted down in a pool of fraud and their chief executive officers (CEOs)—Jeff Skilling, Bernie Ebbers, and Dennis Kozlowski—wound up with long prison sentences. Meanwhile, dot-com companies saw their stock prices collapse, as Cisco lost 83 percent of its value and Amazon went down 89 percent. Those two quickly rebounded, while many others never recovered.

Boom years in stocks followed, driven by aggressive traders, high leverage, and minimal liquidity. Corporations were forced to respond to demands for short-term earnings and increased cash returns to shareholders via stock buybacks. Widespread lack of fiscal responsibility led to the global financial crisis, triggered on September 14, 2008, by the bankruptcy of Lehman Brothers. Its collapse was quickly followed by the insolvency of leading financial institutions, including Citigroup, Merrill Lynch, AIG, and dozens more, causing credit markets to shut down completely.

There followed a decade of recovery until the 2020 arrival of the COVID-19 pandemic. It shut down economies all over the world until governments stepped in with massive deficit funding to ameliorate the damage. In 2022, Putin's Russia launched a brutal invasion of Ukraine, starting the largest war in Europe since World War II. Meanwhile, climate disasters like rampant forest fires, tornados, and earthquakes occur with increasing frequency as the planet's mean temperatures continue to rise.

What's next? None of these major crises were predicted, beyond a handful of after-the-fact "I told you so" claims. As leaders, the question for us becomes: How should we lead through these unexpected events?

At the end of the 20th century, students at the U.S. Army War College predicted the world of the 21st century would contain *volatility, uncertainty, complexity,* and *ambiguity*—VUCA for short. The last 2 decades have proven how prescient they were. This raises the question: What qualities do leaders need to navigate crises successfully? For that, we propose VUCA 2.0: Vision, Understanding, Courage, and Adaptability (Figure 12.1).

In leading through crisis, think of yourself as captain of the ship. Because of all the uncertainty, you need to have a clear *vision* of where you are going. As Stephen Covey writes, "Begin with the end in mind." That is your destination. No doubt your ship will be buffeted by winds and storms. To navigate through them, you need to have a deep *understanding* of how things work—the knowledge that comes from years of experience. Then you need to summon the *courage* to lead your team through the storm without vacillating in the face of uncertainty. Because you will face unexpected events, you must have *adaptability* in your tactics yet be unwavering in your vision.

VUCA	VUCA 2.0
• Volatility	• Vision
• Uncertainty	• Understanding
• Complexity	• Courage
• Ambiguity	• Adaptability

Figure 12.1 VUCA and VUCA 2.0

Indra Nooyi: Performance with Purpose

Vision, understanding, courage, and adaptability describe the leadership of CEO Indra Nooyi as she built PepsiCo for 12 years through consumer challenges, stock market criticisms, and activist investors trying to break up the company. Born in Chennai, India, she graduated from Madras Christian College and then came to America to study business at Yale. Afterward, she worked for storied enterprises, including Johnson & Johnson, Booz Allen Hamilton, Boston Consulting Group, Motorola, and ABB, before joining PepsiCo in 1994.

When Indra became CEO of PepsiCo in 2006, she laid out a bold vision, Purpose with Performance, which had four goals: (1) return value to shareholders; (2) nourish people and societies; (3) minimize impact on the environment; and (4) cherish employees. Indra says, "It was incumbent to connect what was good for the business with what was good for the world."

> Every company has a soul, made up of all the people who comprise the enterprise. Employees do not want to park their persona at the door. They want to work for a company where they can bring their whole selves to work, a company that cares about the world.

To nourish people, Indra focused on advancing healthier eating and drinking habits by increasing zero- and low-calorie options with innovation and marketing of good-for-you products like juices, teas, and oatmeal while retaining its traditional fun-for-you products like Pepsi Cola and Frito-Lay chips. To balance PepsiCo's portfolio, Indra created a nutrition group led by food scientists that focused on reducing sodium and sugar in company products.

While her new mission was well-received internally, the financial community was skeptical. Their focus was clearly on short-term earnings, which to them meant soda and chips. One sarcastic portfolio manager asked Indra, "Who do you think you are? Mother Teresa?"

Indra faced her first major crisis in 2011 when Pepsi fell behind Diet Coke to the #3 position for the first time as market share slipped.

Immediately, investors' knives came out, charging that PepsiCo had lost focus on its core business. In Indra's first 5 years, PepsiCo stock had grown only 3 percent, while Coke's stock rose 42 percent.

In response to investors' criticisms, Indra made a series of tactical changes without wavering from her vision. She invested $600 million more in marketing its soft drinks, tacitly acknowledging that Pepsi needed to refocus more on its core business. She also made a series of leadership changes, most notably replacing the head of North American beverages.

Her changes led to a steady recovery, and PepsiCo stock responded accordingly in 2012 and 2013. Then activist investor Nelson Peltz, owner of Trian Partners, saw the opportunity for a short-term gain with an aggressive proposal to break up the company, spinning off its beverage business and merging its snacks business with Mondelez—a company he controlled. To pursue his plan, he purchased $1.5 billion in PepsiCo stock (1 percent ownership) and launched an active media campaign to tout his proposal.

After reviewing the proposal with her board, Indra turned Nelson down. She went on CNBC and made her case convincingly. She had a surprise supporter in Warren Buffett, who told CNBC, "If I owned control of PepsiCo, I'd keep both businesses. One of them (snacks) is a terrific business. The other (beverages) is a perfectly good business. Why break them up?" Then he added a dig at activists, saying, "I believe in running a company for the shareholders that are going to stay, rather than ones who are going to leave."

Over lunch, I asked Indra, "Why are you so concerned about a 1 percent stakeholder?" She responded thoughtfully that many of her largest funds might be persuaded to back Peltz's proposal to garner near-term gains. The following February, Nelson renewed his campaign with a 37-page letter he sent over Indra's head to the PepsiCo board. Presiding director Ian Cook took the lead 10 days later, forcefully shutting off any interest in Nelson's proposal, writing, "Our focus is on delivering results for our shareholders, not new, costly distractions that will harm shareholder interests." Two years later, Indra and Nelson settled.

In the end, Indra's tenacity, long-term focus, and Performance with Purpose strategy carried the day. Her responses to the 2011 criticism led to 7 years of outstanding results. These were also reflected in PepsiCo's stock price, which climbed 78 percent, more than doubling archrival Coca-Cola's stock gains of 31 percent.

Indra's story shows that, when results are lagging, the best leaders stay fully committed to their long-term vision while making tactical adaptations. In the end you will win out, as Indra did, if you bet right and don't deviate from your goal. In making transformative strategic moves that anticipate societal changes, leaders need to stay on course, warding off or adapting to intervening events with tenacity and the courage of their convictions.

Leading through Crises

Inevitably, all leaders will face one or more crises during their time at the helm. Just as no mariner ever became an expert sailor in calm waters, leaders who try to avoid challenges won't be prepared to confront greater challenges when they are on top. Often there is no way to prepare for a specific crisis except having had prior experience in challenging times, but there are 7 lessons for leading in crisis that all leaders should follow (Figure 12.2).

1.	Face reality, starting with yourself
2.	Dig deep for the root cause
3.	Engage with frontline teams
4.	Never waste a good crisis
5.	Get ready for the long haul
6.	In the spotlight, follow your True North
7.	Go on offense, focus on winning now

Figure 12.2   7 Lessons for Leading in Crisis

Lesson 1: Face Reality, Starting with Yourself

Let's contrast Indra Nooyi during PepsiCo's crisis with General Electric (GE) CEO Jeff Immelt. Indra faced shareholder crises that she successfully navigated. She faced the reality of PepsiCo's lost market share in 2010 and made tactical adjustments by increasing soft drink marketing with an additional $600 million investment but never deviated from her purpose.

In contrast, Jeff Immelt never acknowledged his crises, which included poor acquisitions, performance failures, and a $15 billion undisclosed insurance liability. Rather than address its over-dependence on GE Capital, Jeff instead quintupled the size of GE's consumer finance business, overleveraging its balance sheet. When the banks crashed in 2008, Jeff had to call President George W. Bush to get bailed out along with the banks.

Meanwhile, Jeff sold GE's insurance business in 2004 while keeping the long-term liabilities but failing to disclose them, forcing his successor to take a $15 billion write-off in 2017. He finally sold the remaining parts of GE Capital in 2015, taking a $16 billion loss and then using $50 billion to buy back GE stock at double today's price. He paid too much for high-profile acquisitions like Alstom and Baker Hughes while selling off many of GE's traditional businesses at modest prices.

Under Jeff's leadership, GE investors lost more than $300 billion in shareholder value. He tried to turn GE into a high-tech company, but high tech wasn't in GE's DNA. In the end, his initiatives were mostly shut down by his successors. GE's demise proved that the conglomerate model does not work because it lacks a central purpose that unites its employees and a clear strategy that leverages the company's unique strengths. It is built on financial engineering, not on a central purpose, strategy, and sound business practices that enable the company to grow its market position and long-term shareholder value.

Ask yourself, when you faced disappointments and crises in your past, did you face reality? Did you look in the mirror and probe how your actions may have contributed to the crisis? Did you take full responsibility, or did you blame other people or external factors? You can learn from mistakes you make in early crises in leading when the stakes are lower so that you will be prepared to deal with larger crises when you take on greater responsibility.

Lesson 2: Dig Deep for the Root Cause

Oftentimes a new leader is called on to take over during a financial crisis. Xerox's Anne Mulcahy is an exceptional leader who led Xerox through the greatest crisis in its history when the company was facing bankruptcy. Thrust into a position she never anticipated, Anne demonstrated a remarkable ability to rally Xerox's 96,000 employees around a common purpose. Her empowering approach not only averted bankruptcy but also built a healthy culture for her successor, Ursula Burns.

The Xerox board's decision to promote Anne to CEO when her predecessor failed surprised her as well as everyone else. She explains,

> It was like going to war, knowing there was so much at stake. This was a job that would dramatically change my life, requiring every ounce of energy I had. I never expected to be CEO, nor was I groomed for it.

What no one understood when Anne took the helm in 2000 was that Xerox was facing a massive liquidity crisis as revenues were declining, its sales force unraveling, and new product pipeline depleted. The company had $18 billion in debt and credit lines were exhausted. Morale inside the company had plummeted, and its share price was in free-fall.

With just 1 week of cash on hand, Xerox's external advisers were recommending Chapter 11 bankruptcy filing to erase its debt payments. To make matters worse, Xerox's chief financial officer (CFO) was preoccupied with a Securities and Exchange Commission

(SEC) investigation into its revenue recognition practices. It took a lot of digging, but eventually Anne uncovered the root cause of Xerox's liquidity crisis: its accountants booked future revenues without recognizing expenses.

Since this was at heart a financial crisis, how did Anne cope with it when she had no financial background? To ameliorate the gaps in her experience, she asked the treasurer's office to tutor her on finance.

As she uncovered the company's problems, Anne's purpose became clear: not only to save Xerox from bankruptcy but also to *restore it to its former greatness.* Her challenge was to unite the disheartened organization and get leaders throughout the company to step up.

Instead of endless meetings at headquarters, Anne visited customers to stem the tide of customer defections and field-sales resignations. She told the sales force, "I will go anywhere, anytime, to save a Xerox customer." Her customer engagement sent an important signal that solidified the Xerox field organization and restored customer confidence.

In October 2000, Anne candidly told investors that Xerox's business model was unsustainable. The next day, the stock dropped 26 percent. She notes, "This was my baptism by fire."

> *My greatest fear was that I was sitting on the deck of the Titanic, and I'd get to drive it to the bottom of the ocean. Nothing spooked me so much as waking up in the middle of the night and thinking about 96,000 employees and retirees and what would happen if things went south.*

Despite her doubts, Anne provided her team confidence that Xerox could survive, yet she was not immune from uncertainty and stress.

> *One day I came back from Japan and found it had been a dismal day. Around 8:30 pm on my way home, I pulled over on the Merritt Parkway and said to myself, "I don't know where to go. I don't want to go home. There's just no place to go."*

Have you ever felt like that? In my experience, feelings of loneliness and despair are quite common for leaders, but most do not have the courage to admit it. In times like these, you need the support of your colleagues. Anne credits an uplifting voicemail from her chief strategist in helping her come back inspired the next day.

When the company's external advisers argued that Xerox should prepare for bankruptcy to erase its $18 billion in debt, Anne exploded, "Bankruptcy's never a win. I'm not going there until there's no other decision to be made. Our people believed we were in a war we can win."

Anne did win in the end. She staved off bankruptcy by cutting billions in operating expenses and reducing Xerox's bloated staff by 38,000 employees without touching research and development (R&D) or field sales. In launching 60 new products with new color and digital technology, she restored revenue and profit growth.

Lesson 3: Engage with Frontline Teams

In 2017, when Dr. Peter Pisters was named president of The University of Texas MD Anderson Cancer Center, the nation's leading cancer institute, he inherited an organization with morale at its lowest point following two years of financial losses. MD Anderson faced an unprecedented exodus of highly talented faculty members, who left for a variety of reasons including feeling pressure to increase their productivity to fund research.

Returning to MD Anderson after serving as CEO of Toronto's University Health Network, Peter recognized he had to express confidence, humility, and sincere interest in listening and learning.

On his first day as president, he sent a message to the entire organization: "I'm willing to unlearn and relearn through a listening and learning tour, where I can learn from you what is great about our organization and where you believe my attention and our resources need to be focused." He explains,

I visited 200 units in our organization from the frontlines to topflight talent, making rounds in the hospital at night and weekends. Reaching out to frontline

people and seeing notes from patients to their housekeepers gave me first-hand knowledge of the organization.

To improve executive leadership's dynamic throughout the institution, he began meeting with top leaders on a regular basis. Peter says,

> The visibility onsite in operational units and face-to-face meetings helped rebuild the trust. We established a quarterly leadership meeting, leading off with a patient's story, after which everyone is wiping their eyes and understands with clarity what our purpose is and why are we here. Getting out into the organization on a very regular basis builds the trust that's so important to engineer changes.

The effectiveness of Peter's efforts was confirmed in the biennial employee engagement survey, which had a record participation rate of 89 percent and showed double digit increases in engagement, 6 percent reduction in burnout rates, and stunning 98 percent alignment with MD Anderson's mission.

Lesson 4: Never Waste a Good Crisis

On Sunday morning, September 14, 2008, Penny and I were in Newport, Rhode Island, celebrating my birthday, when I joined a Goldman Sachs (GS) board call at 7:30 a.m. Though I was aware of concerns about Lehman Brothers' financial viability, a Sunday meeting was highly unusual. Goldman president Gary Cohen opened the meeting, saying Lehman would go under that day unless last-minute government efforts could save it. He also indicated that other overleveraged financial institutions might also fail in the coming days.

Gary said Goldman was in good shape due to the large amount of liquidity it had built up to prepare for external financial shocks. That was due to Goldman top management's concerns about instability in subprime mortgages that led to a decision to exit the subprime market and increase liquidity by $100 billion. Those actions enabled Goldman to navigate the greatest financial crisis since 1929 virtually unscathed, aided by Warren Buffett's $5 billion investment.

Were Goldman's leaders smarter than everyone else, or just lucky? Neither. Goldman CEO Lloyd Blankfein, himself an exceptional risk manager, led his team brilliantly through the crisis, as did Jamie Dimon of J.P. Morgan. Both firms bounced back quickly in 2009. In the aftermath of the crisis, Goldman faced intense criticism for its high compensation practices and engaging in a controversial mortgage transaction that led to an SEC lawsuit, Congressional hearings, and negative media stories in spring 2010.

Rather than acting defensively as many leaders would, Lloyd formed the Business Standards Committee (BSC), which included 150 senior partners and was led by GS's vice chair. I was asked to chair a four-person board committee to oversee these efforts. This effort involved a top-to-bottom examination of all of GS's business practices, including its committee structures and approval mechanisms, as well as the transparency of communications and professional training. The BSC report, released in January 2011, included 39 recommendations to improve the firm's practices. By being proactive, Lloyd preempted external intrusion and used the crisis to make Goldman a more effective firm in serving its customers.

Lesson 5: Get Ready for the Long Haul

Only 8 months into her tenure as CEO, Corie Barry faced the COVID-19 pandemic, which threatened Best Buy's in-store and in-home business model. Realizing the pandemic could last a long time, she called her team together and formulated three principles for decision-making through the crisis:

1. Make safety of employees and customers Best Buy's highest priority.
2. Avoid layoffs as long as possible, even if stores were forced to close.
3. Make decisions based on long-term value creation.

Corie announced in mid-March that retail operations would be limited to curbside pickup with no customers permitted in its stores, as Best Buy closed 1,026 locations. In addition, Geek Squad's in-home services were suspended, and corporate employees worked from home. A month later, she furloughed 51,300 employees, approximately 20 percent of its workforce. She notes, "Our goal was to come out the other side of this pandemic a vibrant company."

> We held off long enough to bridge employees until the government stimulus kicked in, so we weren't leaving them high and dry; however, I could not offer them any certainty about when the furlough might end. We made the decision for the health and safety of our customers and employees.

Corie and her board also took 50 percent pay cuts, and her direct reports took 20 percent cuts. To preserve cash in case the crisis worsened, Best Buy drew down its entire revolving credit facility of $1.25 billion, in addition to its $2 billion cash on hand. To preserve cash, she also suspended share repurchases, reduced incoming merchandise deliveries, extended vendor payment terms, reduced promotional spending, and ceased capital expenditures.

In the early stages of a crisis, leaders never know how long it will last, nor do they understand its full implications. By November 2020, Corie realized that Best Buy had not only successfully navigated the crisis but also accelerated its new business strategy of combining in-store merchandising, online purchasing, and in-store pickup. Best Buy discovered the competitive advantage of its Geek Squad could be expanded through remote service as well as in-home. By preparing for a long-term downturn and broadening its buying options for customers, Best Buy gained market share through its crisis management.

Lesson 6: In the Spotlight, Follow Your True North

CEOs and company leaders are just one incident away from being thrust into the spotlight. That's what Starbucks chair Howard

Schultz and CEO Kevin Johnson learned when two Black customers were arrested in its downtown Philadelphia store, and a video of the incident went viral. Their charge? Trespassing—or as they explained, waiting to meet a friend. Their arrest violated Starbucks' basic value of treating everyone equally. Speaking with Gayle King on CBS television, Howard said,

> When I first saw the video, I was sick to my stomach. I was embarrassed and ashamed. This is the antithesis of what Starbucks stands for. It is undeniable that I am personally responsible. We need to address it transparently and honestly.

Later Howard said he asked his manager, "If those two young men were White, would you have called the police? To her credit, she said, 'Probably not.' Once I knew that, I had a moral obligation to tell the truth."

No doubt Starbucks was in the wrong here, but Howard followed his True North and reaffirmed Starbucks' values. He went immediately to the scene, apologized to the men, made a financial settlement, and acknowledged his accountability publicly. Starbucks then closed all 8,000 of its U.S. stores for a day of racial-bias training.

By taking full responsibility for the incident followed by specific actions, Starbucks was able to minimize the damage. Obviously, it would have been better to avoid this situation, but people make mistakes. When they do, your job as a leader is to take responsibility and initiate corrective action immediately.

Lesson 7: Go on Offense, Focus on Winning Now

Emerging Leader: Jenn Hyman

Jenn Hyman did not build the iconic Rent the Runway (RTR) brand by being timid. Intelligent and confident, she cofounded the company to solve a problem nearly every woman has encountered: "a closet full of clothes, but nothing to wear." Over the course of a decade, Jenn raised more than $340 million and recruited celebrities like Beyoncé and Gwyneth Paltrow as supporters and board members. Eleven years in, the company's subscription service was growing more than 100 percent year over year.

Then COVID-19 hit, and RTR faced rapid revenue declines. As Jenn explains, "You don't really need to have a new outfit every day if you're sitting at home in your pajamas." She acted quickly, cutting everything from capital expenditures to inventory, cutting budgets, and reducing headcount by 40 percent. She then raised $100 million in debt and equity to ensure the business could continue operating regardless of how long the pandemic endured.

Transparency helped Jenn earn trust during an uncertain period when she was forced to make difficult choices to stabilize the business. She says,

> I had to communicate that we were in a crisis. We were reinventing our business model under the hardest external conditions the company has ever experienced. Crisis situations present an opportunity to flex a new kind of leadership muscle and learn new skills—how to deeply connect, motivate and inspire, develop resilience and grit, and ruthlessly prioritize with fewer resources.

Jenn articulated to her team her resolute belief that Rent the Runway's "Closet in the Cloud" would be even more resonant in a post-COVID-19 world. She says, "Once we made the cuts needed to survive, we used this time to transform the business and ensure we came out stronger than before." She laid out a bold strategy to achieve this:

- Reinventing RTR's core subscription model in favor of tiered pricing customized to consumers' usage
- Using demand downturn to restructure operations and execute process improvements to strengthen efficiency

- Launching a resale vertical, adding revenue, and creating a new funnel for attracting new subscribers
- Shifting its product acquisition toward capital light channels where designers have more of a partnership model with RTR

Jenn anchored her strategy in the original mission of the business but envisioned post-COVID-19 as "a second founding moment" for the company:

> Fashion is an undemocratic industry in which only 1 percent of people could access the things we aspire to. Our mission is to say to women, "You can have whatever you want." That was a galvanizing idea for our founding team. There was a rebellious spirit of: we're going to take this elitist industry and turn it on its head. We weren't going to let a once in a 100-year pandemic destroy this vision.

By affirming its mission of democratizing fashion for everyone and creating a more competitive business model, Jenn used the pandemic to RTR's advantage. In October 2021, Jenn took RTR public, becoming the first company to make an initial public offering (IPO) with a female founder–CEO, chief operations officer (COO), and CFO.

Bill's Take: Crisis Is the Real Test for Leaders

As a leader, you will inevitably face a crisis during your career that becomes the defining moment of your tenure. When you are following a plan and things are going well, it is relatively easy to perform and get people to follow your lead. When the crisis comes, whether from internal issues or external sources, your leadership is truly tested.

In a crisis there is no playbook about what to do, nor are the root cause and its implications clear. That's when you need to pull your team together, face the crisis objectively, consider worst-case possibilities, and develop a flexible plan to navigate it.

Throughout my career I have faced many such crises and have observed how differently leaders handle them. It is surprising how often people we thought were strong leaders in good times fail to step up to the challenges. That's when the real leaders take charge to bring people together to find a way through.

Crisis reveals courage. Leaders who are more concerned about external appearances may lack the courage to take decisive action when the way forward is unclear because their fear of failure takes hold. Courageous leaders don't worry about looking good; they just want to rally people to get through it. They are willing to face all obstacles and lead people to a better place.

As an emerging leader, you need to test yourself in lower-stake situations to prepare for greater responsibilities when the stakes are higher. The only way you can develop courage is by testing yourself in the most difficult circumstances. My advice is: seek these opportunities; don't hold back from them. When greater crises emerge later in your career, you will be prepared not only to lead your team through them but also to have the courage to make bold moves that enable you to emerge as a winner.

Idea in Brief: Leading in Crisis

Recap of the Main Idea
- Crisis is the real test for every leader.
- All leaders inevitably face crises during their time at the helm.
- To navigate through a crisis, you need to be unwavering in your *vision* with deep *understanding* of how things work, summon the *courage* to lead your team through the storm, and be flexible and *adaptable* in your tactics.
- The 7 *lessons* to follow in a crisis are:
  1. Face reality, starting with yourself.
  2. Dig deep for the root cause.

3. Engage with frontline teams.

4. Never waste a good crisis.

5. Get ready for the long haul.

6. In the spotlight, follow your True North.

7. Go on offense, focus on winning now.

Questions to Ask

1. Ask yourself, when you faced crises in your past:

   a. Did you face reality?

   b. Did you look in the mirror and probe how your actions may have contributed to the crisis?

   c. Did you take full responsibility?

   d. Or did you blame other people or external factors?

2. Envision a future crisis. How would you respond? Do you have the right team to navigate it? Do you have the right purpose and strategy to use as your destination?

Practical Suggestions for Your Development

- Be transparent with your team about the challenges your organization faces and encourage them to contribute to solutions.

- Meet with employees, customers, and advisers to understand the problems and hear different perspectives.

- Develop decision-making principles and long-term plans to navigate the crises.

- Use the crises to transform your business and your organization to enable you to strengthen your market position for the future.

13

THE MORAL LEADER

Doing well and doing good are not mutually exclusive.
—Marc Benioff, CEO, *Salesforce*

In this final chapter, we propose a challenge for your leadership: to be a moral leader who upholds your values, exemplifies integrity, and demonstrates courage to make a positive impact on the world.

Aristotle postulated three qualities of great communicators: logos, ethos, and pathos. Though logic and empathy are required characteristics of today's leaders, what is most necessary is ethos, or morality. In today's era there is a crying need for moral leaders. Think of Mahatma Gandhi, Abraham Lincoln, Mother Teresa, Nelson Mandela, Winston Churchill, and Martin Luther King Jr. as great moral leaders. They set a standard that few of us believe we can achieve.

Yet the virtues they demonstrated are within our grasp. You can become a moral leader by discovering your True North, behaving authentically, and following your North Star to pursue your purpose. When you do so, you inspire people to follow your leadership, and you become a role model for others.

Dov Seidman, business leader, foremost thinker, and advocate for moral leadership, observes, "Leadership is how leaders touch hearts, not just minds, how they enlist others in a shared and significant endeavor, and create the conditions where everyone can contribute their fullest talent and realize their deepest humanity."

Moral leaders are driven by purpose and animated by courage and patience as they wrestle with issues of right and wrong and inspire others. Moral authority must be earned by who you are and how you lead. No longer can you have power over people; you only can have power through people.

Dov says that wrestling with these issues requires reframing them in moral terms and pausing for deep reflection:

To be a moral leader, you need to pause and reflect on the world you're in, the dilemma you're facing, and how you are handling it. That pause is essential to ensure your behavior is aligned with your values by framing the issue in moral terms.

Chip Bergh: Levi's Moral Leader

Levi Strauss chief executive officer (CEO) Chip Bergh is an example of today's moral leader. Prior to becoming CEO in 2011, Chip attended Lafayette College, served in the U.S. Army, and worked for Procter & Gamble. When he took over, Levi's had declining sales, high debt, and a weakened 168-year-old brand that was losing its relevance. Never one to flinch from challenges, Chip believed he could reinvigorate the brand and restore the company's financial strength by leading through his humanitarian values and principles. In 2019, he brought the company back to public markets after 39 years of private ownership. In 2021, despite the COVID-19 pandemic, the company reported multidecade record revenues and profitability.

When I spoke with Chip as he passed the 10-year mark as CEO, he was ebullient about how he could make a difference and how he was addressing today's most challenging issues. Chip believes Levi's iconic brand stands for authenticity, and that must be reflected in its leadership and employees.

If a brand doesn't act—if the words and pictures don't go together—that brand is in trouble. We believe in taking stands on important issues and those stands have an impact, not just on the company but on the Levi's brand.

Our brand, one of the most iconic in the world, had a near-death experience a decade ago. For me, making this company great is a noble cause. Enabling people to be their true authentic selves is what the Levi's brand is all about.

Chip models authenticity in his interactions with Levi's employees. For example, he hosts a monthly "Chips and Beer" session that is webcast globally. After a brief update on company news, he shifts to an open-mic format that enables employees to ask about anything. He believes his high level of transparency builds trust among employees: "People recognize I'm approachable."

Chip wants Levi's to be a company where employees bring their authentic selves to work every day. He explains, "The COVID-19 pandemic had such an epic impact, so I want people to tell their grandchildren someday how the company treated them during this time, especially when we had to close our stores, and gave everyone who got laid off 12 months of health care."

He also believes leaders must be authentic in how they speak out about important public issues, observing that social advocacy has always been the Levi's way. "In a world that is increasingly divided, CEOs have an obligation to weigh in. We have clout, and we have a voice. If we stand on the sidelines, we're not fulfilling our roles as leaders," he says.

In recent years, Chip has been outspoken about hot-button issues like ending gun violence, climate change, and paid family leave. He notes, "Young consumers today are socially aware and read through the B.S."

We target Gen Z consumers, so we must understand their mindset. Climate change and gun violence are very important to them, so we take clear stands. We can't stand for everything, or we stand for nothing. So we try to stand for things that matter most. My lens in deciding on where to take stands is, will we be on the right side of history 30 years from now?

Chip believes, "A diverse organization will outperform a homogeneous one every time." Following George Floyd's murder, he had a moment of reckoning when his team took a hard look at Levi's diversity and realized, "The ugly truth is we aren't where we need to be." Chip responded by meeting with Black employees to understand their experiences working at Levi's, pledging to share annual updates on diversity, equity, and inclusion (DEI) statistics, conducting wage equity audits, and appointing a Black leader to the company's board.

He is also working to strengthen voting rights, giving employees time off to vote and donating $3 million to provide fair access to the polls. When Georgia legislators passed more restrictive voting laws, he called them "racist." Today, he works with legislators in other states to prevent passage of similar bills.

Chip is a big believer in the "pause principle" he learned from Dov Seidman. In addition to keeping a daily journal, he pauses to ask:

- Did I make a difference in someone's life today?
- Was I helpful to my team today?
- Am I thinking about where we're going and looking around corners?
- Am I living my values?
- Am I leading by example and making a difference in how I lead?

Do you take time for a pause each day? Ask yourself these probing questions, and you will find your days are aligned with your desires and they will help you become a more moral leader. Alternatively, you may find that mindfulness or meditation accomplishes this as well.

Through his actions and his voice, Chip Bergh is a role model for all of us to be moral leaders. He has passion for his purpose of making Levi's a powerful force in the world. He is courageous in taking on politically charged issues, as he inspires and elevates his employees. He concludes, "This company has driven profits through principles, as we manage for the long-term."

The New Stakeholder Capitalism

The courage and vision of moral leaders like Chip Bergh provides a refreshing contrast to the transactional, short-term mindset that has dominated the business and financial world since the 1980s. As short-term traders, hedge funds, and activist investors gained power—compensated with high fees and 20 percent of gains—they had an insidious effect on capitalism. Focused on driving short-term gains and share buybacks rather than investing in companies for long-term returns, they created a frenzy to maximize short-term shareholder value.

By influencing companies to cut research and other long-term investments, this pressure impacted the economic value and the future viability of firms like General Electric (GE). In 2001, GE was the world's most valuable company. Under the management of CEO Jeff Immelt, its shareholder value declined by $300 billion, the largest decline in history. With no mission and no clear values, GE is a vivid example of the pitfalls of Milton Friedman's doctrine that "the social responsibility of business is to increase its profits"— and of the failures of 20th-century leaders who adhere to it.

Though publicly held corporations are legal entities chartered *by society for serving society*, such fierce shareholder pressures over the past 30 years convinced many businesspeople that their role is solely to manage assets to maximize near-term returns. In 2019, the Business Roundtable (BRT), composed of the top firms in America, took a momentous step when it shifted from shareholder primacy to stakeholder capitalism.

Led by J.P. Morgan's Jamie Dimon, 181 CEOs in the BRT committed "to lead their companies for the *benefit of all stakeholders*— customers, employees, suppliers, communities, and shareholders." Jamie notes, "Major employers are investing in their workers and communities because they know it is the only way to be successful in the long term." Johnson & Johnson's (J&J) Alex Gorsky, a principal author of the new statement, adds, "It reflects the way corporations can and should operate today, affirming the essential role corporations can play in improving our society when CEOs are truly committed to meeting the needs of all stakeholders."

This change was met with skepticism by some in the financial community and media, but it has been widely embraced by CEOs and their leaders as the way they have always wanted to operate— absent short-term shareholder pressures. They are convinced that serving all stakeholders creates greater long-term value for everyone and avoids debacles like GE.

In my experience, many proponents of maximizing shareholder value never understood *how* companies create sustainable shareholder value—or they don't care because they are simply short-term traders of stocks, not long-term investors in companies. Creating sustainable value must start with the alignment of all stakeholders around a shared mission and values in service to a corporation's customers and all those who have a stake in its success.

An organization's purpose and values engage employees and provide the inspiration for them to innovate and to provide superior service to customers. This creates satisfied customers, which in turn increases revenue. Growing revenues increases profits and provides opportunities for reinvestment in employees, innovation, and customer service. That creates sustainable shareholder value, creating a virtuous cycle as all stakeholder interests are aligned (Figure 13.1).

Leading an organization with a multistakeholder model is not easy, as leaders must make difficult decisions and trade-offs in attempting to meet the needs of all their constituencies. It is difficult to satisfy all stakeholders as their goals are often conflicting. Investors, employees, customers, social activists, and government leaders will inevitably apply pressure on decision-makers for their interests to take precedence. Sustaining value creation over long periods of time requires wise judgment and deliberate action from leaders operating with a moral compass. These decisions were

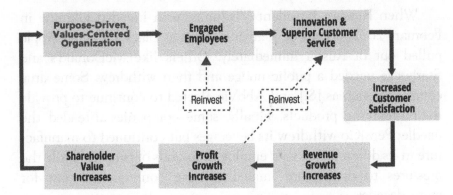

Figure 13.1   Sustaining Growth and Performance

especially difficult during the pandemic when rapid changes had to be made with limited information.

Best Buy CEO Hubert Joly catalogues five approaches that different leaders use in decision-making:

1. Just perform.
2. Do no harm.
3. Be a "net positive" contributor, doing more good than harm.
4. Be a force for good in the world.
5. Address some of society's greatest challenges.

The first three approaches were typical of 20th-century business leaders. Today's leaders are committed to contributing through the last two ways. In pursuing their North Star, moral leaders like Chip Bergh are taking on the great issues of our time.

When Should Leaders Take on Public Issues?

Increasingly contentious media coverage and pressure from shareholder activists and social activists raise a vital question: When should CEOs speak out and take action on public issues? These decisions are extremely complex as usually there is no clear "right" answer.

When Russian President Vladimir Putin invaded Ukraine in February 2022, dozens of companies such as BlackRock and Apple pulled out of Russia immediately. Others like McDonald's and Starbucks needed a public nudge and then withdrew. Some drug companies such as J&J and AbbVie elected to continue to provide their lifesaving products. Finally, some companies threaded the needle; PepsiCo withdrew its beverages but continued to manufacture in its dozen plants that employ thousands of people. While the pressures to decide are immediate, the consequences last for many decades.

Deciding to get involved in a public issue is not an easy choice for leaders, as inevitably you will be criticized regardless of what you do. You cannot speak out on everything, or you lose impact. Even if you decide not to be involved, there can be serious consequences. Disney's Bob Chapek found this out by ignoring the Florida legislation restricting discussion of sexual identity issues in public primary school education, which upset his LGBTQ+ employees and many others. Although he later came out against the bill, the damage was done. Meanwhile, his predecessor, Bob Iger, who ran Disney for 15 years, took a public stand against the legislation.

Moral leaders should focus on issues that relate directly to their purpose and values. When Merck's Ken Frazier resigned so publicly from the President's Council following the Charlotteville unrest, he did so from his moral convictions, but he also gave up his seat at the table to influence the president.

To make these difficult decisions, you need the framework of your own purpose and values as well as those of the company. Does being involved violate my deepest values or my organization's? Is it contrary to my North Star or the company's purpose? How can I do the least harm? How can I do the most good?

Let's look at some moral leaders who are addressing important issues through their leadership.

- Making capitalism work for everyone (Marc Benioff)
- Sustaining our environment (Paul Polman)

- Ethical banking that helps people and communities (Richard Davis)
- Building inclusive communities (Glen Gunderson)
- Reimagining health care (Brad Smith)

Will you take on one of these issues, or perhaps you will address educational opportunity for all, women's rights, or income inequality? You cannot change the whole world, but you can have a powerful impact by picking an issue that calls to you and using your voice and your position for the greater good.

Making Capitalism Work for Everyone

Marc Benioff is the quintessential example of how a moral leader uses the duality of "doing well by doing good" to lead his company. He sees his role in leading Salesforce as using capitalism to serve everyone who has a stake in the company, even the homeless on the streets of San Francisco.

Marc's career started at software giant Oracle where he entered with a bang, winning the company's Rookie of the Year award his first year. At work, he thrived with his high energy, extreme drive, and customer focus. Outside of work, he volunteered in the community. He says this separation was disorienting: "I was working in schools, doing philanthropy, and giving back, but I was two people, businessperson Marc over here, and spiritual philanthropist Marc over there." He says Oracle was "too much Milton Friedman—only about shareholder return."

Then Marc took a sabbatical to visit an Indian ashram. He had an epiphany when guru Mata Amritanandamayi challenged him to give back to others.

> I said to myself, "I want to be one person—the same Marc everywhere and totally integrated. When I start a company, philanthropy, giving, and generosity are the company's values from Day One." That was a powerful moment.

When Marc founded Salesforce in 1999, he saw a market opportunity to transition software to the cloud and envisioned customer relationship management (CRM) software that could tailor one-to-one digital customer relationships. He made values of trust, customer success, innovation, and equality central to Salesforce's culture. Then he baked service into Salesforce's DNA through a 1–1–1 model, where the company donates 1 percent of its stock, 1 percent of its product, and 1 percent of employee time to volunteerism.

Marc has built Salesforce into an incredible success, worth $250 billion. The company is the clear leader in customer relationship management (CRM); it is Salesforce's culture that stands out. Marc explains,

> Research shows companies that integrate a broader mission into their corporate culture outperform their peers, grow faster, and deliver higher profits. Salesforce is living proof that new capitalism can thrive, and everyone can benefit. Doing well and doing good are not mutually exclusive.

Marc has the courage to make hard decisions when Salesforce's values are tested. Values are just words, he says, until you turn them into consistent behaviors. When then Indiana governor Mike Pence signed a bill discriminating against LGBTQ+, Marc publicly said Salesforce—which was Indiana's largest tech employer at the time— would disinvest from the state. Other CEOs followed his lead, including Cummings and Eli Lilly. When Pence called him, Marc threatened the business community would issue "rolling economic sanctions" against Indiana. Shortly after, Pence changed the law.

In his hometown of San Francisco, Marc advocated taxing large technology companies to address homelessness. Criticized by other tech CEOs, Marc said, "This is a small amount to help clean up our city, and we are making billions."

> Our female and LGBTQ+ employees, homeless, public schools, and the planet are key stakeholders that form the company's fabric. You're knitting a

beautiful quilt. If you bring it together, you can have great shareholder return and fabulous stakeholder returns. We're here to improve the state of the world and love each other, not just make money.

Marc constantly wrestles with issues of fairness and justice, such as inequality. He wrote "We Need a New Capitalism" in the *New York Times*:

To my fellow business leaders, we can no longer wash our hands of responsibility for how people use our products. Profits are important, but so is society. If our quest for greater profits leaves our world worse off, we teach our children the power of greed. It's time for a new capitalism—fair, equal, and sustainable capitalism that works for everyone where businesses give back and have positive impact.

By design, Marc's outspokenness challenges other CEOs to keep pace. He believes business is the greatest force for change and thinks the business community must play a larger role in addressing great issues while humanizing business. Through his leadership, Marc is having an impact by demonstrating how the multi-stakeholder approach to capitalism works for everyone.

Sustaining Our Environment

For the past decade, Unilever's Paul Polman has been the leading business voice for sustainability. Early in his tenure, Paul recognized sustainability is Unilever's North Star and published the "Unilever Sustainable Living Plan" as the basis for Unilever's strategy. He made bold commitments and tracked them rigorously, holding his leaders accountable for individual commitments and making them publicly available. In doing so, Paul built on the company's roots and the legacy of cofounder Lord Leverhulme, who used Sunlight soap to help eliminate malaria in Britain.

Paul transformed Unilever by making sustainability commonplace in every product, which in turn created competitive advantage.

He also acquired sustainable brands like Seventh Generation and Sir Kensington's. To transform his leadership team, Paul created the "Unilever Leadership Development Program" that trained thousands of leaders in authentic leadership.

Completing his decade as CEO, Paul left in 2019 and formed an organization called IMAGINE with Valerie Keller as cofounder to galvanize industry leaders around the United Nations' 2030 Sustainable Development Goals. Paul and Valerie are working with CEOs to make sustainability core to their business strategies, starting with the food and apparel industries.

Through personal relationships, Paul is influencing CEOs and other leaders to pay greater attention to environmental issues and make firm commitments for change. Paul's recent book, *Net Positive*, advocates that organizations contribute more to the environment than they use.

Most emerging leaders are believers that we must change our behaviors to reduce the impact of climate change. What actions will you take to address these challenges?

Ethical Banking That Helps People and Communities

Richard Davis is the one of the most ethical bankers of the past quarter-century, never deviating from his principles to make more money. He avoided the high risk, high reward transactions that created the 2008 banking crisis. His U.S. Bank came through it unscathed.

Richard had an unusual career philosophy early in his U.S. Bank career. He stayed at lower levels within the organization, making lateral moves in frontline jobs and turning down several vertical promotion opportunities where he would have made more money. That background led to his love of being with frontline employees in the bank, especially tellers. "My strong suit in leading people is knowing whom to listen to," he says. "When you're on top, it's hard to understand the working lives of frontline people—the people talking to your customers—unless you're out there personally with them."

As CEO of U.S. Bank, Richard faced his greatest challenge when he chaired the banking industry association during the 2008 and 2009 Great Recession. He met with President Barack Obama to explain the importance of only making creditworthy loans. He welcomed Dodd-Frank banking legislation and tighter Federal Reserve regulation, saying, "They created a fair playing field."

Richard envisions the local banker as the community leader, who knows the community's needs and brings people together to improve outcomes. As CEO, he was the business leader of the Twin Cities community, taking on leadership of the YMCA, United Way, Minneapolis Orchestra, Art Institute, and Minnesota Business Partnership. He led efforts to build the city's new football stadium, which now bears U.S. Bank's name, and brought Super Bowl LII to Minneapolis. He says, "You can't have a healthy bank if your community is falling apart."

Richard limited his time as CEO to 11 years, "so I could finally do my service mission that I dreamt about as a teenager." Now as CEO of the Make-A-Wish Foundation, he transformed the organization during the COVID-19 pandemic by envisioning alternatives to airplane travel for very sick children.

Banking and finance are critical to everyone as "the fuel in the tank" that enables us to create financial stability and security as well as using our net worth to enhance our lives and create healthy communities. What is required are ethical bankers like Richard Davis who put their clients' needs ahead of just making money.

Building Inclusive Communities

Glen Gunderson spent his early years in for-profit enterprises. He passed up more lucrative opportunities to lead YMCA of the North because he was inspired by its mission to "put Christian principles into practice through programs that build healthy spirit, mind, and body for all." He has built the Y into the third largest in the world, serving 400,000 people, many of whom are socially disadvantaged.

The COVID-19 pandemic and George Floyd's murder forced Glen to rethink the Y's role in the community as locations had to be closed and team members were laid off. Taking on issues like food insecurity, evictions, and job losses, he used the Y's locations to distribute food to needy families and provide childcare while reaching out to isolated seniors and offering classes virtually.

Now Glen is transforming the Y from swim and gym facilities into programs that foster well-being in spirit, mind, and body for everyone. He is a visionary who created the Y's Equity Innovation Center in 2018. Following George Floyd's 2020 murder, it became a vital site for honest dialogues among community leaders about how to address the community's pain and develop solutions to these issues.

Nonprofit leaders like Glen are essential in bringing people together to build inclusive communities and address challenging issues like race relations and the pandemic. If you are working in a for-profit company, you can learn a great deal by serving on community boards, as I have throughout my career.

Read More
Klaus Schwab, Executive Chairman, The World Economic Forum

Discover how Klaus's passion for fostering world peace led him to establish a gathering place for leaders to find common ground.

Emerging Leader: Brad Smith Reimagining Health Care

After graduating from college, Brad Smith turned down a high-paying job at McKinsey to be the driver for U.S. Senate candidate Bob Corker. Why take one third of the pay? "It seemed more interesting," Brad says. That led to stints as a White House staffer and running an education think-tank in Tennessee.

When his ailing grandmother was suffering from a serious illness, Brad discovered inequities in how care was delivered. His experience inspired him to create Aspire Health, a palliative care company that takes responsibility for outcomes rather than just fee-for-service billing, with former Senator Bill Frist as board chair. Brad expanded the business into 25 states, serving hundreds of thousands of patients.

After selling Aspire Health to Anthem for $440 million, Brad was asked to return to Washington in the Department of Health and Human Services. "The timing wasn't ideal, but I realized I might never get this call again." He was just two months into his new job when the COVID-19 pandemic hit, and Jared Kushner asked him to move to the White House to help tackle the pandemic's challenges.

Brad says, "I went from problem to problem, setting up a structure and solution before moving onto the next thing. I realized that by staying behind the scenes, there were tremendous opportunities for service." Even while leading COVID-19 briefings from the White House podium, meeting regularly with the President, and serving as deputy director of the Domestic Policy Council, Brad kept a low profile—due to his humility and his desire to get things done.

Now back in Tennessee, Brad is starting a collection of new health-care businesses. He says,

> Health care has a tremendous impact on people's lives. We're focused on the most vulnerable patient populations. I've served in government, founded a company, and run a nonprofit. You can help people in all those sectors—the question is, where can you have the greatest impact?

Brad says, "Moving between sectors gives you humility about how much you have to learn." His career illustrates the benefits of going where you are called and doing every job well, no matter how small or how great. It also shows that taking the unconventional road can lead to opportunities you never dreamed of.

Bill's Take: Your Leadership Makes the Difference

Believing that innovative organizations need new leaders every decade, I imposed a 10-year limit on my tenure as Medtronic CEO. I was 58 when I turned over the reins to my successor and completely unsure what lay ahead. It reminded me of rappelling down a rocky cliff wall with no end in sight.

For 8 months, I considered everything—including government service, another CEO role, or running the Aspen Institute. Then I moved to Switzerland to teach at two great Swiss institutions. While there, Enron, WorldCom, and Tyco collapsed, creating the corporate governance crisis.

That's when I saw the vital need to transform organizations with authentic leaders who lead with a moral compass. I recognized the enormous impact that leaders can have on millions of people by addressing society's greatest challenges. I decided to devote myself to developing emerging leaders dedicated to building sustainable organizations that make the world a better place. By contributing to this leadership transformation, I believe I can make a greater difference than by focusing on any single organization.

This leadership transformation requires moral leaders to step up to leadership in organizations and throughout society. Moral leaders are introspective and cultivate high levels of self-awareness and emotional intelligence. This doesn't require religious faith, although many moral leaders are inspired by religion and spirituality. They pursue causes that inspire them with an energizing life force, giving them the courage to take on difficult challenges.

Moral leaders don't require position power. Anyone can become a moral leader by using their voice and writing to inspire others, as Warren Bennis and Jim Wallis have done. Their character and their actions set such a powerful example that people follow them, as they teach and coach people to develop their moral character. Since retiring from Medtronic, my satisfaction comes from the accomplishments of the emerging leaders like you whom I have taught and worked with—some of whom tell their stories in these pages.

Now the torch of leadership is passed to you as the emerging moral leaders who take on the challenges of leading in today's complex world. My clarion call is to lead with your heart as well as your head to make this world better for everyone. Start with your organization by acting with moral clarity as you discover your True North and follow your North Star. Your reward will be the satisfaction of knowing you used your gifts to leave a legacy of which you can be proud.

Idea in Brief: The Moral Leader

Recap of the Main Idea

- Moral leaders in business, government, nonprofits, and other walks of life are vitally needed to address society's greatest challenges.
- Today's business leaders recognize their responsibilities go beyond the bottom line to use their organizations to make positive contributions to society.
- Creating sustainable value must start with the alignment of all stakeholders around a shared mission and values in service to a corporation's customers, employees, shareholders, and all those who have a stake in its success.
- You cannot solve all the world's problems, but you can have meaningful impact when you focus your leadership on one or more major issues.

Questions to Ask

1. Do you meet the criteria of a moral leader? What areas of your leadership do you want to develop?
2. What great challenges are you taking on?
3. How is your organization focused on making a positive impact on society's challenges?

4. How can you serve all your stakeholders? What trade-offs will you have to make?

Suggestions for Development

- Make a list of the different stakeholders in your business. Underneath each, list out tangible ways you're creating value for each of them.

- Survey your employees on the impact they think the business has on the world, using their feedback to reframe the purpose of the organization:

  a. In what ways does our purpose address the world's problems?

  b. How inspired are you by our purpose?

  c. How would you change the purpose to be more meaningful?

  d. How important is it that our business is sustainable?

  e. What steps could our company take to be more sustainable?

  f. How should we measure the impact our company has on improving the world?

References

Introduction

Covey, Stephen M.R. 2008. *Speed Of Trust: The One Thing That Changes Everything*. Free Press.

Korn Ferry. 2021. "Future of Work Trends in 2022: The New Era of Humanity." *KornFerry.com*. https://www.kornferry.com/insights/featured-topics/future-of-work/2022-future-of-work-trends.

Ibarra, Herminia. 2015. "The Authenticity Paradox." *Harvard Business Review*. https://hbr.org/2015/01/the-authenticity-paradox.

James, William. 1878. *Letters of William James*.

Chapter 1

Bennis, Warren, and Robert Thomas. 2002. *Geeks and Geezers*. Harvard Business Review Press.

McGrane, Bill. 2010. *All Rise: The Remarkable Journey of Alan Page*. Triumph Books.

Chapter 2

American Academy of Achievement. 2012. "Oprah Winfrey Interview." https://achievement.org/achiever/oprah-winfrey/#interview.

Brooks, David. 2019. *The Second Mountain*. Random House.

Foster, Chad. 2021. *Blind Ambition: How to Go from Victim to Visionary*. HarperCollins Leadership.

Fu, Ping. 2013. *Bend, Not Break: A Life in Two Worlds*. Portfolio.

Harry, Prince. 2021. *The Me You Can't See (TV Mini Series)*. Video. https://tv.apple.com/us/show/the-me-you-cant-see/.

Miller, Arthur. 1953. *The Crucible: A Play in Four Acts*. Viking Press.

Chapter 3

Brown, Eliot. 2021. *The Cult of We: WeWork, Adam Neumann, and the Great Startup Delusion.* Crown.

Carlson, Nicholas. 2012. "Mark Zuckerberg's Secret IMs from College." *Business Insider.* https://www.businessinsider.com/exclusive-mark-zuckerbergs-secret-ims-from-college-2012-5.

Fain, Travis. 2020. "Durham Businessman Going to Prison for Bribery; Former Congressman Gets Probation for Lying to FBI." *WRAL.com.* https://www.wral.com/nc-mega-donor-gets-7-years-for-bribery-former-congressman-gets-probation/19244019/.

Frier, Sarah. 2021. "The 'Ugly Truth' about Facebook." *NYTimes.com.* https://www.nytimes.com/2021/07/09/books/review/the-ugly-truth-sheera-frenkel-and-cecilia-kang.html.

Guardian Staff. 2020. "Facebook Refuses to Remove Doctored Nancy Pelosi Video." *The Guardian.* https://www.theguardian.com/us-news/2020/aug/03/facebook-fake-nancy-pelosi-video-false-label.

Gupta, Rajat. 2005. Speech at Columbia University, New York.

Horwitz, Jeff, and Deepa Seetharaman. 2020. "Facebook Executives Shut Down Efforts to Make the Site Less Divisive." *Wall Street Journal.* https://www.wsj.com/articles/facebook-knows-it-encourages-division-top-executives-nixed-solutions-11590507499.

Isaac, Mike. 2017. "Uber Founder Travis Kalanick Resigns as C.E.O." *NYTimes.com.* https://www.nytimes.com/2017/06/21/technology/uber-ceo-travis-kalanick.html.

Khorram, Yasmin. 2021. "Jurors in Elizabeth Holmes Trial Can Hear Some Evidence about Extravagant Lifestyle as Theranos CEO." *CNBC.com.* https://www.cnbc.com/2021/05/23/elizabeth-holmes-jury-can-hear-limited-evidence-of-ceo-lifestyle.html.

Lashinksy, Adam. 2017. *Wild Ride: Inside Uber's Quest for World Domination.* Portfolio.

Lindberg, Greg. 2020. *Failing Early & Failing Often: How to Turn Your Adversity into Advantage.* Independently Published.

Mezrich, Ben. 2019. "Inside The Cage Match Between Mark Zuckerberg and the Winklevoss Twins." *Vanity Fair.* https://www.vanityfair.com/news/2019/04/inside-the-mark-zuckerberg-winklevoss-twins-cage-match.

Newcomer, Eric, and Brad Stone. 2018. "The Fall of Travis Kalanick Was a Lot Weirder and Darker Than You Thought." *Bloomberg.com.* https://www.bloomberg.com/news/features/2018-01-18/the-fall-of-travis-kalanick-was-a-lot-weirder-and-darker-than-you-thought.

Paulson, Jr., Henry. 2010. *On the Brink: Inside the Race to Stop the Collapse of the Global Financial System.* Business Plus.

Pelley, Scott. 2021. "Whistleblower: Facebook Is Misleading the Public on Progress against Hate Speech, Violence, Misinformation." *CBSNews .com*. https://www.cbsnews.com/news/facebook-whistleblower-frances-haugen-misinformation-public-60-minutes-2021-10-03/.

Raghavan, Anita. 2013. "Rajat Gupta's Lust for Zeros." *NYTimes.com*. https://www.nytimes.com/2013/05/19/magazine/rajat-guptas-lust-for-zeros .html.

Randazzo, Sara, and Heather Somerville. 2021. "The Elizabeth Holmes Trial: Patients Describe Alarming Test Results." *Wall Street Journal*. https://www.wsj.com/articles/the-elizabeth-holmes-trial-patients-describe-alarming-test-results-11637272480?mod=ig_theranoscoverage.

Rosenberg, Matthew, Nicholas Confessore, and Carole Cadwalladr. 2018. "How Trump Consultants Exploited the Facebook Data of Millions." *NYTimes.com*. https://www.nytimes.com/2018/03/17/us/politics/ cambridge-analytica-trump-campaign.html.

Schechner, Sam, Jeff Horwitz, and Emily Glazer. 2021. "How Facebook Hobbled Mark Zuckerberg's Bid to Get America Vaccinated." *Wall Street Journal*. https://www.wsj.com/articles/facebook-mark-zuckerberg-vacci nated-11631880296.

Woodward, Alex. 2021. "Zuckerberg Dismisses Facebook's Role in Polarising US, Blaming 'Political and Media Environment.'" *Independent*. https:// www.independent.co.uk/news/world/americas/us-politics/facebook-mark-zuckerberg-testimony-b1822496.html.

Chapter 4

Baugh, Natalie. 2019. "BYU Alum's Company Works to Strengthen Communities around the World." *The Daily Universe*. https://universe.byu.edu/2019/11/01/ byu-alumn-company-cotopaxi-impacts-the-world-for-good/.

Bryant, John Hope. 2009. *Love Leadership: The New Way to Lead in a Fear-Based World*. Jossey-Bass.

Huffington, Arianna. 2015. *Thrive: The Third Metric to Redefining Success and Creating a Life of Well-Being, Wisdom, and Wonder*. Harmony.

Jung, C.G. 2017. *Modern Man in Search of a Soul*. Martino Fine Books.

Maslow, Abraham. 1943. "A Theory of Human Motivation." *Psychological Review* 50(4): 370–396.

Nadella, Satya. 2017. *Hit Refresh: The Quest to Rediscover Microsoft's Soul and Imagine a Better Future for Everyone*. Harper Business.

Smith, Davis. 2021. "How Davis Smith Founded Cotopaxi and Built One of the Most Recognizable Outdoor Brands." *Utah Business*. https://www .utahbusiness.com/davis-smith-cotopaxi-founder-story/.

Toegel, Ginka, and Jean-Louis Barsoux. 2012. "Self-Awareness: A Key to Better Leadership." MIT *Sloan Management Review*. https://sloanreview.mit .edu/article/self-awareness-a-key-to-better-leadership/.

Whyte, David. 1992. *The Poetry of Self Compassion*. Many Rivers Press.

Chapter 5

Gergen, David. 2022. *Hearts Touched with Fire: How Great Leaders Are Made*. Simon & Schuster.

Hsu, Tiffany. 2018. "'Our Values Are Not for Sale,' Says Delta C.E.O. as Airline Considers Ending Divisive Discounts." *NYTimes.com*. https://www .nytimes.com/2018/03/02/business/delta-nra-discount.html.

Rushe, Dominic. 2017. "African American CEO Kenneth Frazier Quits Trump Panel after Charlottesville." *The Guardian*. https://www.theguardian .com/us-news/2017/aug/14/kenneth-frazier-quits-trump-business-panel.

Chapter 6

Alighieri, Dante. 2003. *The Divine Comedy (The Inferno, The Purgatorio, and The Paradiso)*. Translated by John Ciardi. New American Library.

Bloomberg, Michael. 2001. *Bloomberg by Bloomberg*. With Matthew Winkler. John Wiley & Sons.

Cook, Tim. 2015. "EPIC's Champions of Freedom Event." Speech, Washington, D.C.

IBM. 2004. *Our Values at Work*. https://www.zurich.ibm.com/pdf/hr/ Our_Values_at_Work.pdf.

Chapter 7

Kopytoff, Verne. 2020. "Nike CEO John Donahoe Went on a Vision Quest. Here's What He Learned." *Fortune*. https://fortune.com/2020/11/10/ nike-ceo-john-donahoe-vision-quest-learnings/.

Chapter 8

Greenleaf, Robert. 2008. "The Servant as Leader." The Greenleaf Center for Servant Leadership.

Jobs, Steve. 2005. Commencement address, Stanford University, Stanford, CA, June 12. http://news.stanford.edu/news/2005/june15/jobs-061505.html.

Mandela, Nelson. 1994. *Long Walk to Freedom: The Autobiography of Nelson Mandela*. Little, Brown.

Chapter 9

Barcott, Rye. 2012. *It Happened on the Way to War: A Marine's Path to Peace*. Bloomsbury UK.

Cook, Tim. 2015. "Commencement Speech at George Washington University." Speech, Washington, D.C.

Joly, Hubert. 2021. *The Heart of Business: Leadership Principles for the Next Era of Capitalism*. Harvard Business Review Press.

Chapter 10

Colvin, Geoff. 2014. "Mary Barra's (Unexpected) Opportunity." *Fortune*. https://fortune.com/2014/09/18/mary-barra-general-motors/.

Compass Real Estate. 2017. *Robert Reffkin: Compass' Mission*. Video. https://www.youtube.com/watch?v=p4N0AIt3FFM.

Gergen, David. 2001. *Eyewitness to Power: The Essence of Leadership: Nixon to Clinton*. Touchstone.

Glazer, Emily. 2021. "Where the CEO of Compass Found His Direction." *Wall Street Journal*. https://www.wsj.com/articles/where-the-ceo-of-compass-found-his-direction-11625889602.

Hoffman, Bryce. 2013. *American Icon: Alan Mulally and the Fight to Save Ford Motor Company*. Currency.

Kotter, John. 1990. *Force for Change: How Leadership Differs from Management*. Free Press.

Media.GM.com. 2014. "Mary Barra's Oral Testimony for U.S. House Hearing." *Media.GM.com*. https://media.gm.com/media/us/en/gm/news.detail.html/content/Pages/news/us/en/2014/Jun/0617-barra-testimony.html.

Putre, Laura. 2020. "The Barra Era: A Look Back and What's Ahead for GM." *IndustryWeek.com*. https://www.industryweek.com/leadership/companies-executives/article/21144226/the-barra-era.

Reffkin, Robert. 2020. "How to Build a Great Team." *LinkedIn.com*. https://www.linkedin.com/pulse/how-build-great-team-robert-reffkin/.

Reffkin, Robert. 2021. *No One Succeeds Alone: Learn Everything You Can from Everyone You Can*. Harvest.

Whitehurst, Jim. 2015. *The Open Organization: Igniting Passion and Performance*. Harvard Business Review Press.

Chapter 11

JPMorgan Chase & Co. 2020. "2020 Workforce Composition Disclosure." *JPMorgan Chase & Co.* https://www.jpmorganchase.com/content/dam/jpmc/jpmorgan-chase-and-co/documents/workforce-composition-disclosure.pdf.

Alesci, Cristina. 2017. "Xerox's Ursula Burns: Business Is Made for Men." *CNNMoney.* https://money.cnn.com/2017/02/03/technology/american-dream-ursula-burns/index.html.

Burns, Ursula. 2021. "How I Saved Xerox from a Near-Death Experience." *Built In.* https://builtin.com/corporate-innovation/xerox-ursula-burns.

Burns, Ursula. 2021. *Where You Are Is Not Who You Are: A Memoir.* Amistad.

Cohen, Mikaela. 2021. "Ursula Burns and Darren Walker Tackle Diversity in Corporate America." *CNBC.* https://www.cnbc.com/2021/06/16/ursula-burns-and-darren-walker-tackle-diversity-in-corporate-america.html.

Eavis, Peter. 2022. "Board Diversity Increased in 2021. Some Ask What Took So Long." *NYTimes.com.* https://www.nytimes.com/2022/01/03/business/corporate-board-diversity.html.

Ignatius, Adi. 2021. "I'm Here Because I'm as Good as You." *Harvard Business Review.* https://hbr.org/2021/07/im-here-because-im-as-good-as-you.

Johnson, Stefanie, David Hekman, and Elsa Chan. 2016. "If There's Only One Woman in Your Candidate Pool, There's Statistically No Chance She'll Be Hired." *Harvard Business Review.* https://hbr.org/2016/04/if-theres-only-one-woman-in-your-candidate-pool-theres-statistically-no-chance-shell-be-hired.

EDMGroup. 2020. "Merck Sustainability Report 2020." *EMDGroup.com.* https://www.emdgroup.com/en/sustainability-report/2020/.

Alliance for Board Diversity. 2018. "Missing Pieces Report: The 2018 Board Diversity Census of Women and Minorities on Fortune 500 Boards." *Deloitte.* https://www2.deloitte.com/content/dam/Deloitte/us/Documents/center-for-board-effectiveness/us-cbe-missing-pieces-report-2018-board-diversity-census.pdf.

Alliance for Board Diversity. 2020. "Missing Pieces Report: The Board Diversity Census of Women and Minorities on Fortune 500 Boards." 2020. *Deloitte.* https://www2.deloitte.com/content/dam/Deloitte/us/Documents/center-for-board-effectiveness/missing-pieces-fortune-500-board-diversity-study-6th-edition-report.pdf.

Stankiewicz, Kevin. 2021. "Former Xerox CEO Ursula Burns Says Biased Criteria Is Holding Back Board Diversity." *CNBC.* https://www.cnbc.com/2021/06/15/ex-xerox-ceo-ursula-burns-says-biased-criteria-is-holding-back-board-diversity.html.

Zahn, Max, and Andy Serwer. 2021. "Yahoo Is Part of the Yahoo Family of Brands." *Finance.Yahoo.com.* https://finance.yahoo.com/news/becoming-xerox-ceo-shouldnt-have-been-shocking-ursula-burns-134518764.html

Chapter 12

CBS Mornings. 2018. "Starbucks' Howard Schultz Was 'Sick' to His Stomach When He Saw Arrests Video." Video. https://youtu.be/0h1BJN9X-ys.
Nooyi, Indra. 2021. *My Life in Full: Work, Family, and Our Future*. Portfolio.

Chapter 13

Benioff, Marc. 2019. "Opinion | Marc Benioff: We Need a New Capitalism." *NYTimes.com*. https://www.nytimes.com/2019/10/14/opinion/benioff-salesforce-capitalism.html.
Johnson, Todd. 2019. "A Denim Renaissance." *BizJournals.com*. https://www.bizjournals.com/sanfrancisco/news/2019/12/20/2019executive-of-the-year-chip-bergh-had-led-a.html.
Mackey, John, and Rajendra Sisodia. 2014. *Conscious Capitalism: Liberating the Heroic Spirit of Business*. Harvard Business Review Press.
Marquardt, Andrew. 2021. "Leadership in Crisis: Levi's Leaders Focused on Company Culture and Empathy to Make It through 2020." *Fortune*. https://fortune.com/2021/02/24/levi-strauss-covid-chip-bergh-ceo-chro-tracy-layney-business-leadership-pandemic/.
McGregor, Jena. 2019. "Levi's CEO Chip Bergh Wears His 501s in the Shower." *The Washington Post*. https://www.washingtonpost.com/business/2019/03/22/five-questions-levi-strauss-ceo-chip-bergh/.
Mohan, Pavithra. 2018. "Levi CEO Chip Bergh Wants You to Give Your Employees Time to Vote." *Fast Company*. https://www.fastcompany.com/90253672/levi-ceo-chip-bergh-wants-you-to-give-your-employees-time-to-vote.
Moore, McKenna. 2020. "Levi's CEO Chip Bergh on Why He Takes a Stand on Gun Control, Diversity, and Getting Out the Vote." *Fortune*. https://fortune.com/2020/09/01/levis-ceo-chip-bergh-gun-control-get-out-the-vote-gotv-retail/.
Rosenbaum, Eric. 2019. "Levi Strauss CEO Chip Bergh on Taking Big Risks with an Iconic Jeans Brand." *CNBC*. https://www.cnbc.com/2019/11/19/levi-strauss-ceo-chip-bergh-on-taking-big-risks-with-the-jeans-brand.html.
Seidman, Dov. 2011. *How: Why How We Do Anything Means Everything*. Wiley.
The Economic Club of Washington, D.C. 2019. *Marc Benioff, Founder, Chairman & Co-CEO, Salesforce*. Video. https://www.youtube.com/watch?v=ohZP0zJxnG0.
The HOW Institute for Society. 2020. *CEO Chip Bergh Admits Levi Strauss Has a Diversity Problem But He's Got a Plan to Fix It*. Video. https://youtu.be/y32SCTOxQ7s.

About the Authors

Bill George is executive fellow at Harvard Business School (HBS), where he has taught leadership since 2004. He is the author of four best-selling books: *Authentic Leadership*, *True North*, *Discover Your True North*, and *7 Lessons for Leading in Crisis*.

He was chair and CEO of Medtronic, the world's leading medical technology company. Under his leadership, Medtronic's market capitalization grew from $1.1 billion to $60 billion, averaging 35 percent a year. He joined Medtronic in 1989 as president and COO, was CEO from 1991 to 2001, and was chair of the board from 1996 to 2002. Earlier in his career, he was an executive with Honeywell and Litton Industries and served in the U.S. Department of Defense.

He has served as a director of Goldman Sachs, ExxonMobil, Novartis, Target, the Mayo Clinic, and World Economic Forum USA. He received the 2014 Bower Award for Business Leadership and was elected to the National Academy of Engineering in 2012. He has been named one of the Top 25 Business Leaders of the Past 25 Years by PBS, Executive of the Year by Academy of Management, and Director of the Year by National Association of Corporate Directors.

Bill received a BS in industrial engineering with high honors from Georgia Tech and his MBA with high distinction from Harvard University, where he was a Baker Scholar. He has received honorary PhDs from Georgia Tech, Mayo Medical School, University of St. Thomas, Augsburg College, and Bryant University. He and his wife, Penny, reside in Minneapolis, Minnesota.

Zach Clayton is founder and CEO of Three Ships, which owns a collection of digital marketplace businesses that enable brands to efficiently connect with consumers and help them buy with confidence. The company's businesses have more than 300 employees. He received a BA from University of North Carolina–Chapel Hill, where he was a Morehead Scholar and Phi Beta Kappa honoree, and his MBA with high distinction from Harvard Business School, where he was a Baker Scholar.

Zach serves on the boards of the Dix Park Conservancy, With Honor, and Business for Educational Success and Transformation NC. He has supported Bill on editorial projects since business school and benefited tremendously from the ongoing journey of trying to better understand and apply the concepts in *True North*. He, his wife, Katie, and their four children live in Raleigh, North Carolina.

Acknowledgments

We are deeply indebted to many people who contributed to the *Emerging Leader Edition* of *True North*. First to Lauren Schwenk, who served as our chief of staff on this project. She brings great skill, speed, and thoroughness to research, writing, editing, and design. We couldn't have written this book without her.

We also appreciate the encouragement and support of the Wiley team, led by Jeanenne Ray, in this book and all books in the *True North* series. The pioneering work on leadership by the late Warren Bennis and David Gergen provided the intellectual basis for many of the ideas here. We are indebted to Peter Sims and Diana Mayer, who contributed so much to the original *True North* in 2007.

From Bill: The new ideas in the *Emerging Leader Edition of True North* have been greatly enhanced by our leadership group at Harvard Business School (HBS), especially the research, leadership theories, and brilliant teaching of Dean Nitin Nohria, Hubert Joly, Scott Snook, and Tom DeLong, along with other HBS colleagues for their insights and wisdom: Michael Porter, Krishna Palepu, Mihir Desai, Ranjay Gulati, Amy Edmondson, Das Narayandas, Len Schlesinger, Frances Frei, Srikant Datar, Rob Kaplan, Jay Lorsch, and the late Clay Christensen. Thanks also to Diane Weinhold and Stacy Walcheski of the George Family Office, who provided helpful support and project management. The insights, counsel, and encouragement of my wife, Penny, have made this book possible.

From Zach: Thanks to my colleagues at Three Ships who have read this book, worked to apply its ideas, and journeyed together toward becoming more authentic leaders. I particularly appreciate

Aarti Sura, Lauren Prosser, John Morgan, John Clayton, Seth Lytton, Walker Fuller, and Steve Noel, who each provided constructive feedback on this new edition. David Cusick, Shane Dutka, Derek Gould, Sarah Haupt, Casey Head, Christian von Kantzow, Marc Lewis, Andres Riobueno, Rebekah Sedaca, Anna Skender, and many others have engaged with the content and shaped it through our leadership development small groups. Thanks also to my awesome assistant, Lily Revels. I have the best colleagues in the world, and I am grateful for the many gentle nudges (okay, strong steers?) they provide. Finally, when I describe my wife, Katie, I always include the word *wise*. She is an amazing person, wife, and mother. I am deeply grateful for her generally—but also specifically for our discussions on leadership development and her willingness to talk about *True North* on so many dates!

Index

Page numbers followed by *f* refer to figures.